Edited by Brett Goldstein with Lauren Dyson

Beyond Transparency

Open Data and the Future of Civic Innovation

Beyond Transparency: Open Data and the Future of Civic Innovation

Edited by Brett Goldstein with Lauren Dyson

Code for America Press, San Francisco, CA.

© Code for America 2013. Some rights reserved.

Read this book online at codeforamerica.org/beyond-transparency

Editors: Brett Goldstein, Lauren Dyson, and Abhi Nemani

Assistant Editor: Rachel Lehmann-Haupt

Cover Designer: Angel Kittiyachavalit

Web Designer: Angel Kittiyachavalit

Web Producer: Mick Thompson

Interior Layout: Christopher Derrick for Unauthorized Media

ISBN-13: 978-0615889085

Table of Contents

Preface

By Brett Goldstein

The rise of open data in the public sector has sparked innovation, driven efficiency, and fueled economic development. And in the vein of high-profile federal initiatives like Data.gov and the White House's Open Government Initiative, more and more governments at the local level are making their foray into the field with Chief Data Officers, open data policies, and open data catalogs.

While still emerging, we are seeing evidence of the transformative potential of open data in shaping the future of our cities. It's at the city level that government most directly impacts the lives of residents— providing clean parks, fighting crime, or issuing permits to open a new business. This is where there is the biggest opportunity to use open data to reimagine the relationship between citizens and government.

And as momentum grows and norms are set, we reach a critical turning point in the trajectory of the movement. As a community, we need to be reflective, mindful, and adaptive. We must take stock of what's worked so far and what we still need to learn in order to ensure we are driving towards meaningful, sustainable outcomes.

Beyond Transparency is a cross-disciplinary survey of the open data landscape, in which practitioners share their own stories of what they've accomplished with open data. It seeks to move beyond the rhetoric of transparency for transparency's sake and towards action and problem solving. Through these stories, we examine what is needed to build an ecosystem in which open data can become the raw materials to drive more effective decision-making and efficient service delivery, spur economic activity, and empower citizens to take an active role in improving their own communities.

How This Book Came to Be

The idea for this book originated while I was in my role as Chief Information Officer for the City of Chicago. I was often flooded with requests of how to replicate the Chicago "success story" with open data. Some essays had been written to talk about implementations using specific vendor platforms. This was valuable, but I felt it required a broader approach. The more I thought about it, the more I came to believe that the moment was right for a "guidebook" of sorts that documented the successes and lessons learned of open civic data so far.

I had become acquainted with Jennifer Pahlka, founder of Code for America, through the City of Chicago's engagement as a Code for America Fellowship city in 2012. We had built a trusting relationship through our discussions related to Code for America's work in Chicago, and continued to get to know each other at the ongoing stream of open government and civic innovation conferences, meetings, and events that we both frequented. As I pondered how to push forward this idea of marking a milestone in civic open data, Jen was an obvious ally.

I reached out to Jen with a big idea: let's write a book on open data. For two busy professionals, this seemed like a herculean task, but a plan came together that leveraged the resources of Code For America along with the insights of key players in the data space. Jen was enthusiastic and pulled together a team from Code for America to support the project. Within a few weeks, we had an initial list of contributors signed on. Within a few months we had chapter drafts in hand and a working outline of the book. A good idea coupled with agile execution—in many ways, the way this book was created embodies principles of the open data movement in and of itself.

What Does This Book Seek to Do?

Beyond Transparency is a resource for (and by) practitioners inside and outside government—from the municipal chief information officer to the community organizer to the civic-minded entrepreneur. We aim for this book to accomplish a few specific things.

For a local government looking to start an open data program, we hope the lessons outlined here will help them do exactly that.

We want to spark a discussion of where open data will go next—and how we, as practitioners, can be smarter, more effective, and more broadly impactful.

We want to help community members (technologists and otherwise) outside of government better engage with the process of governance and improve our public institutions.

And we want lend a voice to many aspects of the open data community. In this book, you'll see perspectives from many different participants that comprise an open data ecosystem: public servants, community organizers, NGOs, technologists, designers, researchers, journalists, and citizens. With *Beyond Transparency*, we've brought together a diverse cross-section of the field's top innovators and leaders to share their stories of what has been achieved with open data so far, what they've learned along the way, and how we can apply those lessons to realize a more promising future for America's cities. As they look back on what's been accomplished so far—and what is yet to come—emergent themes resonate throughout their stories.

As the title of this book suggests, the community is realizing the need to look beyond the rationale of transparency and instead align open data efforts with policy objectives, applying it to solve problems that really matter and make better decisions about how to allocate scarce resources. We also hear again and again the need for citizen-centered design that borrows principles from the User Experience field to move from data that is open to data that is truly usable and accessible by the public. Many practitioners cite the need for open data standards—across various types of civic data—to increase interoperability and make impact scalable. These are just some of the ideas and lessons that emerge from the stories gathered here.

As we look forward, this is an exciting point in time. We have proven the value of open data. We have shown it can be done in short order, in cities of all sizes, from Chicago to Asheville, North Carolina. And now it is up to all of us to carry on the work that has been started.

Acknowledgments

Thank you to my wife Sarah—as I continue to pile on projects, her tolerance is remarkable. Thank you to Lauren Dyson and the rest of Code for America team who helped bring this vision to fruition. Thanks to Mayor Rahm Emanuel, whose support laid the foundation that allowed open data in Chicago to become what it is today. And above all, thank you to the community of practitioners whose work is featured in this book. Your ingenuity, hard work, and commitment to innovation illuminate a path forward to a stronger public sphere powered by open data.

PART I:
Opening Government Data

Editor's Note

In the first section, we consider the challenges and outcomes of opening government data through a series of practical case studies.

In Chapter 1, civic software developer Joel Mahoney tells the story of how opening government data changed the conversation around Boston's school assignment policies, which have been a topic of debate since the 1960s. Open data, he argues, not only contributes to a more informed public discourse, but can play a key role in upholding core democratic values, like aligning policy with societal goals.

Next, in Chapter 2, we turn to the City of Chicago, which pioneered one of the most comprehensive municipal open data programs in the country. Brett Goldstein, who was Chicago's first Chief Data Officer, tells the story of building Chicago's open data efforts from the ground up. Providing a first-hand account of the internal workings of city hall, he shares what they learned about building sustainable technical infrastructure for open data.

In Chapter 3, we examine another angle of Chicago's open data initiative. Daniel X. O'Neil, Executive Director of the Smart Chicago Collaborative, has worked closely with the City of Chicago's open data team and local open data activists to advance the city's progress in this space. He breaks down the key components of data, policy, developers, capital, and products that have allowed a sustainable open data ecosystem to develop in Chicago.

Emer Coleman—founder of the London Datastore, one of the flagship open data efforts in a major city—tells us about open data in a non-US context in Chapter 4. She gives a personal perspective on the establishment of the Datastore, the policy context that preceded it, and the challenges of data release in the public sector.

Finally, we examine how open data can have big impact in smaller cities—not just highly resourced urban areas. In Chapter 5, Jonathan Feldman, Chief Information Officer of Asheville, North Carolina (population 85,000), writes about open data as a long-term investment and explores some of the challenges and opportunities specific to smaller local governments. Through a case study of how Asheville's emerging open data efforts can save city resources, he urges other small cities to consider the pragmatics of open data.

CHAPTER 1

Open Data and Open Discourse at Boston Public Schools

By Joel Mahoney

I am a firm believer in the people. If given the truth, they can be depended upon to meet any national crisis. The great point is to bring them the real facts.

—*Abraham Lincoln*

Inside the Maze

In March of 2011, the City of Boston had a problem: the *Boston Globe* had just published a special multimedia series titled "Getting In: Inside Boston's School Assignment Maze" that offered a critical view of Boston's school assignment policies (*Boston Globe*, 2011). The report profiled thirteen families entering the Boston public school system, and traced their hopes and frustrations as they navigated the complicated school selection process. The following quotes from interviews with the families are indicative:

> I don't have a lot of faith in the process being logical, so I just hope that in that mess we somehow get something that works out.

> —Malia Grant

> Just the word 'lottery' when it comes to schools—what, you just roll the dice and take a shot with your kid and hope for the best? That's pretty much where we're at.

> —Steve Rousell

Ultimately, it's possible that we will leave the city if things don't work out the way we want them to.

—Andy Berg

The report used interactive maps, school performance data, and personal stories to paint a compelling picture of the complexity of the school assignment process. It also showed that the stakes—in terms of citizen satisfaction and trust in government—were high.

These complaints weren't news to the School Department. The school assignment policies dated back to the Racial Imbalance Act of 1965, which required forced integration in Boston public schools, and provoked riots and protests throughout the city (Hoover Institution, 1998). The opposition was so persistent that it made the cover of Time Magazine in 1971. It led to a District Court ruling in 1974, which found Boston Public Schools to be unconstitutionally segregated, and imposed forced busing on the city to remedy the situation. It wasn't until busing was abandoned in 1988 that the issue was finally resolved; by that time the school district had shrunk from 100,000 to 57,000 students, only twenty-eight percent of whom were white (Hoover Institution, 1998).

What appeared to be a logistical issue—distributing a large number of students to a limited number of schools—touched on challenging social questions of race, equality, and opportunity. Should diversity be pursued at the expense of neighborhood cohesion? Should desegregation be enforced at a local level when wealthier parents could leave the city? Should cities be responsible for determining the proper balance? As indicated by the Supreme Court's landmark decision in Brown v. Board of Education in 1954, these questions had a long and contentious history. The simple act of sending a child to school involves some of society's most divisive issues.

By highlighting the school assignment problem in their 2011 report, the *Boston Globe* brought a longstanding issue back into the public spotlight. The report sparked high-level conversations in City Hall and made it difficult for the School Department to ignore the problem. The criticism demanded a response.

Coding for America

In January 2011, Code for America began work in Boston as part of an eleven-month engagement with the City. I was part of a five-person Fellowship team tasked with building innovative applications around public education, partnering with The Mayor's Office of New Urban Mechanics and Boston Public Schools (BPS). Our goal was to make educational services "simple, beautiful, and easy to use," to quote my teammate Scott Silverman.

Our main project was a "trust framework" that would allow developers to build innovative services on top of student information—a kind of "app store for students." By the time the *Globe* article was published in March, however, the viability of the project was in doubt: BPS lawyers were taking a conservative stance toward the possibility of opening data, so we shifted our focus to other projects that would be less reliant on open data.

After the *Globe* report was published, however, we sensed an opportunity to make progress with the city around the sensitive topic of open data. In an early meeting with the School Department, the Superintendent suggested that we build an application to help parents through the school discovery process. We realized that the project would be an excellent opportunity to clarify the eligibility rules in context, especially considering the existing tools—a twenty-eight-page parent handbook, and a home-grown BPS website called "What Are My Schools?"—left much to be desired. In July of 2011, we began work on a project that allows parents to enter a home address and grade level and see a personalized list of eligible schools. We called it "DiscoverBPS."

Our research showed that parents had two primary concerns: school quality and school location. To address those concerns, we included detailed information on commute distances and times (by foot and by bus), as well as MCAS scores, teacher-to-student ratios, school hours, after-school programs, and other performance metrics. We built "walk-shed maps" to help parents make sense of the complicated walk-zone policy (which gave a higher precedence to students who lived within a certain radius of a school), and we added historical acceptance rate data for each grade level in each school. This latter statistic proved to be the most controversial: the School Department worried that the odds of admission would add to the sense of "gambling with your child's future." We countered that it was impossible for parents to make informed decisions without relevant information, and that transparent data would make the lottery process more comprehensible. Even after we received permission to publish the data, the School Department thought that the phrase "odds of admission" would be inflammatory, and asked us to refer to the statistic as "applicants per open seat" (which meant that we had to present the number as a ratio instead of a percentage). Apparently, "open data" had shades of grey.

DiscoverBPS launched in November of 2011 and has received upwards of 15,000 unique visitors since then, with a substantial increase in traffic during school registration months. For context, about that same number of people register for school in Boston each year. It won praise from parents and school officials, who felt that the intuitive UI and data-driven content made the complicated school selection process more intelligible. The most significant feedback, however, came a year and a half later, when Superintendent Carol Johnson told me that DiscoverBPS had "changed the way [the School Department] relates to parents." In thinking about the goals of Code for America—improving citizen engagement by making government services more open, efficient and participatory—I can't imagine a much higher form of praise.

Algorithmic Regulation

It is important to note the backdrop for the Superintendent's remark: I met her at a town hall meeting in February of 2013 where BPS officials were presenting proposals to overhaul Boston's school assignment policies. These plans had been a topic of discussion for years, but had finally become a reality after Mayor Menino committed to resolving the problem in his "State of the City" speech in January of 2012:

> The Boston Public Schools have come a long way in the last twenty years. When I became mayor, many parents considered sending their children to only a handful of schools. Today, more than 100 of our schools have waiting lists because they are so popular with

parents. Our graduation rate has never been higher, and our drop-out rate hasn't been lower in two decades.

But something stands in the way of taking our system to the next level: a student assignment process that ships our kids to schools across our city. Pick any street. A dozen children probably attend a dozen different schools. Parents might not know each other; children might not play together. They can't carpool, or study for the same tests. We won't have the schools our kids deserve until we build school communities that serve them well.

I'm committing tonight that one year from now Boston will have adopted a radically different student assignment plan—one that puts a priority on children attending schools closer to their homes. I am directing Superintendent Johnson to appoint a citywide group of dedicated individuals. They will help design the plan to get us there and engage the community on this transition.

I know I have talked about changing the student assignment plan before. We have made many improvements over the years. 2012 will be the year to finish the job. (City of Boston, 2012)

This directive laid out the School Department's agenda for the next year, including the town hall meetings like the one I attended in February where BPS officials presented the new assignment proposals and solicited feedback from parents. Most of these proposals aimed to solve the busing problem by dividing the school district into smaller assignment zones (see http://bostonschoolchoice.org/explore-the-proposals/original-bps-proposals/). Boston had traditionally consisted of three zones: North, West, and East. The new proposals ranged from nine to twenty-three zones. Like any redistricting effort, there was no easy way to redraw the lines: the number of schools would still be the same, and some parents or groups would always feel short-changed. The meetings were contentious, and parents vented frustrations about the current and proposed assignment systems. And although the Superintendent's comments were complimentary, when I was sitting in the town hall session, where a long line of parents were venting frustrations about the school selection process it was hard to believe that a website like

DiscoverBPS could really have an impact on such deep and intractable problems.

Interestingly, the winning proposal was not on the School Department's original list. It was submitted by Peng Shi, a doctoral student at MIT studying the use of algorithms to address social problems, who had started attending the town hall meetings out of curiosity. Like us, he came to the conclusion that the problem centered on school quality and location, which he believed were poorly addressed by fixed geographical zones. His solution used an algorithm to ensure that each student had access to a guaranteed number of high-quality choices (as defined by the School Department using test scores and other metrics), no matter where in the city the student lived. According to a *New York Times* article on the topic by Katharine Seelye (2013), "He started saying things like, 'What I'm hearing is, parents want close to home but they really care about quality… I'm working on something to try to meet those two goals.' He didn't have a political agenda."

Peng proposed his algorithm to the School Department and they included it in their proceedings. Parents were receptive to the idea, and the School Committee eventually voted it into policy in March of 2013 (the algorithm will be put into effect at the end of 2013). The decision was an historic development in a fifty-year debate.

As Seelye's article noted:

> That it took a dispassionate outsider with coding skills but no political agenda to formulate the model is a measure of the complexities facing urban school districts today. Many such districts, like Boston's, are plagued by inequities, with too few good schools and children mostly of color trapped in low-performing schools. Overcoming that legacy here has been so emotionally charged that previous attempts to redraw the zones have failed (though in 2005 the district did change the algorithm it uses to assign students). (Seelye, 2013)

This description would have applied equally well to our work in Boston as Code for America Fellows.

Data and Discourse

The Boston school assignment story shows the power of open data to shift the public discourse around social issues. The Boston Globe made its case against the School Department using data made publicly available by the School Department (along with parent interviews, etc.); the School Department responded by opening up new data in DiscoverBPS, and by engaging in an open dialogue with parents around proposed solutions. This process involved town hall meetings and a website called www.bostonschoolchoice.org, which includes an entire section devoted to "Raw Data." As Chris Osgood, co-chair of the Boston Mayor's Office of New Urban Mechanics noted, this data allowed third parties like Peng Shi to make informed contributions to the process. The open data served as a kind of API endpoint into the school selection debate.

The Superintendent's comment that DiscoverBPS "changed the way [the School Department] relates to parents" reflects the critical role that user-friendly interfaces to open data (such as DiscoverBPS) play in facilitating that discourse.

By changing the way the school department relates to parents, DiscoverBPS also changed attitudes within the school department about the role—and value—of technology. Based on the success of version 1.0 of DiscoverBPS, the City recently retained me to develop version 2.0 of the software, which will include new data and new tools for parents. I am now continuing conversations at BPS that began in 2011, and have noticed a greater tolerance toward the use of open data, as well as toward the tools and technologies that make open data possible (the BPS IT department is currently building a RESTful API to expose a canonical repository of school and student information). Lastly, the School Department's choice of an assignment policy that can only be administered by a computer strikes me as a hugely symbolic step toward embracing technological solutions—consider what it means that the School Department can no longer pin assignment zone maps on the wall, since the algorithm generates a unique list of eligible schools for each address.

Conclusion

Our work in Boston shows how open data can catalyze change around even the most contentious social issues. At first, we tried to affect change directly by opening up all student information in an app store, but encountered resistance around privacy issues, and had to take a roundabout approach. By instead applying open data to real and existing problems, we were able to demonstrate the immediate value of the data, and make meaningful contributions to a longstanding public debate.

Two and a half years later, the School Department is investing in the continued development of DiscoverBPS, and is demonstrating a deeper understanding of the role that open data can play in governance.

Democracy relies on our ability to frame policy—and regulation—around our broad societal goals. Open data plays an important role in this process by encouraging constructive public discourse, and by proving a transparent measure of progress towards those goals. Indeed, as Abraham Lincoln noted, with "real facts" even the most challenging social issues can be met.

About the Author

Joel Mahoney is an entrepreneur and former Code for America Fellow. He is the creator of DiscoverBPS.org, which helps Boston parents to find the best public schools for their kids, and the co-founder of Open-Counter.us, which helps entrepreneurs to navigate business permitting. His work on DataDonor.org explores the use of personal data as a new medium of charitable contribution.

References

Boston Globe Staff (2011). Getting In: Inside Boston's School Assignment Maze [Multimedia series]. The *Boston Globe*. Retrieved from http://www.boston.com/news/education/specials/school_chance/index/

City of Boston. (2012). The Honorable Mayor Thomas M. Menino: State of the City Address, January 17, 2012. Retrieved from http://

www.cityofboston.gov/Images_Documents/State_of_the_City_2012_
tcm3-30137.pdf

Hoover Institution, Stanford University (1998). Busing's Boston Massacre. Policy Review, 98. Retrieved from http://www.hoover.org/publications/policy-review/article/7768

Seelye, Katherine Q. (2013, March 12). No Division Required in This School Problem. The *New York Times*. Retrieved from http://www.nytimes.com/2013/03/13/education/no-division-required-in-this-school-problem.html?_r=0

CHAPTER 2

Open Data in Chicago: Game On

By Brett Goldstein

Before I joined Chicago's government administration, I knew very little about open data. I certainly had been immersed in the world of data and analytics for some time, but I didn't substantively understand the concept of "open" as it applied to this context. In fact, because I'd worked at the Chicago Police Department in the Counterterrorism and Intelligence Section, open data seemed completely counterintuitive. So when Mayor-elect Rahm Emanuel's transition team reached out to me to discuss ramping up an open data program at the City of Chicago, I had to do some quick and hasty internet research to be properly prepared.

During the mayoral campaign, Mayor Emanuel had held an event at Microsoft that highlighted the importance of open government, citing open data at the heart of his vision for a more transparent Chicago. The mayor then asked me to serve as the city's first Chief Data Officer (CDO) and to implement his vision of a more transparent government that not only makes its data available to the public, but also uses data analysis as a tool to inform policy and improve services.

The new administration started on May 16, 2011, with open data as a top priority from day one. The weekend prior, the policy group had gathered to discuss the strategy for the first hundred days and open data was listed as an early goal. My mission was to take the bones of the city's existing program and make it a cornerstone of the city's transparency initiatives. My first step was to assess what existed and then decide where I wanted to take the vision and direction as the CDO for the City of Chicago.

Before we dive into the details of what ensued, it is worth discussing the simple point that Chicago was the first major municipality to appoint a CDO. This was a clear and immediate statement about the importance of these initiatives to the new administration. Mayor Emanuel had decided early on that he wanted a team that used the city's vast and rich data resources as a tool and that empiricism would inform policy. To achieve that goal, he created a senior-level post within his office that would focus on exactly that. By creating a CDO as his proxy for a data-driven and transparent government, Mayor Emanuel laid the foundation for Chicago to go from lagging behind other governments to being at the forefront of open civic data and transparency.

The City of Chicago did have an existing open data program so I wasn't starting from scratch. Prior to the new administration it was managed by Danielle DuMerer, a project manager in The Department of Innovation and Technology (DoIT). The city had already secured the Socrata platform and kicked off some basic dataset projects—specifically, publishing logs of the Freedom of Information Act (FOIA) requests submitted by the public, as well as an assortment of facility and geographic datasets.

DuMerer had substantially engaged the local open government community with the city's open data. However, the prior administration had not identified the open data program as a top priority among other competing issues, and even with DuMerer's efforts the program struggled to gain significant traction. But once the new administration came on board with a clear mandate from Mayoral Emanuel to make open data a priority, the city's open data program began to immediately change.

In the first two weeks as the city's Chief Data Officer, I did my best to learn the ins and outs of the program I had inherited. I found it frustrating that the data platform had already been chosen. While I appreciate the turnkey efficiency of Socrata's platform, I knew that a proprietary application would become a long-term financial investment. I am also a strong believer in utilizing open source technologies and was disappointed that we were doing little to support the community around CKAN, a widely used open source open data catalog. But because I needed to deliver results immediately, I was not in a position to make a sharp pivot. It wasn't practical to consider other alternative platforms at that point.

There were also the upcoming Apps for Metro Chicago contests, plans for which had been initiated during the prior administration. The John D. and Catherine T. MacArthur Foundation was funding three thematic competitions to encourage businesses and software engineers to use City of Chicago and Cook County open data to create useful applications for residents. We greatly appreciated the philanthropic support of this initiative, but the competition imposed a hard timeline to roll out our program.

It would have been simple to give it just enough attention to meet the requirements of the project and not offend the supporting foundation, allowing us to focus on the ideas coming from the new administration. However, we ended up seeing this competition as a great way to help launch the new open data program in Chicago and it helped us get momentum quickly. (MacArthur has continued to be a fantastic supporter of these forward-thinking programs.) Kicking off the Apps for Metro Chicago competition so soon after the start of the new administration was consistent with the strategy of rapidly expanding the existing open data program.

We immediately found that while technology was relevant to the project, clear executive sponsorship allowed for this initiative to rapidly accelerate. We achieved a couple of key milestones early on that ended up laying the foundation for the future of the program.

First, the city released its crime incidents dataset. Historically, crime data was hard to obtain in Chicago. While Chicago had been a leader in front-facing technologies, its raw data was not easily accessible. The Chicago Police Department's CLEARpath website offered ninety days of historic incident-level crime data via a mapping interface and was a great start in terms of information access. However, if third parties wanted to use the data, they had to do a substantial amount of scraping.

Crime data is historically one of the most demanded datasets and is often too limiting in a few different ways: it is of too short an interval to provide utility for anything other than immediate-term situational awareness; the data is aggregated at a unit of analysis that is too dilutive (à la district, ward, or precinct); and/or the data is not machine-readable.

Chicago endeavored to solve all of these issues in one swift move. The designed release sought to open all incident-level crime data from January 1, 2001, to the present and update the dataset on a twenty four-hour cycle. Holding 4.6 million records, Chicago's published dataset would be the largest automatically updating set of incident-level crime data ever released.

The technology behind the release was not complex, but nor was it trivial. Crime data is recorded in the Chicago Police Department's transactional system and then replicated into their data warehouse. Our approach was to fire an ETL (a set of database functions for moving data from one place to another) from an internal utility server to pull data from the police warehouse and load it into the city's data portal via Socrata's API.

However, along the way, a couple of critical items needed to happen in order to ensure that the data was secure and could be rendered into a releasable form:

- The addresses needed to be block-reduced to protect privacy.

- Spatial coordinates also had to be scattered to assist with privacy protection.

- Updates needed to be captured and replicated into the dataset as the source system records were updated.

- Since the crimes dataset was to be one of their first large datasets, the Socrata platform needed to be able to efficiently handle uploads, updates, and queries.

We successfully completed all of these steps, experiencing some pain along the way, but the process eventually came together. As of April 2013, the dataset includes nearly 5.2 million records, continues to be automatically updated daily, and serves as a good example of the implementation of open data.

This data release brought substantial attention to Chicago's open data program, much of which was due to the press around that release. Sophia Tareen, a reporter with the Associated Press, covered the story. She wrote a thoughtful piece on the enormity of the release and noted that it was a clear turning point for Chicago (Tareen, 2011). While written locally, the article was sent out en masse by the AP and, within a few hours, became an international story. As a result, Chicago's open data program became very real and was validated by the broader community. We learned that there is enormous benefit to a high-profile release of a high-interest dataset early on. I view this as another seminal moment for the program, providing a solid foundation from which to launch. This release worked very well for Chicago, and I suspect it would work for other jurisdictions as well.

Second, the Apps for Metro Chicago competition provided a framework to engage the Chicago community. The competition demonstrated that many Chicagoans were deeply excited about open data and really wanted to engage with government to build tools to help their neighbors. In order to achieve the latter, we had to provide data in machine-readable formats, and it needed to be consistently refreshed. Prior to the re-launch of Chicago's data portal, data had been made available, but usually in the form of a PDF, which technologists know can be somewhat less than friendly.

Our release of street sweeping data during the Apps for Metro Chicago contest window exemplifies this change. While at a Google-hosted open data hackathon in 2011, Scott Robbin approached DuMerer and I to ask about the city's street sweeper dataset. He was interested in building an application that would notify users the night before their street would be swept. I thought this was a fabulous idea, since I had personally received a series of tickets for failing to move my car. However, the path from idea to implementation required some of the city's data. The street sweeping schedule existed, but it was not published in a format easily used by software engineers or technologists. The Department of Streets and Sanitation had taken an Excel spreadsheet and created a calendar, using the software's formatting tools. The resulting spreadsheet was then printed to a PDF and posted on the City of Chicago's website. This format made it impossible to reverse engineer. Fortunately, in situations like these, interns are great at assisting with the tedious, but critical, work of converting an unusable file into one that can serve as a data source. We posted the resulting file on data.cityofchicago.org. From there, Scott produced an excellent site, sweeparound.us, which has assisted many of us in being mindful of the city's cleaning schedule.

The sweeparound.us story exemplifies a couple key lessons that continue to hold true. First, we, as a city, needed to learn to produce data in machine-readable formats as part of our standard business practices. Second, a variety of communities demonstrated an enormous appetite for government data, including civic developers, researchers, and journalists. We saw the emergence of the civic developer community both in the philanthropic and for-profit models. Places like Chapin Hall at the University of Chicago had been struggling for years to extract administrative data for the purpose of research. Open data programs make it substantially easier, removing the need to negotiate non-disclosure or other types of agreements. Open data also has also stimulated new research. A Ph.D. candidate tweeted her gratitude at finally being able to finish her dissertation, and more traditional organizations have now embarked in multi-year studies, based on what has been released on the City of Chicago's data portal.

The last lesson is one coined by Tim O'Reilly (2010): "Government as a Platform." I did not completely understand this idea for some time, but now it's one I greatly appreciate. Chicago's data portal is designed to provide raw data in machine-readable formats. By providing an API to this data, any developer can access, use, or integrate all of this raw material for whatever purpose they can imagine. As the City's Chief Information Officer and CDO, I purposely tried to avoid getting into the app development business and, instead, preferred to grow the portal to offer both diversity and depth. This strategy prevents us from being in the business of maintaining apps that require various programming skill sets and ongoing financial resources. Instead, a standards-based data portal allows us to be the platform, as O'Reilly suggests, and support the innovative ideas cultivated by various communities.

Successfully Implementing an Open Data Program

After two years of building a successful program in the City of Chicago, there are a series of critical points that can be leveraged as other cities consider implementing or expanding open data.

Architecture

Building a large, useful, machine-readable, and meaningful data portal is a non-trivial technical task. First, of course, comes the question of platform. You will need to reflect on your staff's capabilities, along with available funding to make this decision. Here are some points to consider.

If you need a turnkey solution, there are few options are available. Socrata is the dominant platform, and they are good at what they do. They provide a ready-to-go data portal. For organizations who cringe at the idea of building their own servers and using open source, this is the method that is going to work best for you. However, as we will discuss later, in order to have a sustainable open data platform, you are going to need to do some rather advanced work.

Beyond the platform comes the source of the data. For programs that are still in their most basic stage, using a turnkey approach can make this work incredibly easy. Your data may reside in something as simple as a spreadsheet. You can upload that information into Socrata directly and be ready to go in seconds, but it rarely remains that simple once you get beyond the basics.

Much of the data that you have will come from transactional or warehouse systems, and if your world is like mine, many of them are quite aged and somewhat cryptic. You will need to find ways to extract the data, understand what it means, and load it into the platform. This is somewhat less turnkey than you might originally think.

You also need to consider how much data you will be moving and how that will impact your enterprise network, storage, and systems. If you are simply dealing with something like a salary list, which is small data, the issue is trivial. However, what if you want to load something like GPS coordinates of your assets? In Chicago, that would be approximately ten million rows a day. That would stress most environments.

Sustainability

It may seem odd to call out this very specific point, but I suspect it is one of the most critical: the sustainability of the overall design. An open data program that relies on a human to keep it updated is fundamentally flawed. Considering that one of the goals of open data is transparency, it's important to ponder the role of the middleman. I like to joke that people are often shocked when I tell them we do not vet the data before it gets released onto the portal. There is, in fact, no little dude in the basement of City Hall that checks every row of data before it goes out the door. That is the beautiful part of the design behind the portal.

Ninety nine percent of the data that goes onto data.cityofchicago.org arrives there automatically. Each one of the datasets has an ETL job that connects into the source system, takes the data, transforms it as appropriate, and loads it into the platform. This happens daily or more frequently. In some cases, we overwrite the entire set. For others, like crime incidents, we do an incremental update that adds new records and catches changes to existing records. This type of architecture accomplishes a series of critical points.

First, it is scalable. It is impossible to have millions of rows of data available based on manual refreshes. This makes little sense and will not be timely. Second, as mentioned before, it keeps the platform honest. Lastly, it creates sustainability. The program ceases to become about a single individual and, instead, becomes a programmatic area within the technological organization.

Fear

There is a strong institutional fear of open data. In a culture of "gotcha" journalism, the idea of something being disclosed that could embarrass an administration is a common worry and, therefore, barrier. It is often a reason to not release data. My experience with this highlights a couple critical points.

We have released millions of rows of data to date, and so far, it has gone very well. Every time the internal constituency has been concerned about a release, we have been able to push it forward and go public without incident.

It is critical that you develop a strong relationship with your open government community. By fostering this dynamic, you are able to create a "let's make it work together" ethos. I explained that if every mistake I made got blown into a major incident, it would stymie our collaborative goals. In Chicago, they took this to heart. We created a team effort, working with Joe Germuska from the Northwestern University Knight Lab, and formerly of the *Chicago Tribune*, along with Daniel X. O'Neil of the Smart Chicago Collaborative. We would regularly convene via Twitter, email, phone, or at meet-ups. This worked out particularly well as we strived to conquer large and complicated datasets. These are the types of datasets that are very hard to release perfectly the first time.

Often, you will see a dynamic between government, the press, and the open government community that can be less than pleasant because of this "gotcha" concept I mentioned prior. Government releases something that has an error in it, and it becomes a "thing." Maybe there is substantial press around the error or, even worse, it is viewed as being deceitful. Within this framework, there are typically only two strategies that can be taken by government. The first is to not release any data, which is not the optimal track for any of our interests. The second is to ensure that the data is one hundred percent perfect before it goes out the door.

The one hundred percent perfect model is fine when the data is small. If you are posting a spreadsheet with one hundred rows and it is not terribly wide, you can go through each and every line to ensure that it's perfect. You can even scale the exercise to thousands of lines using a variety of mechanisms. However, what happens when the dataset includes millions of rows and covers a decade? Even with scripts and audit techniques, you cannot reach the one hundred percent confidence mark. This leaves most people in a quandary. When you want to release big and important data and you cannot ensure it is one hundred percent correct, it leads to all sorts of drama. It becomes a no-win situation.

This is where we changed the dynamic in Chicago so that we would be able to move the open data program into high gear. It came down to me personally developing a series of relationships within the community and investing the time to ensure that people understood and believed in what we were trying to do. Historically, a high-level member of the administration does not show up at an open government meet-up to discuss open data, but this was what ultimately enabled me to build trust between these entities. It also helped to have contacts like Joe, within the news organization, that allowed for the relationship building. These people believed that our open data plan was bigger than the single story and that we were building a broader system.

Becoming Part of Day-to-Day Operations

As the open data program in Chicago became a robust and useful platform, the question came as to how we should take it to the next level. In the beginning of 2013, the mayor decided that he wanted to make a policy commitment to ensure the sustainability of the program. He issued an Open Data Executive Order (2012-2) that mandated that each department would designate an Open Data Coordinator, the city would create and sustain the position of Chief Data Officer, and there would be annual accountability as to the release of open data for transparency and sustainability (Emanuel, 2013).

The release and exposure of this executive order served to reinforce the hard work that had gone into the creation of the program. The ordering is one that would remain an open question for administrations that are looking to move forward in the realm of open data. Does it make sense to issue the executive order or legislation prior to the beginning of the initiative, or does it make sense to allow for some traction and then create that framework around it?

My preference is around the latter, but, clearly, I am biased. My thoughts focus on the ability to iterate and develop in an incubator environment before it becomes part of the system. Open data programs will have to evolve and grow in different ways in various cities. Lessons that apply to Chicago may not be relevant for a different city. The autonomy to try, explore, and adapt makes a lot of sense and is certainly a model that can be conducive to success. It is critical to create a viable program before becoming overly prescriptive about its functions.

The Bare Minimum to be Successful

In order for an open data program to be truly successful, it requires two key items that are, in fact, also a broader lesson for many government initiatives. The first is the clear and vocal support of the executive sponsor—whether this is the president for the federal program or, in the case of Chicago, the mayor. With the unequivocal support of the mayor, roadblocks disappeared as it became clear that all parties would be accountable for the success—or lack thereof—of the program.

The second is financial support. A mandate with a lack of supporting funding in government is not, in fact, a mandate. There is a common saying in municipal government: "Control is based on a budget line." Whoever controls the budget line controls the project. Chicago committed funding (not a large amount, but funding nonetheless) and resources to ensure that this could be successful. In the case of Chicago, this was able to fund the Socrata platform as a foundation and the ongoing work that was required for ETL development. Without a data platform and some sort of automated way to continue to keep it fresh, it is not a true program that will be sustainable beyond the individual.

I will, however, note the corner case that invalidates my second point, and this is, of course, a model that I admire: the scrappy do-it-yourself shop. In this scenario, the program is based on the open source CKAN model. The entity can build out their open data system on top of that platform. Seeing that they already have shown the innovation to work with open source software, it may be the case that they have the ability to write their own ETLs or leverage some of the great open source ETL tools that are available on the internet. From there, it would be a function of what sort of infrastructure could be built out. There is absolutely no reason a low-cost cloud solution couldn't be implemented.

This type of presence does not require a substantial amount of security, as you are not really worried about accessing the data. Rather, you simply want to preserve its integrity.

This corner case is somewhat interesting, as one can envision a scenario where one partners a strong executive sponsor with a scrappy technologist. Given access and mandate, it would be extraordinarily low-cost for a successful initial foray into the open data space. This is an area that we should be mindful of and find ways to support.

Chicago is an excellent case in showing how one can build an open data program where it is not expected. The role of the strong executive sponsor is critical to a program's success, and Mayor Emanuel played that part. Building close partnerships with the community and strategic media attention were also key components of our success. Through tenacity and sustainable execution by the team, Chicago has been able to put forth an initiative that has become the gold standard in open data. These lessons from Chicago's rapid scaling up of our program will help inform the next generation of open data initiatives, as new models for growth and sustainability of open data emerge.

About the Author

Brett Goldstein is the former Chief Data and Information Officer for the City of Chicago. In 2013, he was named the inaugural recipient of the Fellowship in Urban Science at the University of Chicago Harris School of Public Policy. Before his appointment as Chicago's first Chief Data Officer, he founded the Chicago Police Department Predictive Analytics Group. Previously, he spent seven years in the startup world building online real-time restaurant reservation service OpenTable. Goldstein is currently pursuing his PhD in Criminology, Law and Justice at the University of Illinois-Chicago.

References

O'Reilly, Tim. (2010). Government as a Platform. In *Open Government*. Retrieved from http://ofps.oreilly.com/titles/9780596804350/defining_government_2_0_lessons_learned_.html

Emanuel, Rahm, City of Chicago. (2013). Open Data Executive Order (No. 2012-2). Retrieved from http://www.cityofchicago.org/city/en/narr/foia/open_data_executiveorder.html

Tareen, S. (2011, September 14). Chicago to publish crime stats online. The Washington Times. Retrieved from http://www.washingtontimes.com/news/2011/sep/14/apnewsbreak-chicago-to-publish-crime-stats-online/?page=all

CHAPTER 3

Building a Smarter Chicago

By Daniel X. O'Neil

Introduction

As the open data and open government movement continues, there is a lot of talk about building local ecosystems for the work. The general idea is that there has to be a mildly magic combination of data, policy, developers, capital, and products to enable the kind of growth that is necessary to take the movement to the next level—where there is a mature market for open government products that serve real community needs and lead to sustainable revenue.

The thing about building an ecosystem is that when it is done deliberately, it can be a slog. Building a developer community from scratch, convincing local government to publish data, getting venture capitalists to take a look at open government projects—all of this is tough work that takes time.

By looking at the Chicago example, however, we can see that there's often more built than it first seems. The components can be found, in varying degrees, in any unit of government. The trick is to find, cobble, and congeal these pieces together.

What follows is an illustrative, incomplete, and idiosyncratic look at the ecosystem in Chicago. It is meant to provide a thumbnail take on how the ecosystem developed here, while sparking fires elsewhere.

Data: An Era of Incidental Transparency

The story starts with Citizen ICAM (Information Collection for Automated Mapping), the granddaddy of all crime mapping applications, created by the Chicago Police Department in May 1995. I wrote about

this system back in 2006 because I wanted to understand the archae-
ology of this distinctly unique (and relatively difficult to use) interface
(O'Neil, 2006). You can learn a lot about software by its backstory.
Here's the first sentence of a July 1996 National Institute of Justice
report on Citizen ICAM:

> To better understand the nature and extent of criminal and social
> problems in the community and improve allocation of resources, a
> growing number of crime control and prevention organizations are
> turning to computerized mapping. (Rich, 1996)

The impetus behind the project ("Citizen" is the first word in its name)
was the Chicago Alternative Policing Strategy (CAPS) program. Here's
another snip from the 1996 report:

> ICAM was developed as part of CPD's far-reaching and ambitious
> community policing strategy. Unlike many other community-po-
> licing programs that are limited to a single unit in the depart-
> ment, the Chicago Alternative Policing Strategy (CAPS) is de-
> partment-wide. The strategic plan for reinventing CPD describes
> CAPS as a "wholesale transformation of the department, from a
> largely centralized, incident-driven, crime suppression agency to
> a more decentralized, customer-driven organization dedicated to
> solving problems, preventing crime, and improving the quality of
> life in each of Chicago's neighborhoods.

> In fact, CAPS is really a city program with strong support from the
> Mayor's office and close involvement of city agencies, which have
> been directed to give top priority to "CAPS service requests" that
> affect crime and neighborhood safety. (Rich, 1996)

This twenty-year-old project is a model for where we need to be now—
and where the movement seems to be heading. It starts with deep input from residents to form a "customer-driven organization."

In the technology world, we call these people "users."

Adrian Holovaty's ChicagoCrime.org—widely considered a major
impetus in the open data movement—simply would not have existed

without Citizen ICAM (Holovaty, 2008). At the same time, Chicago-Crime.org was certainly not well-formed public data. For instance, all data was retrieved by scraping with obscure URL calls that ignored the user interface, which limited searches to a quarter-mile radius.

Another example is transit data "published" by the Chicago Transit Authority in the context of their proprietary Bus Tracker system. I covered this extensively in a January 2009 blog post (O'Neil, 2009). The upshot is that Harper Reed scraped all data driving the app, cached it, and served it to developers. This led to a blossoming of transit-focused apps.

The culmination of this work is the publication of the CTA's own API, a document wherein Harper and I are explicitly called out for helping them develop it:

> Special thanks go to Harper Reed and Dan O'Neil for their support and encouragement, and to the independent development community, for showing such great interest in developing applications with CTA data, leading to the creation of this official API. Thank you. (Chicago Transit Authority, 2011)

This is the kind of inside/outside game that is also essential to the ecosystem. You have to work with government institutions to make their data fluency and data policy better.

A last example of early data in Chicago (and perhaps the first explicitly conscious publication of data in the city) is the wealth of Geographic Information Systems (GIS) data published by the City of Chicago. This was another early reason why ChicagoCrime (and, by extension, EveryBlock) could exist. Their policy was formalized in July 2007, but the data had been available long before that (City of Chicago, 2007).

The first section of their documentation, "Data Sharing Principles," has the idea that public information should be public: "Wherever possible, direct requestors to publicly available internet sources of map information."

This is the moment when the governmental provision of data goes from incidental to essential. Before that magic moment, it's important for developers and citizens to look harder for data published in plain sight.

Policy: Enlightened Self-Interest Meets the Movement

As a co-founder of EveryBlock, I spent four years (2007 to 2011) working with sixteen municipalities on publishing data. I saw some fundamental patterns of open data policy development that held true here in Chicago.

First off, I can't emphasize the power of examples enough. In December 2007, I was part of a meeting of open data advocates in Sebastopol, California. The mission was "to develop a more robust understanding of why open government data is essential to democracy."

The output was the "8 Principles of Open Government Data" (Open Government Working Group, 2007). This simple document was a powerful, unimpeachable tool that I used every time I worked with government. It made a significant difference because it gave government-based open data advocates something to point to when they were in their internal meetings. This support of isolated pockets of policymakers was one important pattern I saw here in Chicago as well. Building relationships with public, sharable resources, like the "8 Principles," allowed for shared trust and shared work. This pattern of template sharing is something that works.

There were nascent open data plans and products in the Daley administration, including Chicago Works For You, a project I worked on as a consultant for the City in 2005. Micah Sifry discussed this project in a 2009 article titled "A See-Through Society":

> People are eager for access to information, and public officials who try to stand in the way will discover that the internet responds to information suppression by routing around the problem. Consider the story of a site you've never seen, ChicagoWorksForYou.com. In June 2005, a team of Web developers working for the City of Chicago began developing a site that would take the fifty-five different kinds of service requests that flow into the city's 311 database—

items like pothole repairs, tree-trimming, garbage-can placement, building permits, and restaurant inspections—and enable users to search by address and "map what's happening in your neighborhood." The idea was to showcase city services at the local level. (Sifry, 2009)

Early failures often lead the way to the next policy win—that's another pattern.

Hot topics that receive public attention are fecund areas for open data policy. In Chicago, Tax Increment Financing is a big topic, mainly because it has been an opaque financial instrument, handling huge amounts of money with very little public information about how the system works.

It's no accident that a number of Aldermen sponsored the TIF Sunshine Ordinance in 2009 (Brooks & O'Neil, 2009). Pressure and heat get results.

The last pattern has perhaps led to the most good: when the chief executive of a unit of government wants to make a big push. Mayor Michael Bloomberg of New York won an unusual third term at the same time he pushed for BigApps; San Francisco Mayor Gavin Newsom was planning a run for governor at the same time he worked to open DataSF; and our own Mayor Rahm Emanuel embraced open data when he made a move from the White House to Chicago City Hall.

This is the pattern of powerful, enlightened elected officials in the executive branch deciding that open data is good policy. They back this up by empowering people, like former Chicago CIO Brett Goldstein and CTO John Tolva, to develop and implement that policy.

It's the unique and aggressive policy of publishing data that has brought the movement further here in Chicago.

Developers: Civic Activism

Every city has its own history and its own approach to the world, and I think that is expressed in its technological history as well. Chicago has been a center of civic activism and individual public creativity for decades.

It can be traced as far back as Jane Addams, who created the Hull House in 1889. It was the first "settlement house," cooperative residences for middle-class "settlers" in predominantly immigrant neighborhoods that aimed to reduce inequality in urban areas (Wade, 2004). She was also a tireless scholar who studied the geographical distribution of typhoid fever and found that it was the working poor who suffered most from the illness.

Chicago is the place where the drive for common standards, like the eight-hour workday, was fought (Jentz, n.d.). It was a center for the battle against mortgage redlining (the practice of denying or raising prices for mortgages that has played a role in the decay of cities). Activists used data to understand the predicament and prove their case.

The General Transit Feed Specification (GTFS) is a recent national example of success in putting civic data to use for the public good. Everyone loves CTA bus tracker apps, but few people know that the installation of the GPS satellite technology making that possible is the result of a lawsuit brought by a group associated with the Americans Disabled for Accessible Public Transit (Chicago Transit Authority, n.d.). Their case, Access Living et al. v. Chicago Transit Authority, required "installation of audio-visual equipment on buses to announce bus stop information to riders who have visual impairments or are deaf or hard of hearing" (Equip for Equality, n.d.). When you hear the loudspeaker system announce the next street where the bus is stopping, you have de facto data activists to thank.

This is the place where saxophonists rise from the stage, blare out a ten-minute solo, and calmly fade back into the band. It's the place where slam poetry was conceived—individual poets audaciously grabbing the mic for three minutes and getting judged by the crowd. It's also where improv comedy—with its focus on ensemble and fast thinking—was invented.

These are threads for us in the civic innovation movement here in Chicago. I believe they're embedded in the work. They form examples for us to follow—the quiet humility of the worker in the crowd, the developer among the people.

You can find recitations of particular apps using specific datasets anywhere. Just remember that every city has unique cultural and technological histories. This is the essence of an ecosystem, and it's why they are local.

It's one thing to recognize history and another to build a local movement from it. Here are some of the entities that have helped form and accelerate the work:

- Illinois Data Exchange Affiliates was an early-incarnation open data group that led the way (Illinois Data Exchange Affiliates, 2007).

- Independent Government Observers Task Force was a 2008 non-conference, where many of the leaders of the movement worked together (Independent Government Observers Task Force, 2008).

- Open Government Chicago(-land) is a meetup group started by Joe Germuska (Open Government Chicago(-land), 2013).

- Open Gov Hack Nights are weekly meetings that have been critical to accelerating the pace of development (Open Gov Hack Night, n.d.).

- Digital.CityofChicago.org is a publication at the center of city policy and examples ("Release All the Data," 2013).

Capital: Philanthropy Leads, Capital Must Follow

Without money, there is no sustainability.

As an ecosystem matures, it finds ways to adapt and grow. In technology and data, growing means capital. In Chicago, a main source of capital currently comes from philanthropic sources, though there are some stirrings in the market.

The first open government data apps contest—Apps for Metro Chicago—was primarily funded by the MacArthur Foundation (O'Brien, 2011). The contest was an important moment in the ecosystem—it was the first time that government and developers were brought together in the context of a project with cash prizes.

The Smart Chicago Collaborative, a civic organization devoted to improving lives in Chicago through technology, is funded by the MacArthur Foundation and the Chicago Community Trust. Additional funding came through the federal government's Broadband Technology Opportunities Program, a program designed to expand access and adoption of broadband opportunities in communities across America (National Telecommunications and Information Administration, n.d.).

EveryBlock was funded by a $1 million grant from the Knight Foundation, and then was acquired by MSNBC. This was a test of using philanthropic money and open source as a basis for a business. There have not been many examples since then. This is a problem that needs to be fixed—we need more experimentation, more value.

A digital startup hub in Chicago, known as 1871, has a number of civic startups in their space, including Smart Chicago, Tracklytics, Purple Binder, and Data Made. As these organizations deliver more value, the entire civic innovation sector will attract more capital.

Products: The Next Frontier

In order for the ecosystem to be self-sustaining, we have to create popular, scalable, and revenue-generating products with civic data.

Developers in Chicago are making a renewed focus on users. An example is the Civic User Testing Group run by Smart Chicago (Smart Chicago Collaborative, n.d.). We've spent years trying to get regular residents to participate in the product development process, and now we have more than five hundred people signed up in our first six months.

We have to do this—go beyond anecdote, beyond the cool app that lacks real traction, into creating business models and datasets that add value. We need to make products and services that people can't live without.

This will require a mix of proprietary solutions, open source code, and shared standards. Companies need to follow viable product strategies—moving from one-off apps to sustainable systems. Interoperable data is a critical component to making this happen.

The good thing about this is that there are models to follow in other successful companies right here in Chicago. SitterCity is a vast consumer success story. OpenTable, Groupon, and GrubHub are all Chicago companies that found ways to reduce transaction friction in various markets.

They did this, in the main, with a strict attention to customers. In the civic innovation sector of the technology industry, we call those people "residents." When you are serving people and make popular products, you are necessarily serving a civic need.

We're beginning to focus on this work here in Chicago by adding value to civic data with unstructured public content, by creating systems around predictive analytics, and making baseline services, like Open311, that can serve future product needs.

What's Your Ecosystem?

This is a short take on a complicated subject that, in the end, has to be completely local. Hopefully, it gives some specific examples of how we've built an open data ecosystem in Chicago and points to how far we have to go.

Chicago has contributed, in our small way, but we have to be measured by how we contribute to the entirety of the internet, rather than this civic innovation subset. We're ready to keep going, and we're excited to share our models with the rest of the country and the world.

About the Author

Daniel X. O'Neil is the Executive Director of the Smart Chicago Collaborative, a civic organization devoted to making lives better in Chicago through technology. Prior to Smart Chicago, O'Neil was a co-founder of and People Person for EveryBlock, a neighborhood news and discussion site that served 16 cities until February 2013. He's a co-founder of the OpenGovChicago meetup group.

References

Brooks, M. & O'Neil, D. X. (2009, August 5). Chicago's First Attempt at TIF Sunshine Falls Short. Progress Illinois. Retrieved from http://www.progressillinois.com/2009/8/5/columns/tif-sunshine-review

Chicago Transit Authority. (2011, June 16). Bus Tracker API Documentation. Retrieved from http://www.transitchicago.com/asset.aspx?AssetId=2917

Chicago Transit Authority. (n.d.) Open Data from CTA. Retrieved from http://www.transitchicago.com/data/

City of Chicago, Department of Business and Information Services. (2007, July). GIS Data Sharing Policies and Procedures. Retrieved from http://www.cityofchicago.org/dam/city/depts/doit/general/GIS/GIS_Data/Data_Sharing/GIS_DataSharingPolicy.pdf

City of Chicago. (2013, April 1). Release All the Data. Chicago Digital. Retrieved from http://digital.cityofchicago.org/index.php/release-all-the-data/

Equip for Equality. (n.d.). What is the Access Living et al. v. Chicago Transit Authority Class Action Settlement Agreement? Retrieved from http://www.equipforequality.org/programs/transportationrights/ctasettlement.php

Holovaty, A. (2008, January 31). In memory of chicagocrime.org. Retrieved from http://www.holovaty.com/writing/chicagocrime.org-tribute/

Illinois Data Exchange Affiliates. (2007). The Business Case for Real-time Sharing of Government Data. Retrieved from http://downloads2.esri.com/campus/uploads/library/pdfs/132035.pdf

Independent Government Observers Task Force. (2008). Independent Government Observers Task Force: A Non-Conference. Retrieved from http://igotf.org/

Jentz, J. B. (n.d.). Eight-Hour Movement. The Encyclopedia of Chicago. Retrieved from http://www.encyclopedia.chicagohistory.org/pages/117.html

National Telecommunications and Information Administration. (n.d.). BroadbandUSA. Retrieved from http://www2.ntia.doc.gov/

O'Brien, J. (2011, June 24). Apps for Metro Chicago Illinois Competition Launched. Chicago Tonight. Retrieved from http://blogs.wttw.com/moreonthestory/2011/06/24/apps-for-metro-chicago-illinois-competition-launched/

O'Neil, D. X. (2009, January). Harper Reed: "The power is not the mashup. It's the data." Retrieved from http://www.derivativeworks.com/2009/01/h.html

O'Neil, D. X. (2006, February 18). History of Citizen ICAM. Retrieved from http://www.derivativeworks.com/2006/02/history_of_citi.html

Open Gov Hack Night. (n.d.). Open Gov Hack Night Registration, Chicago. Retrieved from http://opengovhacknight.eventbrite.com/

Open Government Chicago(-land). (2013). Open Government Chicago(-land). Retrieved from http://www.meetup.com/OpenGovChicago/

Open Government Working Group. (2007, December 8). 8 Principles of Open Government Data. Retrieved from https://public.resource.org/8_principles.html

Rich, T. F., National Institute of Justice. (1996). The Chicago Police Department's Information Collection for Automated Mapping (ICAM) Program. Retrieved from https://www.ncjrs.gov/pdffiles/icamprog.pdf

Sifry, M. L. (2009, January 15). A See-Through Society. Columbia Journalism Review, January/February 2009. Retrieved from http://www.danielxoneil.com/2009/01/15/columbia-journalism-review-a-see-through-society/

Smart Chicago Collaborative. (n.d.). Civic User Testing Group. Retrieved from http://cutgroup.smartchicagoapps.org/

Wade, Louise Carrol (2004). "Settlement Houses." Encyclopedia of Chicago. Chicago Historical Society. Retrieved from http://www.encyclopedia.chicagohistory.org/pages/1135.html

CHAPTER 4

Lessons from the London Datastore

By Emer Coleman

I've worked for local government in London since 2005. In March 2009, I moved to City Hall to undertake a yearlong research project funded by the Greater London Authority (GLA), Capital Ambition, and the Department of Communities and Local Government. The purpose of the project was to examine how policy was working across the London Boroughs, particularly regarding their use of new media and technology. It also meant analyzing their use of qualitative research methodologies. This project built on research previously undertaken by Leo Boland, who had recently taken on the role of Chief Executive of The Greater London Authority.

Boland and I co-authored an article published in 2008 in the journal *Public Money & Management* entitled "What Lies Beyond Service Delivery? Leadership Behaviors for Place Shaping in Local Government" (Boland, L. & Coleman, E., 2008). We noted how governments were struggling to create cognitive shifts around areas such as waste minimization and obesity, as well as the co-production of services. We were particularly influenced by the view that:

> A public sector that does not utilize the power of user-generated content will not just look old, outdated, and tired. It will also be far less productive and effective in creating public goods. (Leadbeater, C. & Cottam, H., 2007)

We accepted that the big challenge for public service reform was not just to make public services more efficient and reliable—like next-generation consumer web services, such as Amazon.com—but to make them communal and collective, which means inviting and encouraging citizens to participate. To us, open data seemed a vital component of that invitation to participation.

Some important policy milestones had paved the way. In 2008, at the central government level in the United Kingdom, the Power of Information Taskforce (headed by then Labor Minister Tom Watson) ran a competition asking, "What would you create with public information?" The competition offered a substantial prize fund for the winner. In London, Boris Johnson, as part of his election manifesto for mayor, had committed to publishing an open register of interests for all mayoral advisors, and providing a search function on the mayor's website that would enable all Londoners to instantly find information about all grants, contracts, and programs over £1,000. And on President Obama's first day in office in 2009, he made great inroads by issuing the Open Government Directive committing to three principles—transparency, participation, and collaboration—as the cornerstone of his administration.

The City Hall Perspective

The importance of strong political leadership cannot be underestimated in the drive to opening up public data. In the process, however, it is interesting to see how public officials can sometimes undermine that leadership. Mayor Boris Johnson had brought with him to City Hall a cadre of mayoral advisors, all of whom had close ties with the Conservative party (then in opposition in government) in the UK and all of whom were of a generation that understood the power of technology.

Individuals like Guto Harri, Communications Director, and Dan Ritterband, Marketing Director, were close to Steve Hilton, former Director of Strategy for David Cameron. Hilton is also the husband of Rachel Whetstone, the Global VP of Public Affairs and Communications for Google. This group of people all encouraged the Mayor to support an official open data portal for London, called the London Datastore, in order to fulfill his manifesto pledges. They were also keeping a keen eye on the national position being adopted by Conservative Campaign Headquarters before the 2010 General Election.

The 2010 Conservative Party Manifesto made explicit reference to open data under the heading "Change Society to Make Government More Transparent," though no reference to the role of open data was mentioned in two additional related manifesto categories. Reading between the lines from a policy point of view, it seemed that the open data focus of the Conservatives was on transparency rather than the disruptive opportunities that open data offered. It didn't focus on open data's potential role in stimulating economic activity or harnessing disruptive technologies that could benefit citizens. However, there was enough of an open door and the right winds of change to make the establishment of the London Datastore a possibility.

Definition

In 2007, a working group convened by Tim O'Reilly and Carl Malamud offered a definition of what constitutes open data. The resulting document cited eight principles that are widely quoted in the open data movement to determine whether data is open or not: complete, timely, accessible, able to be processed by a machine, non-discriminatory, available without registration, non-proprietary, and free of any copyright or patent regulations (Open Government Working Group, 2007). David Eaves, the Canadian open data activist, simplified the definition somewhat in his influential Three Laws of Open Government Data:

1. If it can't be spidered or indexed, it doesn't exist.

2. If it isn't available in open and machine-readable formats, it can't engage.

3. If a legal framework doesn't allow it to be repurposed, it doesn't empower. (Eaves, D., 2009)

I was heavily influenced by Eaves' definition because it offered a very simple explanation of open data, especially in the early days when little was understood about its potential and it was hard to find actual, practical examples to point to.

The Beginnings

I established a small internal group to begin the scoping process for the establishment of the London Datastore. It included members of both the Data Management Asset Group (DMAG) and the Technology Group (TG) within the GLA. The initial proposition by DMAG and TG was to develop a "web portal" using proprietary software. An initial prototype for this had already been built. Given my interest in ensuring that policy development should be a two-way process and mindful of the invitation to participate, I argued for a shift in approach to open up the scoping process to those most likely to use the data in the first place—technologists and those active in the open data movement.

The role of social media, particularly Twitter, is something not to be underestimated when trying to develop a successful model of engagement around government data. Our call to "Help Us Free London's Data" was sent via the London Datastore Twitter account (@london-datastore) on October 20, 2009, linking to the following invitation:

> The Greater London Authority is currently in the process of scoping London's Datastore. Initially, we propose to release as much GLA data as possible and to encourage other public agencies in London to do the same, and we'd like your help! We want the input of the developer community from the outset prior to making any decisions on formats or platforms. We would, therefore, like to invite interested developers to City Hall, so that we can talk to you about what we want to do, get your views, and seek your input on the best way to deliver for London. ("Help Us Free London's Data," 2009)

This invitation drew over sixty developers to our open workshop on the following Saturday in London's Living Room in City Hall. We got some clear messages from the technology community that helped us manage expectations in the months to follow. We heard their deep level of frustration and cynicism from the many years they had spent trying to get public data released, most specifically in the areas of Transport and Crime. We also heard their concerns that the current structures of government might stop the project from going much further.

More importantly, we listened to them when they told us to "go ugly early" and not make the mistake that government often does of allowing perfection to be the enemy of good. They told us that, as long as the data was not in PDF form, they would take it, and they would help us clean it up at no cost to the state. By working together, we could make things better—it was a powerful moment in the data release journey.

I believe that being open from the very beginning was a crucial element of the success of the London Datastore. Said technologist Chris Thorpe, a former engagement strategist for *The Guardian's* Open Platform initiative, in his subsequent blog:

> Being invited into an organization's home for the start of something suggests a good open relationship to come. The presence on a Saturday of several GLA staff involved in the process also shows me they care deeply about it. (Thorpe, 2009)

Until very recently, I worked in government for thirteen years, largely in communications and engagement, and later, in policy and strategy. Many of those years were spent trying to articulate difficult government propositions to an often apathetic or hostile electorate. The emergence of that kind of third party endorsement for a government initiative, from a respected member of the technology community like Chris (or any community for that matter), is something I found very powerful. I believe that is something that government needs a lot more of if it is to have any hope of repairing the democratic deficit that exists around the world. Open is the only way to achieve this.

Once you move into the open, though, you have to continue in the open, and this can end up being where the real tensions of data release play out. Following the launch of the London Datastore on January 7, 2010, I wrote in a blog post:

> On [January] 7, we promised to increase the datasets from 50 to 200 by [January 29], and thanks to the good work of Gareth Baker in the DMAG team in the GLA, we did just that. Since then, we have had a more or less continuous stream of meetings with the functional bodies Transport for London, Met Police, London Development Agency, Olympic Development Authority, and LFEPA. These meetings have been held with the developer community variously represented by Professor Jonathan Raper, Chris Taggart, and Tom Loosemore—and it's been exciting to see the interchange

between those in the developer community and public servants—coming as they do from different cultures.

All of the functional bodies have agreed that the Datastore is a good idea and have committed to freeing up data in the coming weeks and months. We realize that this might not meet the sense of urgency in the developer community—but let's not pull any punches. We knew that negotiations were always going to be time-consuming and, in some cases, difficult. And let's not be coy about it—being comfortable about releasing data requires huge cultural shifts in the public sector. But we have left all of our meetings encouraged and with the definite feeling that the agenda is changing fast and for the better. (Coleman, 2010)

Reading Between the Lines

In reality, however, things were a little less rosy behind the scenes. My blog post was trying to hold a fine line between managing developer expectations and being honest about the challenges I was experiencing at an official level. As a public servant working for the GLA group, I could not possibly be publicly critical of the reluctance and resistance that I was getting at the official level to the release of their data. To do so would have potentially undermined the authority of the mayor and suggested divisions within the Greater London Authority group.

Since I raised expectations in the stakeholder group to a high level very publicly, I now faced the reality that the timeframe for the release of Transport and Crime data was going to be quite long. Even though the mayor had clearly signaled his intent to presume openness by default at the launch of the London Datastore, it was becoming clear that many of his public servants who were charged with implementing his policy were not inclined to comply with his wishes.

The resistance that I was experiencing does not emerge in isolation in response to a particular initiative, but rather is hard-wired into the bureaucracy. It's both to do with cultures of government secrecy generally (Bennett, 1985; Worthy, 2008), as well as progressive attempts by governments to exploit the monetization of state data (Burkert, 2004).

Other commentators suggest that there is a three-tiered driver at play in the release of open government data. "Three groups of actors can be distinguished: civil society, mid and top level public servants. All actors must be engaged in order to ensure the success of the open data project" (Hogge, 2010). Interestingly, within civil society, Hogge identified "civic hackers" as particularly important.

While I agree with her point about civic hackers (I like to call them digital disrupters), I disagree with her selected drivers and would suggest that the three actors that must be engaged are the state, civil society, and the media. When I, as a public official, was unable to state publicly the resistance to data release at an official level, I could brief the digital disrupters in the Datastore network. They could raise issues on their blogs and ask questions publicly through their networks (social and otherwise) that brought external pressure to bear on their local and central government contacts.

Equally, the role of the media cannot be underestimated. Charles Arthur, technology editor for *The Guardian*, played an essential part in the establishment of the London Datastore. He epitomizes the potential of a new relationship between government and media. A long-time proponent of open data, Charles understood the state's nervousness in entering this territory and the importance of reinforcing the good aspects. He gave praise where it was due, rather than adopting the "gotcha stance" that many in the media take when government takes new steps in new directions. He wrote a seminal piece in September 2010 that praised both Transport for London and the Mayor:

> You might think that Boris Johnson's presence pushing this along is just a bit of grandstanding, but that wouldn't be correct. He's actually been in the vanguard of politicians introducing open data. If you have a long memory for public data-related stories, you'll recall that he did a rather neat end-run around the Labour administration's Home Office in 2008, when, as part of his manifesto while running for the office of London mayor, he declared that he would publish crime maps... Johnson did go on to publish them, and London has been in the forefront of cities, which have tried to do innovative things with the data that its local government and authorities collect. (Arthur, 2010)

It's worth noting that from a UK perspective, *The Guardian* publicly praising a Conservative Mayor is notable because while *The Guardian* regards itself as the paper of record, Conservative commentators perceive it as the home of the left.

And Then There Is Happenstance

The world of data release is neither linear nor always planned. For example, we always knew that the release of bus data in London would be a game changer for the city, since so many Londoners rely heavily on the bus network. We had lots of discussions with TfL over many months about releasing bus data that demonstrated the state was still struggling with the speed of technology (even though we were quite far along on the data release journey). In one meeting between me, transport developers, and Transport for London, the TfL officer responsible for releasing the bus dataset laid out a timeframe that included publishing the data on TfL's website, then waiting six months to enable the data to "bed down" before releasing an official API for developers.

There was quite a heated exchange between the developers and the official while they explained that, as soon as the data went live on TfL's website, they would simply scrape the data and build their apps anyway. A few days later, I received a call from the TfL official telling me that he had considered the discussion and would shorten the data release deadline by three months (bearing in mind that TfL had a whole marketing campaign ordered and paid for to coincide with their release).

However, within hours of that conversation ending, I started noticing some interesting tweets suggesting that TfL had released their bus data. What followed was a rather surreal conversation with TfL. It turns out that the link to the data was available internally on the TfL intranet all along, and someone had simply emailed the link externally, whereupon the developers descended and immediately started building their apps.

"You've got to tell those developers to stop accessing that data," the beleaguered TfL official pleaded with me, bemoaning his loss on the planned marketing campaign and worried about the impact the data load would have on the TfL servers. I had to explain that I didn't know all the developers and ask if he ever heard of the whack-a-mole principle.

Once the genie is out of the bottle, there are effects in the system that you simply cannot control. Given that TfL had released so much of its real-time data at that point, whoever made the link to the bus data public probably reasoned there was no reason not to do so. Open begets more open, and the levers of command and control in the organization can suddenly cease to have the power that they once did.

Three Years On

I have to say that I'm now a poacher turned gamekeeper. I recently left government to join Transport API, a startup that is building its business on open data, including that released by Transport for London. As an aggregator of open data, we are at the coalface of building the businesses we predicted could exist if the state released its public data. Our platform provides data to the incredibly successful City Mapper app in London and, with our partner Elgin (another open data company), we are providing intelligent transport solutions to local authorities around the UK at vastly more cost-effective prices and better terms and conditions than those offered by the incumbents.

We are surrounded by many small companies working on similar issues in the Open Data Institute offices in London where we are based. Our colleagues at Mastodon C, who work with big data and health data, were recently lauded by the *Economist* for their prescription analytics demonstrating the vast sums of money that the National Health Service could save by using generic versions of commonly prescribed drugs. There is also mySociety, a nonprofit organization that continues to develop innovative technology solutions, like Mapumental, FixMyStreet, and FixMyTransport. Of course, there is also Chris Taggart, who is building OpenCorporates, the open database of the corporate world. We hope that all our companies will make the world a better, more open, and more efficient place for citizens—and we believe in it so strongly that we are putting our own money where our mouths were almost three years ago.

I also work on a consultancy basis with the Connected Digital Economy Catapult, an initiative of the Technology Strategy Board (TSB) tasked with supporting the acceleration of the UK's best digital ideas to market. Supporting the interoperability of open data is one of its key targets, building platforms to create multiplier effects with that data along the digital economy value chain. That, along with the work of the Future Cities Catapult, also established by the TSB, provides an important emergent new infrastructure, which I hope will give further impetus, support, and capability for even more tranches of data release in the coming years.

I think there are challenges for the private sector that are different— but not dissimilar—to those the public sector faced when open data became part of the policy landscape. The race for ownership of the smart city has been on for quite some time. A 2010 report commissioned by the Rockefeller Foundation (The Future of Cities, Information and Inclusion) bears out my experiences as Director of Digital Projects in City Hall. The report suggests that there is a potential battle between Jane Jacobs-inspired hacktivists pushing for self-serve governance and latter-day Robert Moses types carving out monopolies for IBM or Cisco. It also argues that without a delicate balance between the scale of big companies and the DIY spirit of government 2.0, the urban poor could be the biggest losers.

Big companies, as well as government, need to learn that you have to collaborate to compete, you have to operate on a presumption of openness, and you have to move away from the idea of first to market advantage. There is profit to be made, of course, but that profit need not be at the expense of a better deal for citizens. All of us, state and private sector alike, need to first ask what is best for public value—and then we need to share our assets to achieve those public goods. The next part of this journey is going to be exciting.

About the Author

Emer Coleman was the architect of The London Datastore. She also works as a journalist and consultant and writes about how technology impacts organizational development. She is the founder of DSRPTN, a consultancy specializing in leadership and change, and also the Business Development Director at TransportAPI, a startup powering innovation and change in transport. She was named in *Wired Magazine's* Top 100 Digital Power Influencers List 2011. She holds a BA in History and Sociology from University College Cork and an MPA from Warwick Business School.

References

Arthur, C. (2010, September 3). Another Data Win: TfL Opens Up Bus and Tube Timetables for Developers. *The Guardian*. Retrieved from http://www.guardian.co.uk/technology/blog/2010/sep/03/tfl-time-tables-boris-johnson

Bennett, C. (1985). From the Dark to the Light: The Open Government Debate in Britain. Journal of Public Policy, 5 02), 187-213. doi: 10.1017/S0143814X00003020. Retrieved from http://journals.cambridge.org/action/displayAbstract?fromPage=online&aid=2692668

Boland, L. & Coleman, E. (2008). New Development: What Lies Beyond Service Delivery? Leadership Behaviours for Place Shaping in Local Government. Public Money & Management, 28 (5), 313-318. Retrieved from http://papers.ssrn.com/sol3/papers.cfm?abstract_id=1266379

Burkert, H. (2004). The Mechanics of Public Sector Information. In G. Aichholzer and H. Burkert (Eds.) Public Sector Information in the Digital Age: Between Markets, Public Management and Citizens' Rights. Cheltenham: Edward Elgar Publishing Limited.

Coleman, E. (2010, February 15). Hectic Times. Retrieved from http://data.london.gov.uk/blog/hectic-times

Eaves, D. (2009, September 30). The Three Laws of Open Government Data. Retrieved from http://eaves.ca/2009/09/30/three-law-of-open-government-data/

Greater London Authority. (2009). Help Us Free London's Data. Retrieved from http://freelondonsdata.eventbrite.com/

Institute for the Future & Rockefeller Foundation. (2010). A Planet of Civic Laboratories: The Future of Cities, Information, and Inclusion. Palo Alto, CA: Townsend, A., Maguire, R., Liebhold, M., & Crawford, M. Retrieved from http://www.rockefellerfoundation.org/uploads/files/814a5087-542c-4353-9619-60ff913b4589-sr.pdf

Leadbeater, C. & Cottam, H. (2007) The User-Generated State: Public Services 2.0. Retrieved from http://www.charlesleadbeater.net/archive/public-services-20.aspx

Open Government Working Group. (2007, December 8). 8 Principles of Open Government Data. Retrieved from http://www.opengovdata.org/home/8principles

Open Society Foundations. (2010). Open Data Study. London: Hogge, B. Retrieved from http://www.opensocietyfoundations.org/reports/open-data-study

The Conservative Party. (2010). The Conservative Manifesto 2010. Uckfield, East Sussex: The Conservative Party. Retrieved from http://www.conservatives.com/~/media/Files/Activist%20Centre/Press%20and%20Policy/Manifestos/Manifesto2010

Thorpe, C. (2009, October 25). A Good Way to Start Building a Data Store for London. Retrieved from http://blog.jaggeree.com/post/222676486/a-good-way-to-start-building-a-data-store-for-london

Worthy, B. (2008). The Future of Freedom of Information in the UK. The Political Quarterly, 79(1), 100-108. doi: 10.1111/j.1467-923X.2008.00907.x. Retrieved from http://onlinelibrary.wiley.com/doi/10.1111/j.1467-923X.2008.00907.x/abstract

CHAPTER 5

Asheville's Open Data Journey: Pragmatics, Policy, and Participation

By Jonathan Feldman

Much of the open data conversation centers on policy, politics, or solving community problems. These are great—and needed—beginning and end points, but there is an important middle point that raises two questions: How do we produce open data? And how can we get open data to be a part of the government process?

Today, local, state, and federal governments generally have to go an extra mile to convert "open records" into what we would recognize as "open data." This essentially means open records that are presented in a convenient, automated, and self-service format.

That extra mile is a tough nut. For all of the benefits of open data, this innovation also creates problems along the journey that make it easy for detractors to undermine open data efforts—think the benefits of social media versus Facebook addiction.

For example, legislators passing open records laws might not have thoroughly contemplated that these records would be generally available—instantly—in near-real-time to anyone who requests that data. Is it OK to distribute a list of everyone who holds a pistol permit? Open records laws in North Carolina, where I live, seemed to imply "yes," but a local journalist got into fairly hot water when he planned to post the list and demanded that a sheriff provide these records in accordance with the law (Henderson and Steele, 2013).

What about the general freak out that government employees have when their salaries are published, in time-honored tradition, once a year in the local papers? Imagine the drama at any business when re-al-time salaries are publicly available for all employees. Someone inevitably ends up asking, "Why is Jane making a thousand dollars more a month than me?"

Change in general is hard, as those in IT and innovation understand very well. The seminal works on change—whether you're talking Chip and Dan Heath's *Switch: How to Change Things When Change is Hard* or John P. Kotter's *Leading Change*—are no less relevant to the open data movement than any other innovation.

In Asheville, North Carolina, where I work, building an awareness of the need for change among multiple groups was a key strategy for creating an environment that was supportive of the change. Despite potential new problems that could be created by the presence of robust open data, the lack of open data created significant problems as well.

All municipalities in North Carolina must respond to open record requests per the North Carolina General Statute, Chapter 132. Citizens, businesses, and journalists may all want access to government records, and the traditional process is painful for everyone. Here's how it typically goes:

1. The requester puts a request into a government department. As an illustrative example, let's say that it's business license data and that the requester contacts the city finance department.

2. In order for the request to be tracked and followed up on, the right place to contact is the public information office. (Many cities have found that when departments fulfill record requests on their own, the ball can sometimes get dropped—this is analogous to the modern day IT help desk, which serves to track service requests.) So, in our example, let's assume that the person in the finance department is on the ball and forwards the request to the Public Information Office (PIO) with no further delay. That's not always a great assumption.

3. IT or the government department pulls the requested data.

4. The city's legal function reviews the data to ensure that the city isn't breaking any laws in distributing the data. If certain data must be redacted (confidential, trade secret, secretary of state information, or other data specified in the law), they instruct IT to do so.

5. IT provides the final work product to the PIO, who then distributes it to the requester.

There are a lot of good reasons for this degree of scrutiny and time spent on the request, but the bottom line from my perspective is this: what if this was only done once for each dataset and future requests could be self-service? That was the primary pragmatic benefit we sought from our open data effort.

I am active in Asheville's startup and entrepreneurial community, so I learned that Asheville was home to a company located downtown whose business model depends on access to government records. The company, BuildFax, employs thirty-five people in our community. I spent some time with their CTO and learned that they had gone to extraordinary pain and expense to integrate the disparate record data into their product offering—essentially, property condition analysis for the insurance and mortgage industries. They faced boxes of printouts that needed to be structured, machine-readable data. It was an interesting example of what entrepreneurs in our community might face if they wanted to build value out of the public data our government stewarded.

I also have witnessed firsthand the quiet aggravation that journalists have when faced with delays in record requests, even when they are legitimate delays.

All of these circumstances were occurring in an environment where finding speculative funding for new projects was difficult. The thought experiment goes like this: "Should we do a project that may reduce staff time involved in record request fulfillment, or should we replace an aging patrol car?" As you would expect, and as is appropriate, urgent public safety needs should and do come ahead of IT innovation. So, in a pretty tight budget, these projects don't get funded.

There's another problem: when data is not available to the public, this actually means that government IT or an expensive vendor must do everything themselves. Civic hackers can't hack into data that they can't access, so how can they innovate? These people could code a project as impactful as Linux, but they can't even get started building for government.

Nobody wins.

In a world where nobody talks to one another about these problems, you could imagine the following insane scenario. Journalists and others complain to lawmakers about barriers to getting data from government. Lawmakers pass a burdensome law that cities have an obligation to publish a taxonomy of all data tables that are available. Journalists then ask for "everything," even though the law prohibits them from receiving "everything" (social security numbers, personnel records, certain law enforcement data, etc.). Then, system vendors declare their data taxonomies (sometimes called "data dictionaries") as proprietary and confidential information. Even when contracts are signed by vendors that refer to the state law, they require government IT workers to sign non-disclosure agreements if they want to gain access to the data tables. This is a truly insane rock and a hard place.

The problem is, this is actually how it often works (or doesn't work) in North Carolina.

In a world where everybody talks to each other about these problems, you could well imagine that folks who need something would simply identify what they need and that the different groups would work together to make it happen.

In our community, after a brainstorming meet-up with others from diverse organizations (a local broadband provider, an entrepreneurship group, local businesses, government, the Chamber of Commerce, an IT networking group), a team of organizers formed and launched a conference called Open Data Day (opendataday.com). The idea for the day was this:

- It would be a "big push" to introduce the problems associated with a lack of open data to citizens, journalists, business people, elected officials, and others in the community and region.

- It would clarify that open data is more than just a government IT or civic-minded individual's problem.

- It would feature national speakers from communities that had success stories surrounding the open data problem.

- It would act as a launch event for our city's open data portal.

- It would feature a hackathon that would act as proof of the concept of what could be possible by using the data on the open data portal.

- Above all else, it would make the problem of open data into a community problem, not just a city government problem.

In fact, we did exactly that. We brought in Code for America's Brigade director, Kevin Curry, as well as Robert Cheetham from Open Data Philly and Theresa Reno-Weber, who serves as Chief of Performance Improvement in Louisville, Kentucky. We launched a data portal. With ten community sponsors, twenty workshop speakers, and 130 attendees, it was a memorable event that created relationships and acted as a springboard for other open data and coding activities in the community (notably the formation of a Code for America Brigade—a group of volunteer civic hackers that meets on a regular basis).

I must emphasize that none of it would have happened if not for our community organizers. Because a diverse set of organizers were behind the event, it was perceived as a community event, rather than a city government event. That made a big difference in how it was accepted both at City Hall and by the community itself. (Who really wants to come listen to a city IT department spout off? Nobody, right?)

Many IT folks have a deep level of discomfort with citizen interaction. They leave it to the public information office, city council, or a neighborhood liaison. I don't think that this can create good outcomes in your community any more than you would have a good outcome for an internal city IT project by avoiding any interaction with internal departments. Business technology exists to serve line departments, of course, but ultimately, business technology exists to serve citizens. It is ridiculous to think that you can have a good citizen outcome if business technology leaders avoid interaction with citizens. Of course, in a large community, you cannot expect that you'll be able to interact with each citizen, so citizen groups are important.

Community organizers for our event came from citizen and business groups, and this contributed to momentum, publicity, attendance, and so on. One particularly important group—prior to the formation of a Code for America Brigade in our city—was the community's entrepreneurship group, Venture Asheville, which provided sponsorship, as well as visibility and credibility in the tech startup and coder community. "Meet The Geeks," a networking organization for IT people in town, was another important organizer group.

In terms of outcomes, the community's open data day effort resulted in:

- Journalists being able to candidly speak about challenges that they had in getting data.

- A lower fear level among local government staff regarding the opening of data due to a greater understanding about the consumers of that data and a greater understanding that the benefits outweigh the risks.

- Great local press coverage, which further educated the community (Forbes, 2012).

- A successful hackathon, with the winner being an app that mashed up data from bus routes and public art to steer citizens to visit public art via bus.

- A platform for the launch of a Code for America Brigade called Code for Asheville.

Challenges and problems naturally remain. Open data shows up so much in the ideological world that city staff can still be worried that participating in open data efforts could be construed as political activity (political activity for city staff is generally not allowed). Also, despite education, there's still confusion about the difference between an open record and open data. Technology and automation is never going to declare a record "open" if it is not open by law, but not every stakeholder understands that.

Sustainability

Our experience demonstrates that a "product launch" is an effective way to get the ideas about problems and solutions out into your community. It's easy for big bangs to fizzle out, though, so an ongoing effort is needed, no matter how you begin open data efforts.

It is obviously not sustainable or practical to publish all datasets immediately. It could also undermine efforts if there is a perception that government staff, particularly IT staff, is arbitrarily or capriciously picking datasets to publish—that is, that the government is acting unfairly.

As a natural partnership between the public information office and IT has emerged, we've used a three-pronged approach for open data publishing criteria. This makes sure that the politics and policy stay with elected officials, the publishing choices city staff makes are reasonable, and we are using our time well.

Pragmatics

Does publishing a dataset save staff time? Does it lower the burden of public record requests by automating a frequently requested or time-intensive dataset? Does it decrease the cost of government? Does it make the process easier for citizens? Does it contribute to a business goal of a citizen-facing business unit (for example, police, fire, or development services, to name a few)?

Participation

This criterion asks how many votes a dataset has on the open data catalog site. If two people want it, it's probably not a great candidate in a community of 85,000 citizens. We actually haven't had a nominated dataset receive strong support from the community. When there is clear support for a dataset to be published, though, we'll do our best to get it out there.

Policy

What does our governing board want? If our board says to publish a dataset that hasn't met the other two criteria of "pragmatic" or "participation" to publish, let's do it.

We feel that following these criteria take staff out of making policy decisions, while also not tying staff's hands or delegating everything to a very busy governing board.

The pragmatics criterion is really important. Most cities, especially those with populations under 100,000, don't have infinite resources. Creating self-service data where there is frequent time spent and creating opportunity for others to build on that data simply makes sense from an operational efficiency standpoint. Our data proves that open data saves IT, legal, and PIO time. We track unique events on the open data catalog (that is, we do not count if someone downloads the same dataset twice), and have seen pretty consistent growth from month to month. In 2013, we averaged 144 unique data catalog requests per month, which may not seem like a lot, but let's put that in perspective. Our old way of handling these requests would generally take at least thirty minutes per individual (if not several hours), so by the time legal, PIO, possibly the department, and IT touched the request, we're talking about two hours of fairly expensive and scarce staff time—at a minimum. Even if you were seriously conservative and assumed no legal or department involvement and just accounted for minimum levels of IT and PIO, that's around seventy hours of work for PIO and IT per month.

Really? Almost two weeks of work? Sure, before open data, we probably didn't have that much (indeed, early data showed about seventy catalog requests per month, meaning about a week of work if it was minimum and manual). We've made data more accessible, though, so folks no longer have a barrier to getting it. Therefore, more people are using it, without having to hire more staff to handle it. That's an important outcome as well.

Next Steps

Once you launch a data portal, drum up interest, and create conversations, it's my opinion that the right thing to do is back off a little bit.

This is hard (at least it was for me) because, as an internal advocate for something that you believe in, you've put a lot of work and time into it.

Let me be clear: this is not about backing off because you will have detractors. Any innovation garners its share of detractors, and, sadly, the misinformed citizen's "you-work-for-ME-personally" syndrome is alive and well amongst a vocal minority of citizens. Open data is no different. You will have detractors, and you will have to deal with them.

More importantly, though, there are others who have ideas and want to participate.

Don't stop leading internally. It's important to continue to communicate about the value of open data in the organization and continue to tell the story of how open data and self-service allows staff to focus on more meaningful work than manual data pulls.

Externally, when you create a little bit of a leadership vacuum by backing off just a little bit, you create opportunity. Natural leaders step up. In our community, a couple of government employees volunteer outside of work to help organize the Code for America Brigade (good for them, as well as the community), and more than a dozen non-government employees are also helping to organize, create code, arrange meet-ups, and so on. At least one university professor and one elected official stepped up into leadership roles in the 2013 National Day of Civic Hacking event in our city, called "Hack for Food."

The "Hack for Food" event challenged folks to solve community challenges: a lack of healthy foods in schools, getting healthy food to people who lack access, and ensuring adequate food supply for the region in case of a crisis. The publicity for the event did talk about open data, hacking, and code—all of which were useful tools—but it primarily focused on solving community problems.

The organizers chose a community priority that had previous governmental and community action surrounding it. For example, the Asheville-Buncombe Food Policy Council's mission is to "identify and propose innovative solutions to improve local food systems, spurring local economic development and making food systems environmentally sustainable and socially just." Also, Asheville's city council passed resolution No. 13-17 on January 22, 2013, that supports municipal food policy goals and an action plan around those goals.

The point: no matter what the community priority is, focusing on the priority and not just the tools is helpful in getting folks excited. When the leadership comes from the community, you can bet that something good will happen.

As the community starts to rally, I think that the best place for the internal open data advocate is as a bridge-builder or interpreter. After all, that open data advocate understands both worlds.

For example, not everything fits neatly into the pragmatics-participation-policy filter. When it doesn't, a little bit of bridging can help. In one case, Asheville's Brigade redeployed an open source budget transparency application called Look at Cook. This app is exactly the type of budget transparency app that ambitious government IT folks have been dreaming about for a decade, but could never fund when faced with other needs. It is squarely in the "want to" quadrant, and government IT spends most of their time in the "must do" and "should do" quadrants. The point is, assuming good intentions from citizens and the government; it's something that everybody wants.

The data for the app was not immediately available (and it was not immediately obvious that this dataset fit one of the criteria), but it was an open record, so the Brigade put in an open records request. The budget office was more than willing to provide data, but had some concerns about whether the data as it stood in the ginormous financial database would correlate to the published official records. They made a good point that budget data is always "point in time" and that the organizational chart doesn't always get reflected in the chart of accounts.

For example, when you reorganize Transit from being in Public Works to its own department or when you take IT out of Finance, all of a sudden your organizational chart doesn't match up to your financial chart of accounts in the system. It might take weeks or even months until all of the journal entries and modifications to the accounting tables are done. It generally takes a whole year to replace a financial system, since it's so complex. In order to present a correct financial picture in the budget book, a lot of work is needed to make sure that account X is included in the tally for department Y.

The answer in this case was to provide actual working documents that were used to build the official budget book.

This didn't solve everything by any means (though the app did get deployed), and there might be people who might argue that the point in time database would be interesting to dig into. This is a good example of how citizens and government staff speak a different language and have different perspectives. They need an advocate who understands and has compassion for both sides.

As with the general population, there are outliers in both government staff and citizens (just like there are the Bernie Madoffs, Mark Sanfords, and Anthony Weiners), but generally, we're talking about normal people simply trying to do their jobs and make a difference in the world. Government staff isn't (generally) trying to hide anything. Citizens (generally) aren't trying to play gotcha games with staff. Government staff is (generally) just prioritizing their work based on what their bosses want and what regulatory requirements and processes they're following. Citizens are (generally) simply trying to ask a simple question and get a simple answer. An open data advocate who understands both sides of the coin can help create more of a conversation and less of a series of demands and silence.

But the question then becomes, how come processes don't integrate the need for open data, and how come the bosses don't think open data is a good idea?

Well, I think that they will one day. President Obama's Open Data executive order issued in May 2013 is a great start for federal agencies. For cities, I think that there will be increased adoption as leadership begins to understand that there is significant efficiency to be gained by adopting open data practices and processes—as we've demonstrated in Asheville. As general practices, like procurement, start to integrate the need for a more efficient operation than mere "open records" into the process, open data will become an important requirement. What if

RFPs and RFQs mandated that vendors address "open data" requirements in their proposals from the beginning? Or offered the proposals in a form where it was easy to separate "proprietary by the state law definition" from "public record"?

The bottom line is that good leadership recognizes that wasting everyone's time on redacting, inspecting, and repackaging documents and data is a bad idea.

Good leadership will recognize the pragmatics of open data.

About the Author

Jonathan Feldman is Chief Information Officer for the City of Asheville, North Carolina, where his business background and work as an *InformationWeek* columnist have helped him to develop innovation through better business technology and process. Asheville is a rapidly growing and popular city; it has been named a *Fodor* top travel destination, and is the site of many new breweries, including New Belgium's east coast expansion. During Jonathan's leadership, the City has been recognized nationally and internationally (including the International Economic Development Council New Media, NATOA Community Broadband, and the GMIS Best Practices awards) for improving services to citizens and reducing expenses through IT innovation.

References

Forbes, D. (2012, November 15). Age of Access: Asheville's budding open-data push. *Mountain Xpress*. Retrieved from http://www.mountainx.com/article/46806/Age-of-Access-Ashevilles-budding-open-data-push

Henderson, B. & Steele, C. (2013, March 3). N.C. sheriffs wage fight over gun records. *The Charlotte Observer*. Retrieved from http://www.charlotteobserver.com/2013/03/03/3889773/nc-sheriffs-wage-fight-over-gun.html#.UiZBV2RATy0

North Carolina General Statutes, Ch. 132 (2013). Retrieved from http://www.ncleg.net/EnactedLegislation/Statutes/PDF/ByChapter/Chapter_132.pdf

PART II:
Building on Open Data

Editor's Note

Once government data has been released, what can it be used for and by whom? What are some of the emergent, and perhaps unexpected, applications? In this section, we hear from different users of open data—including entrepreneurs, journalists, community organizers, government employees, and established companies—and discuss examples of what these stakeholders have done with and learned from open government data.

We begin with Chapter 6 by Brightscope co-founders Ryan and Mike Alfred. Their story starts not with open data, but one step before that. In order to build their business, they worked with federal agencies to release and digitize scores of government records. Along the way, they not only created a successful company but also catalyzed an open data-friendly culture within their partner agencies. They share lessons learned for other entrepreneurs seeking to build businesses around government data and discuss the importance of data standards moving forward to reduce barrier of entry to new startups in this space.

In Chapter 7, we hear from another civic startup, SmartProcure, which has developed a model for transforming FOIA into a government improvement platform. Founder Jeffrey Rubenstein discusses how by aggregating, standardizing, and digitizing government purchasing data across jurisdictions, open data can actually become a tool to increase collaboration between government agencies and help them make more informed decisions.

In Chapter 8, we hear from Chicago-based reporter Elliott Ramos about a journalist's relationship with open public data. He describes how the surge of government data made available under Chicago's new open data initiative changed the way he reported on local stories and allowed for new kinds of storytelling to emerge.

Steve Spiker is the Director of Research for the Urban Strategies Council, an organization that has been supporting innovation in Oakland for almost twenty-six years and often uses government-held data for projects. In Chapter 9, he writes about how the city of Oakland's initial foray in open data has impacted the work of local community organizers and researchers—while also cautioning against overly optimistic views of an "open government" based on the release of limited data.

Finally, in Chapter 10, Bibiana McHugh of Portland, Oregon's TriMet agency writes about her experience developing a data standard for transit information with Google that is now used by hundreds of governments worldwide to make it as easy to get public transit directions as driving directions. She discusses the importance of public-private partnerships in bringing open government data to the platforms and services where people are already going for information.

CHAPTER 6

From Entrepreneurs to Civic Entrepreneurs

By Ryan Alfred and Mike Alfred

Introduction

My brother Mike and I never set out to become "civic entrepreneurs." We did not see ourselves as being a part of the "open government" community. We were simply trying to solve a real-world problem, and that problem required improving the interfaces to government data. In this way, I think our story is the story of many civic entrepreneurs.

In the fall of 2007, we were young (Mike was 26, and I was 24), ambitious, and looking for a way to make an impact. We had just started an investment advisory company called Alfred Capital Management. We were managing money for individuals and families in San Diego and working hard to build the company client by client.

A few months prior, our father, Mike Alfred Sr., had introduced us to one of his clients, Dan Weeks, who was an engineering manager at Hewlett-Packard (HP). He had hired our father for some legal advice related to his real estate properties. Dan presented a business plan to Mike and me that attempted to solve a problem that he and his HP colleagues were struggling: building sound investment portfolios within their HP 401(k) plans. It was clear that Dan was incredibly passionate about 401(k) investing. Mike and I liked his engineering background, but we did not think the idea was viable at first.

Through a series of brainstorming sessions over the following weeks and months—most involving a few whiskeys—the possibility of working with Dan to improve retirement plans took on a new life. These sessions turned out to be where BrightScope began to take shape. We felt we had what could be a big idea. By individually rating every company retirement plan in the US, we believed we would drive an overall improvement in the ability of Americans to retire. It was an ambitious goal, the impact of which would reach far beyond our current client base—and that appealed to us.

Defined contribution (DC) plans are a relatively new addition to the corporate retirement plan landscape, rising out of the Employee Retirement Income Security Act of 1974 (ERISA) as an elective retirement savings program for employees. Originally DC plans were thought of as supplemental to company-sponsored, defined benefit (DB) pension plans, but over time, the DC plan firmly supplanted the DB plan as the primary retirement savings vehicle for American workers. As a result, there has been a major shift in retirement responsibility from employer to employee. In a DB plan, the company makes the contributions and the investment decisions, but in a DC plan, these two responsibilities fall squarely on the shoulders of employees. Unfortunately, most employees lack the discipline to save enough for retirement and the skill to build a well-diversified portfolio.

As we researched these structural issues, we uncovered other problems with DC plans. We found voluminous literature on high retirement plan fees, articles about conflicts of interest between plan service providers and plan participants, and a general feeling that DC plans were not being operated in the best interest of participants. At that point, we knew the opportunity was not solely helping participants make smart decisions for themselves, but also in defining what makes a DC plan good or bad, so that we could inspire the companies who sponsor the plans to make them better. Our objective of helping millions more retire in dignity was really a big data problem, and the first step was tracking down the right data.

The search for data quickly led us to the Department of Labor (DOL). Every retirement plan in the country files a Form 5500 annually with the DOL. Think of the Form 5500 as a tax form listing the assets, contributions, fees, and other details of each employee benefit plan. Larger plans, those with more than a hundred participants, are also required to obtain an annual audit. The combination of Form 5500 and the audit reports represented a gold mine of information, but first, we would need access to the data, which would require interfacing with the federal government.

The data we were looking for was not available through the DOL website. A few data companies were selling the 5500 data, but they did not have the additional high-value data from the audit reports. The decision was made to visit the DOL's public disclosure room to ask for the data in person. At that point, we did what any entrepreneur would do in our position: wrote a business plan, raised a little bit of money from friends and family, and booked a flight to Washington, DC.

As it turned out, this was the beginning of our path to civic entrepreneurship with BrightScope. Though we never intended to build a business around "open data" and "open government," that was precisely what we were about to do.

When "Public Disclosure" Is Not Enough

Showing up at the Department of Labor for the first time was definitely a culture shock. We had been to DC several times before, but mostly to visit the monuments as students. We had never been to DC "on business."

I do not think you can overstate the difference between startup culture and federal government culture. Startups are all about speed—fast decisions and rapid development. In DC, you get a sense that everything happens slowly, and every decision is placed under the microscope. The professional staff at the DOL took their work very seriously, but they were held back by a lagging technology infrastructure and years of working through a slow bureaucracy to get work done.

We made our way through DOL security, and the staff directed us toward the public disclosure room. The public disclosure room itself is not much to speak of. It is a small, windowless room covered on two sides with bookcases filled with administrative staff manuals, advisory opinion letters, meeting minutes from advisory board meetings, and a whole host of other items that might be of interest to the public.

A desk lined the left wall upon entering. What appeared to be a

1990s-era IBM PC running a custom DOL version of MS-DOS sat on the desk. It was difficult to use and looked to be gathering dust. While this was the "public disclosure" room, we personally could not imagine many members of the public visiting the room, so the state of the computer did not surprise us.

By this point, Mike had realized that we would need to get some assistance from the DOL staff in order for this trip to be successful, so when an employee entered the room, he engaged him in casual conversation. Before long, both of us were standing behind the desk, looking over the staffer's shoulder as he dug through the DOL database in search of the documents we described.

After thirty minutes of searching, we found what looked like an audited financial statement for the first company we had been looking for. After confirming that the document was in fact open to public inspection, we printed a copy. We repeated this process for ten to fifteen companies, so that we could ensure that the data was consistently available. We ended up leaving with audit reports from some of the companies with the largest retirement plans in the US, including IBM and HP, as well as some smaller companies that our friends worked at—Google and Facebook. We were informed that the reports would cost fifteen cents a page, which we agreed to, and left the DOL feeling buoyed by the fact that the data existed to accomplish our goals.

Our initial excitement about the data was quickly replaced by frustration. Upon returning to San Diego and working our way through the first fifteen plans, we did a quick back-of-the-envelope calculation that with sixty thousand audit reports, an average of fifty pages per report, and a cost of fifteen cents per page, it would cost roughly 450,000 dollars to obtain the complete dataset for a single year. To top it off, the DOL clearly had no way to provide the reports to us in bulk, as evidenced by the manual way in which the DOL staffer had printed the first fifteen reports for us. There were also procedural hurdles. While the DOL instructed filers to avoid putting personally identifiable information (PII), such as social security numbers, on the filings, they would occasionally still find filings with this information and have to redact them. While these redactions were rare, they still caused the DOL to create a policy of manually inspecting every printed page before providing the printed reports to the public.

With little to lose, we put together a list of the sixty thousand plans for which we needed data and filed a formal FOIA request. Within a few weeks, we found ourselves on a call with the DOL FOIA staff. We were told in no uncertain terms that our FOIA request was one of the most onerous requests they had ever received. In hindsight, given their limitations at the time, this assessment seems fair. However, when data is the only thing standing in the way of building a business, it is not what you want to hear.

We managed to work out a compromise with the DOL in which they would print out hundreds of audit reports at a time, put them into boxes, and ship them to us. It was not a sustainable system, but using that approach, we collected enough data to produce our ratings and launch our initial DC plan ratings to the public—and thus, our company BrightScope became a reality.

From Adversaries to Partners

If forced to select a single term to define our relationship with the DOL up through early 2009, the word "adversarial" would certainly be appropriate. We were asking for data that was nearly impossible for the DOL to deliver without some fundamental procedural change investment in technology, yet we would not accept no for an answer.

That status quo of shipping boxes was still in place at the time we launched our public website. After initially choosing a launch date of January 19, 2009, we were wisely counseled to push back a week so we would not get lost in the news cycle of incoming President Barack Obama, whose inauguration was set for January 20th. The administration change seemed irrelevant to our business at the time, but when President Obama made his first order of business the release of his Memorandum on Transparency and Open Government, it grabbed our attention. The memorandum lacked formal teeth, but it was music to our ears:

> All agencies should adopt a presumption in favor of disclosure, in order to renew their commitment to the principles embodied in FOIA,

and to usher in a new era of open Government. (Obama, 2009)

Our business had quickly become heavily dependent on gaining access to public data, but our progress was in fits and starts, surging ahead when a new box of data arrived and then flagging when data was delayed or did not come at all. Almost overnight, we felt a new tune coming out of Washington, a drumbeat of voices intent on making data open, transparent, and accessible, and we felt this could only be good news.

While some felt that Obama's pledge did not cause any change, the DOL, to their credit, began to make steady progress in delivering on opening up their data. What started as the manual printing and mailing of documents transformed into the shipping of external hard drives with thousands of audits. This ultimately resulted in a bulk download utility that was accessible around the clock directly from the DOL website. We went from being constrained by data to having all of the data at our fingertips.

Meanwhile, our public ratings had begun to get serious traction. We received numerous write-ups in the *Wall Street Journal*, the *New York Times*, and other mainstream media, and the traffic to our 401(k) ratings pages was on an upward arc. Starting with just eight hundred plans rated at launch, we had reached fifteen thousand plans by October and thirty thousand plans by the end of December. To process this volume of documents, we brought on new engineers and hired and trained a team of data analysts. Our team quickly expanded from fewer than ten at launch to thirty by the end of the year.

Our relationship with the DOL has transformed over the years. We have spent a tremendous amount of time with DOL staffers and political appointees, who have always taken time out of their busy schedules to meet with us when we are in town. The relationship was facilitated by open government events, which allowed for more casual interaction and discussion of big picture objectives.

In November of 2012, our relationship with the DOL truly came full circle. Impressed with the work we had done analyzing the audit reports, the DOL signed up as a BrightScope client and began leveraging the data for a variety of purposes. What started as a contentious relationship has turned into a true partnership, thanks to the DOL embracing an open approach to data.

Finding Comfort in Transparency

The changed relationship at the DOL is thanks to a combination of a mindset shift on the part of the department and an adoption of technology to solve a business process challenge. They became comfortable with more of their data being open to public inspection, and they started viewing companies like BrightScope as partners in their mandate of safeguarding retirement assets for participants. In some respects, the DOL's new approach reminds me of the original description of the power of open government described in the influential paper "Government Data and the Invisible Hand" (Robinson, Yu, Zeller, & Felten, 2009). In the paper, the authors describe the limited role of government as requiring and enforcing appropriate disclosure, but stopping short of building interactive websites. This is instead focusing on opening up the data to the public so that the private market can engage with the data and ultimately drive its usage and interaction with the public:

> In order for public data to benefit from the same innovation and dynamism that characterize private parties' use of the internet, the federal government must reimagine its role as an information provider. Rather than struggling, as it currently does, to design sites that meet each end-user need, it should focus on creating a simple, reliable, and publicly accessible infrastructure that "exposes" the underlying data. (Robinson, Yu, Zeller, & Felten, 2009)

This way of thinking about government is not new, but it is a fundamental shift from how we traditionally think about government. Asking government to stay focused on data collection and distribution and leaving the building of websites and value-added tools on top of the data to the private sector might seem like chaos to some, but this approach has worked wonders, even within the private sector.

Open government thinker Tim O'Reilly (2010) describes this phenomenon as "government as a platform." BrightScope's plan ratings can be thought of as an "app" on a government platform, leveraging data from the DOL and SEC. Undoubtedly, firms like BrightScope and others will be able to build faster, take more risks, and combine the DOL's data with third-party data in more new, interesting, and cost-effective ways than the DOL could themselves. So, it makes sense for the DOL to focus on platformizing itself and taking advantage of the entrepreneurial energy and innovations of the private market.

Defining Open Data

While BrightScope started with DOL data, as we have grown we have gathered data and information from a variety of public sources, including the Securities and Exchange Commission (SEC), the Census Bureau, and the Financial Industry Regulatory Authority (FINRA). Through the process of identifying high-value datasets and integrating them into our databases, we have encountered all different types of public disclosure. At BrightScope, we are fond of saying that "public" is not a proxy for accessible, usable, or high-value. It is useful, therefore, to describe the best practices of how government agencies and departments currently disclose data and some of the issues their methodologies create. In addition, through this analysis, it is useful to have a common framework with which to evaluate the quality of the disclosure, both in terms of data openness and legal openness.

Technical Openness

When it comes to technical openness, our first belief is that releasing data in whatever state it is in is better than releasing no data at all. Startups have become remarkably adept at working with data and can usually develop processes to transform disclosed data into whatever form and format they need it in. That said, the lower the barrier to adoption, the more engagement you can generate around the data you are releasing.

The following framework comes from Cass Sunstein, President Obama's regulatory czar, and the author of *Nudge: Improving Decisions About Health, Wealth, and Happiness* and *Simpler: The Future of Government*. In a memorandum for the heads of executive departments and agencies on September 8, 2011, he describes a simple four-part test he uses to define "smart disclosure:"

1. Accessible: Free, online and in bulk

2. Machine-Readable

3. Standardized

4. Timely (Sunstein, 2009)

When we first started working with the DOL, the disclosure failed all four tests. The data was not accessible online; it was not available in machine-readable formats; it was not standardized; and it was certainly not timely due to a nearly two-year delay for processing. However, the new DOL disclosure satisfies two of the four requirements. It is available online, both file by file and in bulk for developers, and it is timely, being published within twenty-four to forty-eight hours of the disclosure being filed. The reports are not machine-readable, unfortunately, nor are they standardized, largely due to the fact that the reports are narrative attachments to a document (the Form 5500), so they still require processing. I would still give the DOL high marks for making the most of what they currently receive, though.

Legal Openness

Even once data is technically accessible, it must be open from a legal standpoint for it to be truly "open." The "Open Definition," as defined by the Open Knowledge Foundation, is perhaps the standard in defining legal "openness" as it relates to data and content. Their definition is simple:

> A piece of data or content is open if anyone is free to use, reuse, and redistribute it—subject only, at most, to the requirement to attribute and/or share-alike. (Open Knowledge Foundation)

Opening up data in this way, so that there are no limitations on use, reuse, and redistribution, can be tough to stomach for those with data. Some organizations with important consumer disclosures that they place on the web put strict legal limitations with how the information can be used. One example of this is the Financial Industry Regulatory Authority (FINRA). FINRA operates BrokerCheck, a website that provides tools for consumers to research brokers and broker-dealers. The BrokerCheck website has a prominently placed legal notice making clear its "closed" legal stance:

> The works of authorship contained in finra.org (the Site), ... may not be copied, reproduced, transmitted, displayed, performed, distributed, rented, sublicensed, uploaded, posted, framed, altered, stored for subsequent use, or otherwise used in whole or in part in any manner without FINRA's prior written consent. (FINRA)

This legal language is against the spirit of open government. While the data is online and technically disclosed, it is not legally open and that distinction is important. It is certainly understandable for an organization like FINRA to have concerns about how their data will be used. Ensuring that data is correctly communicated to and interpreted by the public is an important goal, but if that was the only blocking issue, I think it could be overcome. I fear that organizations like FINRA do not open their data because they are concerned with the potential negative impact. As described by Gavin Newsom in his book *Citizenville*:

> [Information] often ends up being used against them. Historically, people who request data or information aren't doing it because they want to solve a problem or create a program. They're often doing it for political purposes, as a kind of "gotcha government. (Newsom, 2013)

We in the open data community need to do a better job communicating why the benefits of releasing open data outweigh the potential negative effects. If we fail to make the case, some of the highest value datasets will either be legally closed or hidden from public view entirely, which would dramatically limit the potential of the open data movement.

Fortunately, I think many government agencies and departments have been able to clear this hurdle. The DOL undoubtedly had internal questions and concerns about the results of disclosing in a legally open fashion, but even with a small dose of engagement from the developer community, that disclosure has yielded huge benefits. Organizations that publish data under a closed license lose the opportunity to cut their costs and leverage the combined skills and abilities of web-savvy engineers and entrepreneurs all over the world.

Lowering the Barriers to the Next Generations of Civic Startups

At BrightScope, we spend a tremendous amount of time collecting, processing, and integrating the data we obtain from our government partners. We recognize, like most data companies, that data requires stewardship to ensure that the data quality is suitable for research, analysis, and public consumption. The challenge for a civic entrepreneur accessing data from the government is that, today, too much of their work lies in the behind-the-scenes discovery, cleansing, and matching across datasets and not enough in building the end tools for their users. By promoting data standards, we can ensure that the work we are doing as civic entrepreneurs and the money invested in our mission is funneled into the higher-value work of creating real tools for consumer decisions.

One example of this for BrightScope comes from the DOL filings. In order to calculate all of the fees consumers are paying within their 401(k) plans, we need to include the hard-dollar fees found directly in the Form 5500, as well as the fees coming from the plan's investment options. This combination of administrative and investment fees becomes what we call "Total Plan Cost." Fortunately, the investment lineup is contained in the audited financial statement. While the audited financial statement provides a list of investment options, it only requires the name of the investment and not an identification number for it. This makes it impossible to directly link the fund to data on mutual funds that is collected and disclosed by the SEC. As a result, BrightScope spends hundreds of thousands of dollars every year parsing out the fund names from the audited financial statement, matching the names to the correct SEC fund ID, and pulling in SEC fund fee data so we can effectively calculate each plan's Total Plan Cost. Each additional data transformation we make opens the door to introducing errors into our database. If the DOL were to simply require plans to file a standardized schedule of assets with the SEC fund ID, then BrightScope could take the hundreds of thousands of dollars we invest in our current process and invest it higher up the value chain instead. Across the federal government, there are literally thousands of examples where a lack of coordination across agencies and departments leads to lost opportunities to make mash-ups of government data tremendously easier for entrepreneurs.

A more prominent example of this phenomenon is all the data released every year across state and federal governments about individual companies. Information about their earnings is available from the SEC; information about their retirement plans are available from the DOL; information about their lobbying activity is available from the Senate Office of Public Records; information about their environmental record is available from the Environmental Protection Agency; and information about federal contracts they have won is available from the General Services Administration. Yet, there is no easy way to link all of these datasets together.

This is actually a broader issue that came to light during the financial crises, in which the debt of failing institutions was hard to track down, and thus, it was difficult for companies to gauge their "counterparty risk." This difficulty—and the rapidly declining risk tolerance of the firms in question due to liquidity concerns—caused a freeze in the OTC derivatives and, ultimately, the credit markets in which banks and others refused to lend because of concern about their existing exposures. This issue has led to calls from industry for an international Legal Entity Identifier (LEI) system in the financial markets. It is designed to handle the hierarchy problem—for example, it is estimated that AIG has over 250 operating subsidiaries and operations in 130 countries. The benefits of LEI are important:

> The Legal Entity Identifier (LEI) program is designed to create and apply a single, universal standard identifier to any organization or firm involved in a financial transaction internationally. Such an identifier for each legal entity would allow regulators to conduct more accurate analysis of global, systemically important financial institutions and their transactions with all counterparties across markets, products, and regions, allowing regulators to better iden-

tify concentrations and emerging risks. For risk managers in financial institutions, the LEI will increase the effectiveness of tools aggregating their exposures to counterparties. (The Depository Trust & Clearing Corporation, 2012)

While LEI is designed to solve a problem in the financial markets, it may also serve the open government community, provided it is either adopted throughout the government or utilities are built that provide mapping from the codes of each individual branch of government to the LEI. This is also not the only approach. Open government advocates, like Beth Noveck (a founder of ORGPedia) and the Sunlight Foundation, have taken the lead on advocating for a better approach, but there is still much work to be done.

Creating open source standards for identification and linking across datasets is not easy, but with every breakthrough, we lower the barriers to adoption of data for analysis and research. The benefits accrue to open data entrepreneurs and also to the very government agencies and departments tasked with regulating the companies, products, and industries that presently lack standards.

Closing Thoughts

While we did not think of ourselves as civic entrepreneurs when we started, our history is really a history of government as a platform and building a business on public data. When we first met and spoke with open government evangelists, like Tim O'Reilly, Jen Pahlka, Alex Howard, Beth Noveck, Laurel Ruma, and countless others, we began to realize how powerful an idea it truly was to provide entrepreneurs with data and access to government. BrightScope is proof that building a viable, for-profit business on top of government data can be a sustainable business model that both benefits government and provides enormous opportunities for entrepreneurs. Now, it is up to the open data community to work to lower the barriers to entry for future civic entrepreneurs.

About the Authors

Ryan Alfred is Co-Founder, President, and COO of BrightScope, a financial information company that brings transparency to opaque markets. Ryan is a noted expert and frequent speaker on financial industry regulation and is actively engaged in the debate in Washington DC about issues relating to retirement. Ryan was named to *Forbes'* Top 30 Under 30 in Finance (2012) and to the *SmartMoney* Power 30 (2011).

Mike Alfred is Co-Founder and CEO of BrightScope. Previously, Mike was the Co-Founder and Portfolio Manager of Alfred Capital Management LLC, an independent registered investment firm located in La Jolla, CA. He has been a Financial Advisor and Portfolio Manager since 2003. A noted and quoted 401k and financial expert, Mike has appeared on CNBC, ABC News, Fox Business News, National Public Radio and in the *Wall Street Journal*, the *New York Times*, *USA Today*, *Forbes*, *BusinessWeek*, and many others.

References

Financial Industry Regulatory Authority, Inc. (2013). Legal Notices. Retrieved from http://www.finra.org/Legal/index.htm

Newsom, Gavin (2013). *Citizenville: How to Take the Town Square Digital and Reinvent Government*. New York, NY: The Penguin Press.

Obama, B. The White House, Office of the Press Secretary. (2009). Freedom of Information Act. Retrieved from http://www.whitehouse.gov/the_press_office/FreedomofInformationAct

Open Knowledge Foundation. (n.d.). Open Definition. Retrieved from http://opendefinition.org

Robinson, D. G., Yu, H., Zeller, W. P., & Felten, E. W. (2009). Government Data and the Invisible Hand. Yale Journal of Law & Technology, 11, p. 160. Retrieved from http://papers.ssrn.com/sol3/papers.cfm?abstract_id=1138083

Sunstein, C. R. (2011, September 8). Informing Consumers Through Smart Disclosure. Retrieved from http://www.whitehouse.gov/sites/default/files/omb/inforeg/for-agencies/informing-consumers-through-smart-disclosure.pdf

The Depository Trust & Clearing Corporation. (2012, November 26). Legal Identity Identifier. Retrieved from http://www.dtcc.com/products/dataservices/lei.php

CHAPTER 7

Hacking FOIA: Using FOIA Requests to Drive Government Innovation

By Jeffrey D. Rubenstein

Turning FOIA On Its Head

> The Freedom of Information Act (FOIA) is a law that gives you the right to access information from the federal government. It is often described as the law that keeps citizens in the know about their government. (www.foia.gov)

Even according to the government's own FOIA website, FOIA is presented as a way for citizens to gain an advantage, but there are two sides to this coin. FOIA can be used as a tool to help government agencies help themselves.

Contrary to popular belief, Google doesn't have the answers for everything. FOIA requests, while typically presented as a way for citizens to extract information from the government, can actually provide the best pathway to help government agencies innovate, work smarter, and become more efficient.

There is an opportunity before us to use FOIA to benefit the government on a massive scale. FOIA is about more than transparency; it can be the basis for true collaboration.

The Problem: Disconnected Data Silos

We live in a world empowered by and accustomed to instant data, instant results, instant answers, and instant analysis. Unfortunately, for those in government, many agencies are forced to operate where the answers they need are either not available or difficult to track down.

Imagine traveling back to a time before smartphones, before mobile phones, before the internet. Suddenly, "Don't Stop Believin'" takes over your universe and your brain desperately wants to know the name of the drummer for Journey. As you reach into your pocket, you find your iPhone. Then, it hits you…there is nothing for your iPhone to connect to in this year, so there is no way to get this information easily. There is no Google to help you yet. You'll just have to wait until you can find the answer, and that may take some time and elbow grease.

When you're used to nothing but two or three clicks between you and the data you need (in case you were wondering, Steve Smith was Journey's drummer during their peak years), having to wait for answers feels horrifically inefficient. We've rapidly evolved from reactive receivers of information to proactive wielders of information.

Government agencies face much tougher questions than names of band members, and the stakes are much higher. Most government agencies do not yet live in a connected world, and they are forced to waste time, resources, and money simply due to the absence of easily accessible (and searchable) information.

This is not to suggest government agencies are devoid of technology; quite the opposite is often the case. The obstacle for most government agencies is not access to technology, but to actionable data. The government may be masters of collecting data, but it took the private sector to invent the masters of data insight and connectivity, such as Twitter, Facebook, and Google.

According to the most recent figures from the US Census Bureau (2012), there are 89,055 official governmental entities in the country. The vast majority of them have their own individualized systems and are, due to data silos, disconnected from other government agencies.

How Do Government Agencies Handle Purchasing?

An area that perfectly illustrates a stunning data disconnect is government procurement. The government, at all levels, has to buy everything; they do not make their own paper, desks, light bulbs, cables, computers, planes, tanks, or carpet. Everything the government needs, they have to purchase elsewhere from government contractors.

The purchasing process is primarily based on price thresholds, and the available pathways are verbal quotes, written quotes, bids, and RFPs (Request for Proposals). The following are examples of typical guide-lines, though each jurisdiction adopts variations and exceptions (most often for construction and IT projects, which have significantly higher thresholds):

- Less than $2,500: Obtain one verbal quote from a government contractor known to be competitive, and it is within the agen-cies' discretion to choose the winning contractor.

- $2,500 to $5,000: Government agencies are usually required to get three verbal quotes, and although low bid is the prevailing priority, these choices are also within the discretion of the pur-chasing agent.

- $5,000 to $10,000: A government agency would typically seek three written quotes. This is usually the highest price range that can still be decided by end-users.

- $10,000 to $25,000: Government agencies typically have to open a bid process, and then every registered (i.e. known) ven-dor gets notified.

- $25,000 and up: Government agencies usually must enter a budgetary action process and issue a call for bids and/or RFPs, which is sent to all registered vendors.

The overwhelming majority (more than 80%) of government purchases is found below the thresholds for formal bids and RFPs. Purchases for low-priced commodity items (laptops, printers, cables, paper, etc.) are usually what you'll find below the bid/RFP threshold.

What Does a Government Agency Want to Know When Purchasing?

When a government agency has a need for a product or a service, they aspire (though currently, rarely succeed) to have answers to the following questions:

- Best price: What is a competitive price? Who has the lowest price?

- Best value: Which vendors are the most responsible and reliable? Who offers the best quality and warranty?

- Choice: Are we reaching as many vendors as we can? Are we reaching out far enough to get the right vendor? (Note: Government agencies routinely cite finding the right qualified bidders as one of their biggest challenges.)

- Piggybacking Opportunities: Are there existing contracts out there that we could piggyback on for a lower price?

- Peer Feedback: What other government agencies have purchased this before and could give me useful insights? Who has existing RFP or bid language that we could use? (Note: Lacking knowledge about the product is another top challenge cited by government agencies, especially for technology purchases.)

- References: What other government agencies have had experiences with the vendors we are considering? Is there something we don't know?

How can a government agency answer these questions in a sector plagued with data silos? The best price may not be what is known locally or regionally, but nationally.

There are cooperative buying services that provide pricing research platforms, such as US Communities (http://www.uscommunities.org) and IPA (http://www.nationalipa.org/), but since inclusion is voluntary, these platforms only provide data from participating government agencies and vendors, and the information they provide does not answer all of the questions a purchasing agent needs to know to find the best value on all products and services they need to purchase.

The Current Challenges of Coordinated Government Purchasing Efforts

There has been no comprehensive database to find other government agencies with detailed purchasing history.

When purchasing agents are only required to get quotes from competitive vendors, without external validation, it can lead to the same vendors being used repeatedly. The nature of the process and the lack of resources typically lead to the same vendors being repeatedly called upon. What if a purchasing agent had access to every purchase made by every agency across the nation? Would they be in a better position to evaluate their purchasing options?

When a government agency must offer a contract through a bid or RFP process, the best vendors might be actively watching for RFP and bid notifications, or they might not. For the ones that do respond, they may provide references, but omit the bad references. There's been no way for government agencies to know about the references that vendors don't share, and there hasn't even been a way for them to know—with certainty—where the best value can be found.

Sole source procurement is another challenge for government agencies because, by definition, a sole source cannot be the best value; it is the only choice. However, sometimes a contractor is presented as a sole source, when, in fact, they are not. While a local search may not uncover this, a national search would have a higher likelihood for success. It could be that a similar product is offered by a vendor in another state. Other times, it could be that there is another (and possibly cheaper) distributor of the exact same product that could have been unknown to the "sole source."

The end result of these data silos is that a majority of government purchases are made at a higher price than the best available rate.

The data has always been available, but it wasn't connected or indexed. In millions of separate data files, the answers to everything a government agency would want to know could be found. Somewhere, a lowest price was entered into a document or spreadsheet. Somewhere, a government agency found a better way, a better source, or a better product that everybody needed to know about but never got shared.

Government Purchase History as an Open Data Solution

There is, however, one place that all government purchases (at all levels) are captured: purchase orders and purchasing cards. While less than eighty percent of government purchase activity uses a bid or RFP, effectively a hundred percent use a purchase order or purchasing card.

Purchasing data contains a wealth of information: date, buyer, seller, product descriptions, line-item pricing, quantities, and more. The problem, until recently, is that this incredible repository of actionable data—the purchase transaction data—existed independently from agency to agency. Most city, county, state, and federal agencies store their purchasing data in different formats and in different systems.

The idea for SmartProcure came from witnessing the same product being purchased at wildly different prices by different departments in the same city. This was a problem that could be solved with a proper database, but no such database existed at the time.

Thus the concept of hacking FOIA began. Instead of trying to build a process from scratch, it was more efficient to use an existing and accepted government practice (FOIA) and use that to proactively obtain purchasing data. Instead of relying on the government to pay for such a database, a decision was made to create the database at no cost to the government. Revenue would be generated from selling access to the database to government contractors. In this way, the government would get the benefit of every agency's data at no cost, and government contractors would gain access to powerful business intelligence.

FOIA requests have helped SmartProcure acquire nearly sixty million purchase orders (and counting) at the local, state, and federal level. Purchasing data is obtained from the government (voluntarily or through FOIA requests), which gets converted into a normalized and searchable format, and the data is given back to the government at no cost. SmartProcure was the first (and still the only) provider of a fully indexed and searchable database of government purchasing information.

Now, empowered by a searchable database of purchasing information from across the nation, government agencies are able get the best value. They can use the information to instantly see all data for every purchase of any product, identify who sells that product, and find the best pricing. They can get quotes from the best vendors, not simply the already-known vendors, as had been the case before searchable government purchasing data became available.

Paul Brennan, a purchasing agent for Rockland County in New York, was using purchasing history to research pricing for a current project. "I used SmartProcure to look for purchase orders for the pavement rollers we needed. I quickly found a contract in Texas at a much cheaper price than I could find here in the northeast, and I was able to piggyback on that agency's contract and purchase two of them at a savings of $30,000," said Brennan.

FOIA requests can help people in government agencies find the right person to talk to. For example, if a purchasing agent were tasked to purchase an unfamiliar item, it would help to talk to someone in another government agency who actually has experience with the item. The purchasing agent can search the purchase history database for the item, find a purchase order, and then look at the contact information for the purchasing agent. That goes beyond pricing data and takes it to connecting the people with the questions to the people with the answers.

Jason Phitides, a purchasing agent for the City of Jacksonville Beach in Florida, was faced with a daunting challenge. "I needed to purchase a 'beach dune walkover,' but I was new to the area and had no idea what it was. I used SmartProcure to search for the item, quickly found other agencies that purchased them, got the contact information for the purchasing agents, and I was able to talk directly to the people that could share relevant knowledge and experience," said Phitides. "Access to this data not only helps me find the best prices, but it helps me do my job better."

Access to other purchasing agents may help give content and context to RFPs that need to be written and released by another agency, thereby saving time and enhancing the quality and specifications included in the RFP. Except for highly unusual items, it is nearly certain that some agency has already done the research and created an RFP for just about any product or service.

When government agencies are separated by data silos, thousands of hours are wasted created new RFPs and conducting research, when a simple search in a purchasing history database could connect agencies in search of this content and research in just a few steps.

FOIA and Spending Analysis

The drive for best price and best value has led to an increase in government agencies needing to analyze their spending in extreme detail. However, with the barrier to entry being an expensive spending analytics platform and a custom feed of the agency's data on the regular basis, the momentum needed to start this type of program is usually not reached. With easy access to spending analytics using a platform similar to SmartProcure or others, a government agency can easily perform a detailed analysis.

An open purchase history database includes actual purchase data at the line item level, and that means government agencies can perform highly detailed spend analytics in seconds. Want to know how much was spent on paper towels? Pencils? Chairs? Staplers? It's easy when they've got the right data.

With an online purchasing database, even just one individual can instantly search all purchase history for any desired data, and easily generate reports. Government agencies—and the people who work in them—can save time, money, and resources.

A quick survey of SmartProcure's purchase history database found more than $4 million in purchase orders where government agencies paid an outside resource to help them analyze their own spending data. This is something that can be done for free with a government purchase history database, and that's a tangible example of how much the lack of information can cost the government.

FOIA and Crowdsourcing

We already know that crowdsourcing works in the public arena, and FOIA requests are a way to bring crowdsourcing to the government arena.

Using FOIA requests to gather, collate, and share information solves two enormous problems at once. First, government agencies want to do better, and they need the best resources to do that. Second, members of the public (e.g., commercial businesses) often have many ways they can help the government but are not connected in ways that allow them to effectively or efficiently help.

Major movements and major decisions for government agencies often have good data and oversight, but the ocean of micro-movements and micro-decisions can lead to a crippling "Latte Effect." With more than 89,000 government agencies hobbled by disconnected data, every time a printer is bought for 10% too much, or a ream of paper for $2 over the best available price, or when a purchasing agent is forced (unnecessarily) to rely on known local vendors and overpay by $30,000… these add up to an enormous collective drain on the economy.

Imagine the possibilities if more organizations found ways to connect solutions and problems by way of FOIA requests. FOIA requests can be used not only to save the government money, time, and resources, but also to connect them to better solutions and increase innovation.

Coordinated FOIA efforts can be a springboard to innovation, helping to build other products without the need to wait for government inertia. The nature of FOIA requests is that a government response is involuntary. One doesn't have to wait for government agencies to collectively decide to do something. You can use FOIA requests to break through the inertia that exists when developing a multi-agency solution.

A good business model using FOIA requests is to take government data silos (there are many to choose from), organize the data into a single searchable resource, then provide that information back to the government agencies in a way that connects them all to each other.

For any problem faced by any government agency at any level, rest assured that somebody, somewhere has an answer. You can use FOIA requests to connect the people with issues to the people with answers. Crowdsourcing with FOIA can provide unprecedented speed and precision.

"Momentum obstacles" plague any government agency stuck in a data silo. Coordinated FOIA requests can entirely sidestep the need for breaking through these obstacles. If no government agency has to pay, and the data brings actionable benefits, the crowd creates itself, and the benefits of crowdsourcing will flow.

Large-scale FOIA request provide a fertile ground for crowdsourcing. There are a billion separate data files that have captured details on activity and/or decisions at every level of government. If you connect them with FOIA you have instantly created a fully interconnected crowd of enormous size. With government purchasing data, for example, the crowd was there all along, but it took FOIA requests to bring everyone together.

Crowdsourcing is about creating a "master mind." The whole is much greater than the sum of the parts. An individual may not know the answer, but crowdsourced data will provide it in seconds. Crowdsourcing also allows large-scale projects to be broken down and distributed among multiple individuals and agencies, further reducing the inertia needed to be overcome to get a necessary—but difficult—project moving forward.

Crowdsourcing with FOIA can transform the more than 89,000 government agencies into a single organism. Each individual and each entity can not only find a good answer, but the best available answer. Not just a competitive price, but the best price. Not just a solution, but the best solution.

The hunger of the incoming generations to solve big problems with data and technology is palpable. In *Generation We*, Eric Greenberg and Karl Weber (2008) defined millennials as those born between 1978 and 2000, which represents 95 million people, making them the largest generation in US history. It is this generation that has grown up in the era of social media and crowdsourcing, and these are the tools that they wish to change government with.

In *US Politics and Generation Y: Engaging the Millennials* (2013), David Rank wrote:

> While the annual survey of our nation's college freshmen revealed a three-decade trend of declining political interest, hitting a record low in 2000, by 2006 more entering freshmen had expressed interest in discussing politics than at any point in the history of the forty-year survey, including the 1960s (HERI 2007). Studies concluded not only that the emerging generation was more politically engaged, but that we needed to recognize new forms of such democratic participation (Bennett 2007a; Dalton 2008; Zukin et al. 2006). (p. 6)

Instead of complaining about the lack of young, top tech talent going into government, a better solution is to leverage FOIA to build systems that pull the best talent into the government arena.

Bringing It All Together

It is time to change everyone's perspective on FOIA. It can be hacked to become a powerful force for positive change by the government and for the government. It's not just about uncovering secret information, as is typically stereotyped. It can also be (and should be) about connecting disconnected information in a way that everybody can benefit.

Recently, there has been an explosion of organizations that have aggregated data to help local governments, and some have been successful in spreading their concept to multiple cities. Hacking FOIA, though, is about taking all of this to the next level. It goes beyond solving a local problem, a county problem, a state problem, or a regional problem. Hacking FOIA goes beyond a singular focus on police departments, or fire departments, or public works, or IT.

Such efforts are laudable, and they should absolutely continue. But hacking FOIA is about solving big national challenges all at once with coordinated data, and at all levels of government using existing processes. It can be done, and is being done.

About the Author

Jeffrey D. Rubenstein is the founder and CEO of SmartProcure. Jeff is an accomplished senior executive responsible for building successful technology companies, most recently building and selling Advanced Public Safety to Trimble Navigation Ltd. (TRMB). Jeff is an attorney, auxiliary law enforcement officer, and has spent his career working with government organizations. He is passionate about leveraging data to build efficiencies between the public and private sector.

References

Greenberg, Eric H., and Karl Weber (2008). *Generation We: How Millennial Youth Are Taking Over America and Changing Our World Forever.* Emeryville, CA: Pachatusan.

Rankin, David M. (2013). *US Politics and Generation Y: Engaging the Millennials.* Boulder, Colo: Lynne Rienner Publishers. https://www.rienner.com/uploads/50b90f1f69e38.pdf

United States Department of Justice. "FOIA.gov - Freedom of Information Act." Accessed September 16, 2013. http://foia.gov

CHAPTER 8

A Journalist's Take on Open Data

By Elliott Ramos

Journalists are bad at math. No, really. We're really bad at math. The joke goes that we all went into media because we're unable to figure out the proper tip on a restaurant check.

Nonetheless, data is not foreign to reporters. We regularly comb financial reports to pump out quarterly earnings or interpret annual municipal budgets. At times, governments, nonprofits, and researchers are kind enough to do the heavy-lifting for us, providing executive summaries, bullet points, and numbers, broken out into figures that can easily be turned around on deadline. In larger newsrooms, there are teams that specialize in computer-assisted reporting (CAR). They may work with graphics and application teams to crunch numbers and visually display them, utilizing interactive graphics, maps, and charts.

I was lucky enough to have worked at places like the *New York Times* and the *Wall Street Journal*, which had graphics editors and special projects managers who coordinated with reporters and editors on long-term projects. These were often the stories that would run on page one and were given additional resources from photo and graphics departments.

Such stories are the news analysis items, features that would be referred to in-house as a "tick tock." While the story carries the byline of one or two reporters, there is often a large team of contributors, some of whom appear with production credits on interactive graphics that are produced and paired with the piece.

News analysis items allow media organizations to break away from the day-to-day rush of breaking news and concentrate on a story to extrapolate the information and get to the underlying reasons for a policy being enacted. These types of stories examine relationships over a period of time to unearth new information or contextualize data that, at first glance, seems too obtuse to the general public.

While recounting personal and dramatic narratives is always a focus, obtaining documents and records is just as important. Big data projects are nothing new to newsrooms. Some of the more renowned ones would end up winning awards and prompting government action or public outcry. The *Sun Sentinel* won a Pulitzer Prize for public service this year for its series on speeding cops, which utilized a database of transponders to determine that many cops were averaging speeds around or in excess of 120mph, posing a significant safety risk (The Pulitzer Prizes, 2013; *Sun Sentinel*, 2012)

Investigative and special projects teams at news outlets can analyze data that is extrapolated from computers or with pencil and paper. While many news outlets are coping with diminishing staffs, reporters and editors have adapted, utilizing workshops and conferences to learn data and digital skills to aid in their reporting. At WBEZ, the Chicago-based public radio station where I work as a data reporter and web producer, we've invited some of these individuals to train and educate our news staff on working with new tools, analytics, and large data.

News organizations (if they have the money) will sometimes employ researchers and database analysts who assist reporters in making sense of government reports, budgets, and almost everything that is obtained painfully via Freedom of Information Act (FOIA) requests. More often than not, reporters will wait tirelessly for a FOIA request, only to get a PDF or paper file, instead of an electronic file, with blacked out portions of police reports, instead of vivid accounts—and sometimes an outright denial, which requires an exhausting appeal.

That's just for the hard-to-get information, though. If a reporter needs a quick figure or the name of a city vendor, it requires calling a public affairs officer, who has to track down an employee to look up said information. It's absurdly cumbersome and makes it harder to have fleshed out details on deadline, much to the chagrin of stressed journalists.

Fortunately, the access to some of that information is now changing.

I experienced firsthand the effects of this shift on journalism when I moved back to Chicago just as the city's open data movement was taking off. As a bit of background, I'm a Chicago native. Born on the West Side, I resided in the largely quiet Northwest Side neighborhood of Jefferson Park, attending Catholic school on the city's North Side in the Lake View neighborhood.

I attended Columbia College in 2002, majoring in journalism with a concentration on news reporting and writing for newspapers. I was an intern web producer at Chicago's CBS affiliate in 2004, a reporting intern at the Chicago *RedEye* in 2005, and a multimedia intern at the *Chicago Tribune* before graduating in 2006. After graduating, I had an internship as a web producer at the *New York Times*, and in 2007, became a senior web editor for the *New York Daily News*.

Eventually, I found my way to the *Wall Street Journal* (WSJ), where my responsibilities varied from producing web content, managing the homepage, and growing the paper's online news presence over the weekends. My responsibilities eventually evolved to include the production of mobile applications.

In the summer of 2010, I was leading a lot of the production for the WSJ's iPad and mobile apps and helped test and launch the international editions for the paper's Asia and Europe iPad editions. Working at the WSJ was a lot of fun. The paper evolved at a fast pace to catch up from being a paper that focused on long-form, "day after" news to one that had to keep pace with financial news competitors that put a premium on the speed of proprietary information.

Chicago is a hard city to leave, though, and I felt the need to return to my hometown in 2011, finding a place at WBEZ, the public radio station I spent much of my college nights listening to while banging out stories for my reporting classes.

During my first year back, I had to reacclimatize to Chicago's news scene. I was lucky that I was coming home under a new mayor, which meant all of Chicago's reporters were starting fresh. Mayor Rahm Emanuel wasted no time in shaking up the city's departments with a flurry of new appointments, which included the creation of the city's first Chief Data Officer and Chief Information Officer, a role filled by Brett Goldstein.

Goldstein and his newly formed Department of Innovation and Technology was quick to tap into the active group of civic hackers and developers, some of whom authored a smattering of blogs that relied on manual data collection at times. One worth noting is streetsblog.org, which was run by a civically active biker named Steve Vance. Vance blogs about transportation and biking issues, but has also created and hosts a number of GIS files, which includes bike crash incidents and bike routes.

Goldstein's employees would actively ask civic developers what they needed. Those developers would start projects, but then say they needed a particular map file or dataset. Goldstein's department would then set into motion the release and automatic updates of those files via the city's data portal site.

I turned my attention to the issue of crime in the city at the same time all this information was released. There was a noticeable uptick in violent crime that year, and news organizations began to capitalize on mapping applications to aggregate crime data. *RedEye* reporter Tracy Swartz made a notable effort by manually compiling data from the Cook County Medical Examiner on homicides in the city.

The data was obtained the old-fashioned way: retrieving reports, which she then compiled into tables to list victim names, age, race, and gender, as well as the occurrence and times of crimes. That dataset allowed the *Tribune* (*RedEye's* parent company) and others to visualize where Chicago's murders were happening, parse it by date, and note whether it was by gunshot or other infliction.

That same year, Goldstein's department began to compile and release datasets, which included crime stats and the city's GIS map files. I was relatively new to mapping at the time. While at the *Wall Street Journal*, my interactions with mapping involved updating paths of hurricane maps or the locations of restaurants the paper had reviewed. That summer, though, there were highly publicized robberies and violent assaults in Chicago's gay entertainment district, called Boystown. I utilized the crime data, with the help of my intern Meg Power, to map out violent crime in the neighborhood.

While there was an increase in robberies, overall crime in the neighborhood was roughly the same or decreasing year after year. You wouldn't be able to tell that from the city's news coverage. A viral video of a fight and consequent stabbing that injured one person on the Fourth of July weekend had news vans parked in front of gay bars for a week.

There was a certain level of hyperbole that would trump crime data at times as a spat of "flash mobs" garnered attention from even national news outlets. The *Wall Street Journal* ran the headline "Chicago Police Brace for 'Flash Mob' Attacks." I covered a contentious town hall meeting on policing, where one resident, clad in designer clothes, described the flower-festooned streets of Chicago's Lake View neighborhood as a "war zone." In the summer of 2011, there were moments where cellphone robberies on the CTA transit were being shared on social media en masse by news outlets.

Both officials and residents would cite data, but interpret it differently. In regards to the city's homicide numbers, does one count a death of an individual by a CPD officer? In regards to crime on CTA, do you count crimes at bus stops? Or do you include all crime or only violent crime as the CTA and police have? (See Ramos, 2012; 2013.)

There were times when crime data was the story ahead of the people affected. I've heard police officials cite homicides using the terms like "down this quarter over last year," as if the city were reporting quarterly earnings to investors. I would see similar reports from news outlets, which would use murder tallies as the main emphasis in lieu of reporting on the social issues that caused the crime. WGN TV recently reported on how the media covered the city's homicides. One of the interviewees coined the term "scoreboard reporting," alluding to regular roundups done by outlets for weekend violence: eight shot last night, eight shot in Roseland, eight shot in Englewood (Hall, 2013).

In 2011, it was surreal to see seasoned newspapers and TV stations respond to relatively minor crimes—long a part of Chicago's fabric—as if a mugging was something new. Some were making Twitter updates in high frequency in order to be the first, capitalizing on the referrals to their websites—and therefore, increased pageviews.

I've personally been a vocal critic about this practice, as it ignores the very real possibility of stoking hysteria and does little to inform the public about the underlying social problems contributing to the crime. I'm not at all saying that crime reporting shouldn't be done, but I take issue with a series of retweets about a person getting their iPhone or iPad stolen before the facts of the case are known.

The result may cause officials or police to rush an effort. It may cause hyperbole, often racially charged, to boil in the ether of social media, when the facts are not yet known. Such was the case when a woman made up a story about being robbed of $100,000 worth of jewelry on Michigan Avenue (Sudo, 2013). One former Cook County Prosecutor recently resigned, alleging she was demoted when she dropped charges in a flash mob case that received a negative media backlash (Dudek, 2013).

That winter, I found another use for mapping as the City Council began to redistrict the boundaries of Chicago's fifty wards. I needed to show the public how the current ward map looked and then do a comparison with the proposed changes. I was easily able to pull the map file from the city's data portal site and post to WBEZ's website by way of Google Fusion Tables, which allowed me to label each of the locations with the ease of editing a spreadsheet.

Getting the map files of the proposals being considered was a bit harder. Those files were not available or posted publicly by the City Council members. What the public did have access to was a massive ordinance proposal that ran dozens of pages. Those ordinances were automatically generated by cartographer software and weren't entirely meant to be read—or make sense—to the general public.

Here is an excerpt of the ordinance text defining part of the boundary of the 13th ward:

> ...Central Park Avenue to West 65th Street; thence east on West 65th Street to the Grand Trunk Railway; thence south along the Grand Trunk Railway to a Nonvisible Linear Legal/Statistical

Boundary (TLID:1 12050833) located between West 74th Street and West 75th Street; thence west on the Nonvisible Linear Legal/Statistical Boundary (TLID:112050833) located between West 74th Street and West 75th Street to South Pulaski Road... (Office of the Chicago City Clerk, 2012)

Some of the descriptions ran as long as five pages for a single ward.

With the help of our political reporter Sam Hudzik, I was able to obtain many of the GIS files necessary to create a series of maps that outlined the proposed changes. We were given the files by the caucuses of aldermen and outside groups, who put forth proposals but were unable to get the revised and eventual approved version from the Council's Rules Committee. The Rules Committee was the body that was involved in the real negotiations about how the city wards were being redrawn. They were unable to provide updated map files because they were constantly changing them all the way up to the final hours of approval.

They even approved the map, knowing that the ordinance, produced largely by software, was littered with errors (so many that an amendment was passed months later to correct the remap). That amendment was fifty-eight pages long.

Oddly enough, in a conversation with a spokeswoman for the city's clerk's office, there was no mandate for the aldermen to make electronic maps available. This is because the laws governing the redistricting weren't updated to account for the use of electronic mapping (even though the aldermen were using GIS mapping to redraw the wards). The fact that I still needed to work with outside sources to obtain files or even file as many FOIAs as I do, explains why some reporters have been skeptical of open data.

In Chicago, reporters have had and currently do have to box with city departments to obtain proprietary data. I had to go a few rounds with the police department when I tried to obtain electronic map files of its gang territory map. The Chicago Police Department originally denied my FOIA request and, after getting it appealed, still gave me the files in flat PDF format. I redrew the entire map manually from the PDFs.

I've talked with colleagues at WBEZ and other news outlets that down-right do not trust the data available through the portal site. Others who do trust it, say they've found it useful, but that a lot of the information they would need is not there.

Do I need to figure out the race or age of a homicide victim? I would have to call the Cook County Medical Examiner's office. Where do I find out the details of an armed battery? Chicago's data portal will tell me when and what block the crime occurred on, but I would still need to call the police to find out who the victim was, if that information was even public.

Many will try to tell a story or narrative, but the information they need might be classified due to privacy concerns, or it might not yet have been cleaned up in a machine-readable format from legacy databases. Typos, formatting errors, and other problems within datasets can make reporters question the accuracy or reliability of using data portals.

For me, that's where it becomes interesting.

What I and other reporters who work with data have realized is that government data is fluid, and the idea of getting information that can account for city functions with a hundred percent accuracy is not there. This also means that when a PR person gives us figures for a story, they are quite literally using the same data. The reporters, however, can put the onus of that accuracy on the agency they're quoting, thus leaving the integrity of the reporter and the news outlet intact.

There are times a FOIA request can be denied because the data request is deemed burdensome. And for some, the reporting stops there, and a sentence is tossed in a story saying the data was unavailable. But it might be a little more nuanced than that. If you're a data nerd, you understand things like database migration, categorizations, and legacy platforms. If you can actually get in touch with a human being who can discuss the nuances or differences between a city department's old and new systems, then a reporter can narrow a request, obtain the raw data, clean it up, and present the differences to the public. An intern and I encountered this with the city's towing data, having to refine messy cells with misspellings and typos into a set of two hundred or so categories, down from over a thousand.

When I do my own data analysis, it can be fear inducing, especially when the data is used to explain complex stories. While the data can be as accurate or as whole as the city can make it, the interpretation of that data relies entirely on me. It's a pretty hard limb for any reporter to climb. There's no news media method of peer review, unlike when a reporter quotes figures or stats from an academic study. While there are forums like Investigative Reporters and Editors (IRE), there's no apparatus in place for journalists to share data, for fear of being scooped by a competitor, compromising those coveted pageviews.

I found that I had to start writing my stories with lengthy methodologies or even explain that it wasn't possible to get an up-to-date record, but that what was available still conveyed an overall trend. This was the case when I mapped out abandoned properties and vacant lots to measure the city's urban blight as juxtaposed to public school closings.

Once, I had to report on the effectiveness of Chicago's recent pot-ticketing program, which was touted as a way for police to focus on violent crime and not lock up nonviolent drug offenders. The ordinance said that pot possession under fifteen grams could be a ticket, but the arrest data the city tracked could only identify amounts above or below thirty grams.

WBEZ isn't a stranger to using data. The station has teamed up with outside groups to gather data for use in its reports. Catalyst, which covers education in Chicago, often teams up with WBEZ to analyze Chicago Public Schools data.

WBEZ is a public radio station, which is a lot different than working at a corporate newspaper. Public radio stations regularly partner with other nonprofits and community groups.

In that spirit, it's through a partnership with the Smart Chicago Collaborative and the Chicago Community Trust that WBEZ began to formalize its data journalism effort. The Smart Chicago Collaborative is a civic organization, which believes it can use technology to enhance the lives of those in Chicago.

They approached the station about doing more data-based journalism. In turn, they would provide a grant that would assist us financially with resources for the project.

Daniel X. O'Neil is the group's executive director. He's been instrumental in connecting the station to resources we didn't even know we needed. On the technology end, we've been slowly building up infrastructure that would give the station's journalists a toolset to aid their reporting. O'Neil also helped connect WBEZ with the data community, which included developers and data scientists. They would lend their expertise, coming into the station and giving training sessions about how to handle and interpret data.

As I started to cover the use of data in the city, I found it to be the most unusual thing I've ever come across. City officials usually work with nonprofit groups for city improvement projects. Aldermen, police, and transportation officials regularly meet for community feedback on city projects, but the way that Goldstein's department interacted with the open data community in Chicago was downright surreal for a reporter.

They were attending hack nights and responding to emails or Tweets faster than most city employees I've ever seen. They even take my phone calls directly when I find an error in a dataset. It was downright unsettling to be talking with city officials, saying it would make reporters' lives easier if we had a particular dataset regularly, then having them respond with, "Let's see what we can do to get you that." My imagination internally cuts away to Star Wars' Admiral Ackbar screaming, "It's a trap!"

While I'm sure that Mayor Emanuel is not going to launch a counter-offensive against the rebel forces of the data community, I'm left wondering what the limitations of data are when information is not entirely available in a machine-readable way.

There is a litany of privacy issues when it comes to health departments releasing datasets on patient information, as well as when police departments release information on crime victims. Also, as one of Goldstein's employees put it, cities don't really deal with a lot of personal data, only incidents and locational data.

This means that while it's helpful to get CTA ridership breakdowns and totals for trains and buses, I'm not expecting a situation where the CTA's security footage is regularly opened up to the public.

A listing of city vendors, contracts, and employee receipt reimbursements is a vastly helpful resource, but a considerable amount of reporting is required to contextualize it. I am regularly pairing datasets from the portal site with datasets obtained via FOIA.

Part of the problem is that this is still relatively new territory. For Chicago's program being a fairly recent development, we're in a lot better shape than other municipalities I've seen. I tried finding similar datasets that Chicago has on other city data portals and was unable to find matching records.

Also, reporters must get more involved with the city in releasing sets. Often, the city won't know that an obscure set is useful or has intrinsic news value unless it's brought to their attention.

I'm also worried that some news outlets, which may be pressed with fewer resources and greater demands to churn out content, may not spend time to contextualize the data. There can be the temptation to take a cursory top ten list of a particular dataset because it's easy to write a story on deadline that involves plucking a number from the data portal site and fitting a few quotes around it.

That said, there still is a great amount of work being done by some tireless reporters in this city and beyond through the use of data. We're in the middle of an information renaissance, and while privacy is a very real fear, giving the Fourth Estate the ability to match a government's ability to process and analyze data may even the odds.

About the Author

Elliott is a data reporter and Web producer for WBEZ, a Chicago-based public radio station. Elliott focuses on reporting from enterprise feature stories to data visualizations. He previously worked as a web editor at the *Wall Street Journal*, where he specialized in managing breaking news online and the production of iPad, Android, and mobile applications as the paper's mobile platform editor. Prior to that, he was a senior Web editor at the *New York Daily News* and interned as a Web producer at the *New York Times*. Elliott graduated from Columbia College Chicago in 2006 with a B.A. in journalism, having interned at the *Chicago Tribune*, *Chicago RedEye*, and WBBM CBS2 News. Elliott is a Chicago native, hailing from the city's Jefferson Park neighborhood.

References

Dudek, Mitch (2013, August 6). Prosecutor says she quit after demotion for dropping charges in 'wilding' case. *Chicago Sun-Times.com*. Retrieved from http://www.suntimes.com/21770721-761/prosecutor-says-she-quit-after-demotion-for-dropping-charges-in-wilding-case.html

Hall, Gaynor (2013, June 24). Media and Violence in Chicago. WGN TV website. Retrieved from http://wgntv.com/2013/06/24/media-and-violence-in-chicago/

Office of the Chicago City Clerk. (2012). Amendment of Title 2, Chapter 8 of Municipal Code on Redistricting of City of Chicago Wards.

The Pulitzer Prizes. (2013). The 2013 Pulitzer Prize Winners. Retrieved from http://www.pulitzer.org/works/2013-Public-Service

Ramos, E. (2012, December 28). Chicago police confirm 500 murders in 2012. WBEZ 91.5 website. Retrieved from http://www.wbez.org/news/chicago-police-confirm-500-murders-2012-104615

Ramos, E. (2013, February 28). CTA, Sun-Times get in data fight [WBEZ web log]. Retrieved from http://wbezdata.tumblr.com/post/44257873024/cta-sun-times-get-in-data-fight

Sudo, Chuck (2013, May 17). Police: Woman Made Up Michigan Avenue Robbing Story. *The Chicagoist*. Retrieved from http://chicagoist.com/2013/05/17/police_woman_made_up_mag_mile_robbe.php

Sun Sentinel. (2012). Speeding Cops in South Florida (data file). Retrieved from http://databases.sun-sentinel.com/news/broward/ftlaud-CopSpeeds/ftlaudCopSpeeds_list.php

CHAPTER 9

Oakland and the Search for the Open City

By Steve Spiker

At the center of the Bay Area lies an urban city struggling with the woes of many old, great cities in the USA, particularly those in the rust belt: disinvestment, white flight, struggling schools, high crime, massive foreclosures, political and government corruption, and scandals. Despite these harsh realities, Oakland was named among the five best places in the world to visit in 2012 by the *New York Times*, something we were simultaneously excited about and stunned by. Oaklanders are proud of our heritage, our diversity, our legacy of great musicians, great food, and amazing art, and our truly beautiful city by the bay.

We're not huge like Chicago, New York, or San Francisco—megacities with large populations and a corresponding large city staff. We don't have a history of prominent leaders in the open government movement. Still, we're on the bumpy, exciting road that open data lays out. This road has many possible paths for our city—some lead to truly open government, and some lead to only minor improvements and "openwashing" (referring to the practice of publishing a few datasets and suggesting the government has therefore achieved openness and transparency).

Our journey shows why open data matters to a city with big troubles and how something as geeky as public records access supports a positive transformation in our city—for everyone, not just for us geeks.

The Start of Open: The Conviction Phase

The event that changed my thinking and changed my organization toward "open by default" was as unexpected as it was transformative. I've had the privilege to work at the Urban Strategies Council since immigrating to the USA in 2006. The Council is a social justice nonprofit that strives to support equity in urban communities and in policies that impact low-income communities, mostly communities of color.

A winding road led me to this exceptional organization. I started out as a land surveyor and planner in the private sector, dabbled in IT consulting in London, then landed in public health, working in spatial epidemiology. In the private sector, I got to interface with government in order to access and submit data ranging from suburban plans to large engineering project data and satellite imagery. Following that, I spent some years in the Western Australian Health Department, where I helped to establish a statewide spatial database to support our workforce and to enable public interfaces into government data. Here, I got to experience the empire building and data possessiveness I've railed against in the years since. In this job, I gained firsthand knowledge of what it's like to create, manage, and be responsible for government data. There I experienced both the desire to control and restrict access to "my data" and the knowledge that this restricted data can do so much more when others have access to it. That job demonstrated a great conflict between securing and managing confidential data and supporting easy access to it.

As I was leaving this role, I was struck by the realization that even after years of dealing with data, people in our department still didn't know our team existed and was available to serve them. In later years, I've realized that this is symptomatic of most government agencies: we do a terrible job of communicating. Our governments are not just struggling to be open and accessible to the public; they also fail to do this well internally.

At the Urban Strategies Council, we have a long history of supporting data-driven decisions in local government, community engagement, and the nonprofit community. In order to do this, we've maintained our own data warehouse to allow us to perform very action-oriented social research and spatial analysis. We negotiate access to government data (often paying dearly for the privilege), we sign non-disclosure agreements, we scrape the data, and sometimes, we're lucky enough to easily find what we're looking for online. We even have a formal goal to support the democratization of data. Like most of our partners in the National Neighborhood Indicators Partnership (NNIP), we've done this through building web mapping platforms that enable policy makers, organizers, and the general public to access complex data in simplified systems in order to support broad use of this data. Like most other organizations, our presumption was that because people always call us asking for custom maps, we needed to give them the tools to make them too. This is a fair response, if slightly disconnected from those others' reality. Oftentimes, people will ask us for raw data. Sometimes, we have permission to distribute data, and sometimes, we can justify the staff time to publish or send the data to those asking, but often, we cannot deliver due to a combination of those two factors.

A rather ordinary meeting of the Bay Area Automated Mapping Association (BAAMA) triggered my change of heart about open data. A Canadian firebrand named Paul Ramsey, who built a great open source spatial database tool we use, called PostGIS, finished a presentation with a slide that boldly declared: "Your use of data is not necessarily the highest use of those data."

This one simple statement gave me the conviction to enable others to do good, to understand issues, and to easily find data and leverage it. It struck me that every time we don't make data openly available, we are limiting some other great improvement from happening. Every time we burn through project funds trying to track down and beg, borrow, or scrape data, we are in fact perpetuating the very thing that we regularly complain about from our government. It was suddenly clear that when we set out to rebuild our mapping and data visualization platform (see http://viewer.infoalamedacounty.org), we had to plan to open our data at the same time. When our new system launched in 2012, we were the first, and I think still the only, system built on an ESRI base that allows users to easily download both our geographical data and the raw data behind the maps. We paired this interface with a cobbled together data portal to help users find our cleaned, value-added raw data too. My reasoning was that if we'd used funders dollars or government contract dollars to acquire, clean, and geocode the data, then we should really be making more use of it than we could by keeping it locked away.

Many of our type of nonprofit or university think tanks face the same issue: we've collated incredible amounts of public and private data, yet we really don't have the funds and staff to take full advantage of it all. I grew increasingly frustrated with this reality; we spent days getting data and doing a single project with it, perhaps reusing it a few times, but the true potential of the data was clearly not being realized. In opening our data, we have seen a change in perception of who we are and a marked increase in visibility. We still struggle to avoid being the gatekeeper—the one with control. Instead, we try to be an enabler, a node on the local network that connects those in need with the people or data they require. This is a rewarding role, but even more rewarding is the shift from being analysts that devote significant time to finding data to analysts who get to think, do more real analysis, and have more impact as we benefit from open data in our region.

I believe that to scale open data broadly across local government, we must rely on government staff and leaders to have a similar moment of conviction as the one I had. We're not serving our community well by restricting access to data. Just as we have policies that mandate certain records be made public when requested, if the person who manages the data doesn't like you or your use, then that policy is often ineffective. Government is limited and mandated through policy, but at the end of every request or every new idea, there is a government official with his or her own ideas, struggles, and problems.

In our push to realize open data across all our cities, we must never forget this fact. We are seeking to reach and impact people, not institutions, with our ideas. Yet, as Aaron Swartz (2012) said, we must fix the machine, not the people. We have to reach and connect with the people in order to fix our broken, closed governments.

Unreasonable Expectations

Oakland's city government had long been seen as a blocker of access to information. Information is routinely not accessible unless you are known and liked by the person on the other end. As we launched our own data system, I realized that Oakland was not going to just open its data on a whim. It needed a big push: an open data policy.

I had never written an adopted policy in local government, so it was rather intimidating to begin such a task. Thanks to the work in New York and San Francisco, there were great policy and directive examples I could pull from the Code for America Commons site, which I reworked to suit Oakland (and also Alameda County). I then summarized the priority datasets from most other "open data" cities and drafted some guidelines for how a city could consider adopting and implementing an open data approach. I was now armed with reusable policies, good examples of how powerful opening data had been elsewhere, some clear steps and directions, and what I thought was a silver bullet use case. Where to now? I have never lobbied before, but if felt like that was the next step.

I met with many Oakland City Councilors and, sometimes, their Chief of Staff, to discuss this new thing that I was convinced mattered in our city. In these one-on-one discussions, I attempted to lay out the key issues, benefits, and the need for Oakland to do this. I also discussed the likely (modest) costs to implement this policy. Two reactions stood out in these conversations. First, I learned quickly, that my silver bullet was not viewed as very shiny, and second, I heard that our city councilors had a variety of problems that open data could help solve.

Discussing open data in every case led, if partly out of terminology confusion, to a discussion about technological struggles that the city faces. This included poor access to internal data, the benefits of open source technology, and the ways the city needed better ways to interact with the public. City councilors were frustrated with a lack of easy access to quality data on city assets and operations that made their job of developing informed, data-driven decisions much harder. These internal gains are not insignificant, and any advocates wanting to push for open data would do well to identify local examples that would meet the needs of government itself. After all, behavioral change is easiest when we can relate to a personal benefit. This was a similar experience when pushing Alameda County to consider open data. Developing a complex internal data-sharing infrastructure is incredibly expensive, slow, and frustrating, but opening data for the public is a quick win politically. It also provides fast access to new data for government agencies themselves, which is something that was not possible previously.

My local example of how open data can enable so much more than government can provide, afford, and imagine, was Crimespotting, one of the earliest and most impressive examples of civic hacking on almost open data. It was what I hoped would be our "silver bullet." Built by a good friend, Michal Migurski, this site took a nightly Excel file from an FTP server and provided an elegant, usable interface that helped residents understand the recent crime activity in their community. At almost zero cost to the city, this was my story to demonstrate how awesome opening all the city's data could be. I was wrong. While it resonated clearly with some city councilors, others actually hated the site, making my job much harder.

The reasons for not liking my "silver bullet" mostly centered on the fact that the site did not give them everything they wanted and that it provided information about unpleasant events that made our city look bad. The second concern is a tough argument to work with, but the first is an opportunity. It became clear that Crimespotting itself is not a bad use of data; it's just that city councilors didn't have good access to clear reporting, summary statistics, trend data, and custom reports for their own districts and police beats. This is a reflection on the lack of data analysts in the city and the limited capacity of certain city departments. It also highlights a trend of outsourcing "problems" to vendors. Vendors can create a system to do crime reporting and analysis, but they are not experts on the issues, so it's hard for them to thoughtfully analyze and communicate the data in a local context.

This presents an opportunity for open data. If the city consistently opens their crime data, others can build the interfaces, tools, and reports that are needed for good policy-making. We've helped provide basic Excel files to the city for short-term help, but this need provided a clear use case for OpenOakland redeploying CrimeinChicago.org for use in Oakland: it meets a local need and leverages open data to show the potential in a way that resonates with local leaders.

After my first experiences doing something that resembled lobbying, one city councilor, Libby Schaaf, became the internal champion to make this happen. Unlike other cities, we did not get strong executive support to immediately implement this law. Instead, we had a resolution approved to "investigate open data platforms," resulting in an approved plan and a contract with Socrata to provide such a platform.

Are We Opening Government?

This left Oakland in a strange position. We have both a community-driven open data platform and a city-supported platform, but we are one of the only cities to have a web portal and no legislation to support it (I recently learned that New Orleans is in the same position). To make this even stranger, Alameda County has done the exact same thing. They have the portal, but no policy to support or sustain it.

On one level, this is a wasted opportunity. It's a rare and beautiful thing when both city/county staff and their elected leaders want the same thing. Both parties have a stake in this and have expressed serious support for open data, yet government staff doesn't think legislation is needed and they are not pushing for it. Our elected officials have yet to follow through with legislation to ratify the use and adoption of open data in both the city and county.

There is an aspect to the open data movement that is not really about transparency. It's not uncommon to find an elected official who isn't enthused about the concept of open government: more transparency and, ultimately, more accountability. The transparency argument was not a convincing one for me locally. However, the promise of supporting innovation, making the city more accessible, and promoting new opportunities, along with better internal access to information, was an effective approach. While my pragmatic side is comfortable with a good decision for any particular reason, my idealistic side finds the positions of many officials unsettling and a reflection of the trend being identified by some as "openwashing."

There is sometimes confusion that the adoption of an open data platform creates open government in and of itself. This is not the case—open data alone is not sufficient to create an open government.

The following message from an Alameda County government Twitter account (@ACData) on April 2, 2013, is an example of this flawed logic in action:

#OpenData + #Hackathon = #OpenGov #ACApps Challenge 2013.1 on 4/27 at #Berkeley High School. http://code.acgov.org #gotcode?

The line of reasoning is that we gave you some of our data (awesome), we want you to do stuff with it (nice, thank you), and hence, we now have Open Government (not quite).

Some role clarification is important here. The staff who are trying to open data and engage citizens are in fact moving toward a reality that embodies true open government. However, there are still bad apples within our local governments who are investigated for fraud, mismanagement, or corruption, or for hiding things from the public. Open data that includes a lot of noncontroversial data is low-hanging fruit and is important, but this is only one small piece of the puzzle that leads to open, accountable government. It's a great starting point that takes minimal investment and leads to good publicity, but if we allow our local governments to paint the picture of this work meaning "we're now open so leave us alone," then we have failed them as much as they have failed to truly understand why open data matters.

There is a lesson here for many other cities and for Oakland. Publishing data is not the end game. It is a big deal though. Oakland is taking an easy road and requires increased advocacy to adopt a strong policy to sustain open data. By keeping elected officials more engaged through this process, we might have avoided this situation where we have a practice, but no policy—the opposite of almost every other city working with open data. The risk for us is that as soon as a senior city official doesn't like something being open, it goes away. Take the city staff salary data, which was originally published but then removed. The words "Coming soon" were then published on the city's earlier data page. This is a patently false statement because the reality is that the data was removed. The same data was still, however, available on the state controller's website.

The Panacea of Data-Driven Cities

It's hard to imagine a new policy, new social service, or new investment decision being made in any company or government without the strategic use of data to inform the thinking and planning. Still, too frequently, cities do not have staff with the skills or the mandate to thoughtfully analyze public and confidential data. Those of us in the private sector would be often horrified to see the type of information provided to city councilors to aid their decision-making. Since ninety percent of the world's data has been created in the last two years, we have no excuse for not looking at reliable data to inform our planning and policy-making. This is the future we dreamed of, where data on almost any issue is readily available and easily analyzed. Only, we aren't there yet.

Opening data in Oakland and Alameda County has raised a lot of questions about the quality and reliability of this data and with due cause. This is a valid fear of bureaucrats, yet it is a fear that has no rightful place in our governments. If our raw data is bad, our decisions can only be misinformed. Opening data, therefore, is in some respects the beginning of a data quality control effort within our local governments. Sunshine reveals many flaws, and open data reveals many flaws in our data collection, management, and use in city government. These realizations may make some people feel bad for a time, but the staffer who has been lamenting the lack of time and funding to properly manage the data in their department now has allies across their community who are also concerned about this lack of attention toward data management.

This has traditionally only been possible with very small, tight-knit groups of "experts" who work with government. These have generally been groups who would not push back hard on government for fear of losing favor and income streams. By opening our data, we can now take advantage of the larger pool of citizens who care about and know about that data; and we can learn from them and improve our processes and practices, which will both benefit the internal users of our public data and the wider public.

The problems that become visible around government data can often have ugly consequences, but they must be seen as growing pains as we move from immature uses of data in government to a place where data-driven decision-making is the norm.

Leveraging the Long Tail of Government

Many critics in Oakland have suggested that open data doesn't explain anything, doesn't make anything clear, and doesn't provide answers. Some also suggest that the community focus on open data and open government is overly focused on technological solutionism. The first group is right, albeit barely, while the second group has not fully comprehended this movement and its intent. Let's take a look at a current practice in government and then consider what open data means for the future.

In Open Government (2010), David Eaves provides a cogent story that elegantly describes how citizen's attitudes towards closed government decision-making have changed in the information age:

> There was a time when citizens trusted objective professionals and elected officials to make those decisions on our behalf and where the opacity of the system was tolerated because of the professionalism and efficiencies it produced. This is no longer the case; the Internet accelerates the decline of deference because it accelerates the death of objectivity. It's not that we don't trust; it's just that we want to verify. (Eaves, 2010.)

He goes on to compare Wikipedia and Britannica, where the authority that is transparent in its process is, in fact, more trusted. Eaves posits that "transparency... is the new objectivity. We are not going to trust objectivity unless we can see the discussion that led to it."

In Oakland, open data would have saved the city from an embarrassing failure surrounding a new crime fighting strategy. It could also have spurred a much richer deliberative process to build a comprehensive approach for an issue, instead of a bad model created in closed access meetings. In 2012, the city announced a crime fighting strategy called the 100 Blocks Plan. Immediately, the community, my organization, and dozens of other organizations raised concerns over a serious lack of detail about this plan. We all questioned just exactly where these hundred blocks that contained ninety percent of the crime were. We met with city staff who looked over our initial analysis, which showed a very different reality than what the city had laid out in its plan. They confidently told us that their data was the same, which clearly was not the case. The city chose not to publish accurate information about a place-based strategy and refused to publish the data used to make this critical decision that affects the safety and well-being of our city.

At this point in time, crime reports were almost open data. Michal Migurski had collected years of data for Crimespotting, and the Urban Strategies Council had also cleaned and published even more of this data. When the official response did not ring true with our perception of good government (the model looked quite wrong and the planning process was secretive) in a city with dozens of organizations with analytical and crime prevention experience, we saw this as a failure to leverage the citizens and professionals who can contribute to public decision-making and planning.

In June 2012, we released our own study of Oakland crime hotspots. Our research indicated that at most, one hundred city blocks (and a buffer) could contain only seventeen percent of violent crimes—not the ninety percent figure publicized by the city. We were frustrated that at a time when other cities were publishing raw data to inform the public, along with quality analysis to help us understand their process, Oakland was doing the opposite. So, we attempted to lead by example. We published our study, including the raw data we used for our calculations, and a detailed methodology, so others could review our findings and correct us if we made serious mistakes (Urban Strategies Council, 2012). (We didn't.) This revelation obviously caused a media frenzy that we had no desire to be involved in, but we did think it was valuable to have an informed discourse in our city about crime and city policies to reduce crime. After defending the official plan and numbers as correct, the city turned around and admitted that the data the plan was based on was, in fact, wrong.

The results of these unfortunate events were in no way intended to make any public officials look bad, but to elevate the level of engagement in public decision-making. We wanted to highlight the need for open data to allow the citizens of our city to understand the thinking behind city decisions—to test any statements of fact themselves. It is no longer an acceptable circumstance for local government to make decisions and ask that we simply trust its goodwill and expert opinion.

Oakland's Mayor Quan told the media that she was at fault and should have vetted the data more. In this suggestion, I believe she was wrong. It is far from the role of a city mayor to conduct an independent review of every single analysis or metric given to them. Any elected official must be able to rely on the quality of analysis from city staff and other experts. What open datasets open up is a future where citizen experts can easily provide qualified perspectives on government decisions, analysis, and statements. This is a democracy that can support the role of citizens in active decision-making.

As I suggested earlier, publishing the raw data itself does not create an informed and expert community; it does not equate to answers being readily available. What it does do is enable far deeper engagement on issues that our communities care about. As Aaron Swartz submitted in Open Government (2010), transparency efforts themselves tend to not work in their current forms. The potential of open data is to enable far more responsive and thorough oversight of political and governmental actions, which ideally, could lead to a future where officials are operating in a space they know is no longer invisible and no longer protected by a layer of public records refusals. Instead, it would create a reality in which hundreds or thousands of their constituents can access and question data that explain their motives and actions.

What Has Data Done for Me Lately?

As the furious rush to build "innovative" and "game changing" civic apps and new tools starts to plateau, I believe we are seeing a slow but steady shift into finding ways that this new treasure trove of open data can actually do something useful. By useful, I mean solve problems, uncover unknown problems, and help illuminate new solutions to old problems. I love geeky apps that make my already comfortable life even better, more connected, and more informed, but this is indeed just a way that new technology and data are empowering the empowered. I've seen data do so much more, and we are starting to see this use trend growing nationally and globally.

Groups such as DataKind, GAFFTA, and Geeks Without Borders, and local research/action tanks, like the Urban Strategies Council, have been doing this well—in our case, for decades. Traditionally, it looks like this: define your problem, identify data to inform the problem/solution, obtain data, analyze it, and communicate results and solutions. Open data takes the pain out of this old equation. It also takes the exclusivity out of the obtain data element and provides for unlimited problem solvers. I believe there will be a future need for sophisticated data shops like ours that can gain access to raw, record-level sensitive data for research purposes, but open data sounds the death knell for the gateway or custodian model of data warehousing. The nonprofit and academic sector has to also realize that we have been as guilty of data hoarding as anyone and that we can enable more by following the lead of the public sector and opening our data wherever we can.

On many urban research and spatial analysis projects, data acquisition can run as high as twenty percent of a budget. In just a few short months of working in Oakland with partially open data from the city and the county, we've already saved dozens of hours of time on two major projects. These saved costs to a community add up, especially in the case where researchers are working for the government on contract.

Working with already open data is a shift away from the typical model, where we have to charge local government for the time it takes us to source and uncover its own data to use for analysis. In the cases when we have to do our own data gathering, we should be making it open by default—otherwise, we ourselves are contributing to the problem of withholding valuable data that could be public. These nonprofit and academic institutions are often as protective and closed by nature as government has been, with the added obstacle of the lack of a public mandate due to being a taxpayer-funded entity. There have, however, been promising instances where foundations have begun opening their data to the world (DonorsChoose.org is one good example).

At Urban Strategies Council, we have been a national example in the adoption of an "open by default" policy for all the data we've held and all that we receive, but this also is a slow road since most nonprofit organizations severely lack data and the technological capacity for general operation, management, and publication of their data. When this does happen (and it must), we will see two major outcomes that are important in the social sector in particular: much more transparency in a sector that typically has little (Carl Malamud's inspiring work to publish 990s does not yield measures on quality or efficiency of programs, unfortunately) and the familiar benefit of rich data resources being unlocked and available. Nonprofits, foundations, and universities do the bulk of community surveys in the USA, and many unknowingly duplicate each other's work because the results are closed and protected. This results in the over-surveying of many communities and in wasteful efforts that would not be needed should raw survey results be published by default, along with the final reports.

In the present scenario, funders receive impact reports from grantees stating they served x people for y service, rarely providing any "where" or any long-term outcomes or impacts, merely demonstrating transactional gains through service delivery. Mandating or encouraging small to large nonprofits to begin opening detailed (but not confidential) data will allow funders to begin evaluating real impact. It will allow those who look at the macro picture to accurately identify gaps in actual service delivery and enable them to evaluate macro level outcomes to help guide future funding priorities. If you currently believe that this is common practice in the philanthropic sector, you couldn't be more wrong. What started as an effort to get government to open up publicly funded data for a myriad of reasons will inevitably result in this same trend in the community development and social sector. We will require transparency over simple goodwill and flowery slogans, and we will push for evidence-based practice over "doing what we've always done because it works."

Into the Danger Zone

One caveat that those of us in the data trade will have to work carefully around is competing standards of open data. Many organizations once required the use of non-disclosure agreements and memorandums of understanding, but these no longer have any meaning when we can now find the data we need online. There is, however, a tricky middle ground appearing. Agencies that once would furnish us with detailed, sensitive data for the purposes of research are both publishing some data openly, while at the same time developing better processes for data requests using the Public Records Act (PRA) or FOIA. This results in some blurring of the lines between open data and confidential data and will require very carefully communicated permissions.

Our local police department recently provided us with a rich homicide investigation dataset, which is something that we have accessed over the years. This time, however, it required a PRA. Our assumption that all records provided via PRA are public and, thus, we can republish this data, turned out to be partly wrong.

The department had only given us the data once more because of our trusted relationship as a community research partner. They did not, in fact, consider this sensitive data to be public. In the confusion over open data and new PRA procedures, however, they did issue the data in response to a PRA, hence, technically releasing the data as public record. This reflects the need to carefully and intentionally review data access procedures in every department housing sensitive information. Opening data provides an excellent opportunity to completely document your data holdings, legal availability, and metadata for each. This kind of attention is necessary to avoid confusion in the process and assumed permissions. In this case, it may be necessary to adopt a research access agreement similar to that used by school districts to ensure PRA and sensitive data are not released incorrectly.

Community Development

There is one important sector of American cities that has barely been affected by open data: community development. This field consists of local government departments (often small ones) and local nonprofits, often Community Development Corporations (CDCs). Both of these types of organizations are hampered by a lack of access to granular data relating to their communities of interest, commonly property data, market trends, development, foreclosures, and data from other sectors. Presently, much of this data is locked in government silos or sold at a premium to the public and other government agencies, despite being public data at its core. The barriers of cost, unclear availability, and confusion over the quality, currency, and the relevance of most property data mean that too many CDC type operations are running data-blind. We've interviewed many local organizations in this field and found that almost every one faces these barriers in a way that affects their effectiveness and impact.

This sector must be data-driven, as the volume of investment it draws nationally is substantial. Decisions of where, when, and how to invest would rarely be made without solid data in the private sector, yet this is all too common in the CDC world. Opening key property and economic development data will add a level of sophistication and rigor to the CDC world that is important. However, it will not automatically create skills or cheap tools to analyze and utilize this data. As funders and government become more focused on evidence-based and data-driven efforts, both sources of investment must accept their role in supporting or providing that kind of capacity.

Who Owns Your Data?

Opening property data will bring a fight over public ownership that opening property data. Presently, in Alameda County, any nonprofit or any city/county agency that wishes to consider the impact of foreclosures on their work or to evaluate the impact or opportunities that foreclosures have created, must purchase this data from private sources. This means every agency, independently. The opening of some data should prompt us to ask about the realities behind other data not being opened. In this case, the source of this data is a county agency: the Clerk Recorder. The Clerk Recorder has a simple mandate that has not changed significantly for some time. When a foreclosure is filed, it comes in paper form. The date, bank or foreclosing agent, and the homeowner are electronically recorded, while other critical details, like amount, address, city, etc., are left on a scanned image. These images are made available to title companies, who provide the once-valuable service of creating digital records, which are then sold back to any government or public agency who needs them. In 2013, this cannot be accepted as good government.

This is not a flaw with the Clerk Recorder, who seems to be a genuinely helpful person based on our interactions. It's a flaw in how we think about assets and resources and a lack of agility in government to adapt as opportunities arise. These corporate data fiefdoms should not survive the broader opening of public data, as people's expectations rise and as government is encouraged to create value where it can. Creating usable data is one of the easiest ways to do so. Can you imagine not being able to answer a simple question like "How many foreclosures did you accept in the city of Oakland this year?" Because the agency itself creates no data, it cannot answer this question directly.

Are You Open for Business?

On the back of the benefits that community development can reap are the even more substantial rewards gained through increased economic development. This is simple in practice, but we've apparently been sleeping at the wheel in cities like Oakland. Our city desperately wants investment and retail, but we've failed to make the path smooth and to help those considering our city make informed decisions. For large corporations, access to local data is, perhaps, less of a barrier to investment because of their access to professional market analysts, brokers, and the like, but for a small to medium enterprise, these services are mostly out of reach.

It should be a no brainer for Oakland to both open its data and encourage the development of tools on top of this data. As of January 2013, in our city, a potential new business owner or investor could not find data or tools online to allow the owner to review business permits, building and development permits, vacant properties, blight, or regional crime comparisons. Compare this with our neighbor city of San Francisco where all these things are simply available. They're available because they are needed and help make the path smoother for new business. When times are tight in local government, like during the past several years, we must get smarter. Releasing all this data is opportunistic and critical. If our city is unable to build the tools to help attract business because of funding or outdated IT procurement approaches, then the data will suffice at a marginal cost. Others can build tools more cheaply and faster. The old adage that says we can't do this because it's expensive is hard to use as a straw man anymore. This change will take leadership from our city to identify an area of internal weakness and engage with the broader community in an effort to develop the tools and analyses that this data makes possible. This would be an incredible demonstration of recognizing the potential in the long tail of government and in how open government can collectively do so much more together.

Conclusion

Every city takes a different path to open its data and progress toward open government. Oakland is off to a slow but exciting start with its data platform and with increased engagement through this data. Yet, it remains to be seen if our city will push through legislation to protect and sustain the worthy efforts of city staff at this point. Our lesson here is that engagement with elected officials must be sustained at a high level to ensure policy matches practice and also that developing strong initial resolutions is the key to avoid watered down plans and slow, uncertain paths forward.

Opening data is increasingly being seen as a single solution that will satisfy the transparency advocates. It is up to those of us who understand how much more is needed to speak truth to this misrepresentation of what open data is and is not. This relies on stronger ties with elected officials and behaviors more akin to community organizing efforts than those of tech startups. More open data provides us all with powerful fuel to demonstrate ways that open government can truly be more effective and more agile, but it will be largely left to those of us on the outside to demonstrate this and to encourage government to embrace open data more broadly.

While the app-developing world is an attractive audience to make use of new open data, there will be incredible gains in efficiency, decision-making, and planning in the community development, social service, and land management sectors that are just as impactful. Software developers are the focus for now, but in time, as this movement reaches the analysts, planners, and researchers who also live on data, this movement will come of age. Soon, more of the latter will experience the joy of responding to a complicated research data request with the phrase "Sure you can have the data. It's open and online for free already!" We can all become enablers, part of a rich platform that creates value and shares for the benefit of all.

I've worked across dozens of cities in the USA and elsewhere, and for decades, the problem was always this: we can't get the government data we need or it's expensive. Enough cities have now demonstrated that this should not be the norm anymore. We enable far more value to be created once we become open-by-default cities: open for business, open for engagement, and open for innovation.

Author's Note

After writing, some positive progress has been made in Oakland. At the request of council member Libby Schaaf, we are beginning crowd-sourcing of new legislation for an official open data policy in the city of Oakland. We've combined what we see as the strongest and most relevant elements of policies from Austin, Texas; Portland, Oregon; Raleigh, North Carolina; and Chicago. We've published the draft for public comment, and so far we have great feedback from other practi-tioners in cities with experience of their own process and locals inter-ested in making this right for us. It's an experiment. It should be fun. Next we hold a roundtable session to review and consider what this means for our city. And then we try to get this passed! Onward.

—*Steve Spiker*

About the Author

Steve Spiker (Spike) is the Director of Research & Technology at the Urban Strategies Council, a social change nonprofit supporting inno-vation and collaboration based in Oakland for almost twenty-six years. He leads the Council's research, spatial analysis, evaluation, and tech work. He is also the Executive Director and co-founder of OpenOak-land, a civic innovation organization supporting open data and open government in the East Bay.

References

Eaves, D. (2010). Open Government. Available from https://github.com/oreillymedia/open_government

New York Times (2012). The 45 Places to Go in 2012. The *New*

York Times, January 6, 2012. Retrieved from http://travel.nytimes.com/2012/01/08/travel/45-places-to-go-in-2012.html?pagewanted=all&_r=0

Swartz, A. (2012, September 25). Fix the machine, not the person. Retrieved from http://www.aaronsw.com/weblog/nummi

Urban Strategies Council. (2012, June 5). Our Take on Oakland's 100 Blocks Plan. Retrieved from http://www.infoalamedacounty.org/index.php/research/crimesafety/violenceprevention/oakland100blocks.html

Urban Strategies Council. (2012, May 22). Our Method: Oakland's 100 Blocks Plan. Retrieved from http://www.infoalamedacounty.org/index.php/research/crimesafety/violenceprevention/oakland100blocksmethod.html

CHAPTER 10

Pioneering Open Data Standards: The GTFS Story

By Bibiana McHugh

In 2005, I was working at TriMet, the public transit agency in Portland, Oregon, as an IT manager for Geographic Information Services. Earlier that year, while traveling, I found it very frustrating to try and find transit directions in the unfamiliar cities I was visiting. This was especially true when transportation agencies that provided differing services or areas were not consolidated. It was much easier at that time to get driving directions from popular online mapping services, and I realized this was probably encouraging car usage over public transit.

In my role at TriMet, I worked with transit data every day, so I knew such data was available and the potential was there. We offered our own online transit trip planning tool, as many agencies do. The trouble was, the average citizen often didn't know where to go to find this information, especially if he or she was unfamiliar with the local transit system. The general public was used to going to certain online destinations for driving directions—Google Maps, MapQuest, and Yahoo were all widely used at the time—but the data they needed to plan a trip using public transit wasn't available where they were looking.

Bringing Data to the Citizens

As a public servant who had worked to improve public transit for nearly a decade, I saw this as a missed opportunity to promote public transit to an audience that might not be aware of the option. When I returned to Portland, I made it my mission to make it just as easy to get transit directions as it is to get driving directions from anywhere in the world. I reached out to several companies to inquire about the idea of integrating Portland's public transit data into their existing navigation products in order to allow users to plan transit trips.

After some persistent follow-up with no response, I contacted Jeremy Faludi after reading his article "A Call for Open-Source Public Transit Mapping" (Faludi, 2005). He introduced me to Chris Harrelson, a software engineer at Google who had the same idea in mind. He and a group of like-minded volunteers had been working on building out a prototype of Google Transit during their twenty percent flexible project time. They had the idea and the basic infrastructure. What they needed to continue was a government partner who could provide service data (routes, timetables, etc.).

In July of 2005, we got together with the team at Google to discuss the project. At first, some of the TriMet staff were hesitant to hand over the data—it's very complex spatial-temporal data that is difficult to handle correctly. But when we saw that Chris' team knew what they were doing, we were very impressed. Tim McHugh, TriMet's Chief Technology Officer, generated the initial data export that same night—the beta version of what would eventually become the first widely used transit data standard.

TriMet already had an existing centralized enterprise database that housed all of the relevant data already pieced together in good form. Having this foundation in place was significant—only because of this was it possible to write an initial script in less than an hour that would export the data required for transit trip planning. We published this schedule data in the form of CSV files based on our existing internal database schema and shared it with Google, as well as publicly on our website, so that any third-party developer could access and use it.

The other component was that our agency leadership gave us support to move ahead with the experiment. Carolyn Young, our executive director, gave us permission to open the data almost as soon as we had the idea. We were lucky that our agency has a long history of supporting open source and open data. TriMet's TransitTracker™ (next arrival times) feed was already open, so outside developers were already using TriMet open data prior to 2005. We had had an open source-friendly procurement policy in place for a decade. These factors meant that the

TriMet culture was primed to be supportive of this type of initiative, which allowed us to move quickly.

On December 7, 2005—less than five months after our initial conference call—the first version of Google Transit was launched with TriMet data that covered the Portland Metro area (Garg, 2005). The launch received an overwhelmingly positive response. As Google Transit went live for the first time, word first spread across Europe. According to the Google Transit Team, they watched in amazement as the number of hits to the site increased exponentially. By morning, as the US awoke, the counts were reaching staggering numbers, even by Google standards.

The day of the launch, I did numerous interviews with local TV stations, newspapers, and even several radio stations. It seemed we were onto something important—something that people cared about. We knew we needed to get other agencies on board so that this could expand beyond Portland.

Scaling Up

We had held a workshop just before the launch of the Google Transit beta, in an attempt to get other agencies and developers on board with the effort to open and standardize this data. Multiple transit agencies participated—including representatives from Seattle, Chicago, and New York, among others—but many were apprehensive. A common concern was that providing data in the standard open format wouldn't benefit the agency; it would only benefit Google.

However, this resistance turned around as soon as everyone saw the positive public response to the launch announcement. Agencies saw that they could benefit from being involved—not just by getting good publicity for their agency, but also by offering a service that was clearly in demand by the public. Department heads started calling us, asking, "How can we be next?"

To scale up to more cities, it was essential that transit agencies standardize and publish their schedule data so that it could be integrated into third-party apps the same way across jurisdictions. We worked with

Google and with several of the interested agencies to develop this standard format, then called the Google Transit Feed Specification (GTFS), based closely off of the first series of data that TriMet had published.

We chose to keep the files in CSV format. We wanted it to be as simple as possible so that agencies could easily edit the data, using any editor. This approach received substantial criticism—it was even called "technically old-fashioned and brittle" (KiZoom, 2006)—but it was important to us to keep the barrier to participation low so that even smaller, less-resourced agencies could join in. As Google Transit team member Joe Hughes put it in his original welcome message on the GTFS discussion list:

> We chose CSV as the basis for the specification because it's easy to view and edit using spreadsheet programs and text editors, which is helpful for smaller agencies. It's also straightforward to generate from most programming languages and databases, which is good for publishers of larger feeds. (Hughes, 2007)

In September 2006, Google Transit launched in five more cities that began publishing their service data in the nascent standard format: Tampa; Honolulu; Eugene, Oregon; Pittsburgh; and Seattle. Shortly thereafter, we published the first version of the GTFS spec under a Creative Commons License ("What is GTFS?" 2012).

Within a year, Google Transit launched with fourteen more transit agencies in the United States and expanded internationally to Japan. As of July 2013, Google Transit has launched in hundreds of cities worldwide ("Google Maps: Transit: Cities Covered," n.d.). Detailed transit instructions, in addition to driving directions on Google Maps, is available in Africa, Asia, Australia, Europe, North America, and South America.

In early 2007, TriMet and other transit agencies began to publish their transit data openly, in a more formal and publicized way, with official sites for developer resources. TriMet and San Francisco's BART, the Bay Area Rapid Transit, were the first agencies, and others soon followed as the benefits became increasingly apparent ("Developer Resources," 2013; "For Developers," 2013).

TriMet's core business is not software development. By making our data open, we were able to leverage external resources to bring benefits to the public. Making transit data publicly available and collaborating with a community of software developers has resulted in hundreds of useful and popular transit applications for TriMet customers and many others. Many have all been developed by third parties offering a wide range of creative and useful tools available on multiple platforms for a variety of users. When I asked Tim McHugh about why he supported opening our data to third-party developers, he explained:

> Due to the large proliferation of transit applications on mobile platforms, the market is able to react quickly to changes and to fill gaps in service. This is something that one government IT department could not develop or support with the same level of spontaneity and flexibility. (McHugh, personal communication, 2013)

One of the first initiatives President Obama introduced was an open government initiative ("About Open Government," n.d.). This resulted in Data.gov, a resource for software developers and a resource for applications in support of open data and open source software. This movement has spread to many cities, states, and countries, bringing many benefits to the public. Having already released open data in transit put us in a good position to respond quickly to the mandate and take advantage of this new momentum from the top.

In addition to online groups, forums, and mailing lists, other sites, like the GTFS Data Exchange (www.gtfs-data-exchange.com), began to emerge to establish communities around the standard and facilitate wide adoption in the industry. Companies that offer support for the production and maintenance for GTFS began to fill an important void in the industry. GTFS began to generate business and business incentives.

Why Standards Matter for Cities

I believe there are several important ingredients that made the GTFS initiative successful:

- A collaborative team that started small and designed for a very specific use.

- Releasing the transit data specification in an open standard; the simplicity of the specification and format.

- A tangible business incentive for the transit agencies and for private partners to participate.

- The contributions and involvement from the worldwide community of users.

The biggest advantage of being part of the GTFS standard for agencies is that their information appears in a global set of search products that are easy to use and visited by millions and millions of people every day. People who do not know a city well, are visiting, or are simply unaware of the agency's services, can benefit and find alternatives to driving. Regular public transit riders benefit from being able to find transit information in a familiar user interface and in the context of other useful information. It's about providing better information and service delivery for citizens, which is ultimately aligned with any agency's mission.

This all comes at a low cost for the city. At TriMet, our process is automated, so there is very little overhead. TriMet has four major service changes a year, in addition to minor changes and adjustments in between. We may update and publish our GTFS data as frequently as twice a month. TriMet has not incurred any direct costs for this specific project, except resource time, which is a very small investment in comparison to the returns.

Now that agencies have made GTFS freely available as open data, hundreds of applications have spawned worldwide. We found that by making our data easily and openly accessible, developers are getting very creative and expanding its use. This is not only beneficial because it expands the number of product offerings available, but it can also have emergent economic benefits for developers and the communities they live in. In addition, because the standard allows for interoperability between cities, applications built to serve one city can be readily deployed to serve other cities for a much lower cost and effort than if the data wasn't standardized.

Early on in the adoption of GTFS, it was suggested that transit agencies charge fees for their GTFS data. However, it became apparent that the return on investment (ROI) was far greater than potential sales on the data. In addition, Public Records requests reminded agencies that making sought-after data openly available was a far better solution than addressing many requests individually. Some developers resorted to screen-scraping the data off transit sites, which was not a stable method that ensured access to current and accurate customer information. It became apparent that open data in a standard format was the solution that was in the best interest of the public.

Lessons Learned for Scalable Standards

Civic data standards are not just limited to the realm of public transit. Data is a central component of every facet of public service, and there is an opportunity for standards in many of them. Emergent efforts include those like Open311, a standard format for civic issue reporting; LIVES, a format for restaurant inspection data; and House Facts, a standard for residential building inspection data. Lessons from our work developing GTFS can help inform how to build a truly scalable and open data standard for cities.

A key to the success of GTFS was that we built around a real use case. We saw a real problem and a way to solve it with data. Because the standard clearly linked to a real-life problem, we were able to articulate a real ROI for adoption. It's important to take the time to think through all the different stakeholders and how they can benefit from participation. Don't underestimate the value of publicity as a tool when pushing to get those first adopters on board. Public agencies are usually accustomed to getting negative media coverage when something goes wrong and no coverage when something goes right. The chance to get positive press for the good work they are doing is often a powerful incentive. It was game changing when TriMet gained national attention at the launch of Google Transit.

Working with a well-known national partner to integrate the data can provide a tremendous amount of the momentum needed to succeed. Working with Google enabled us to show scalable value quickly, as well as gain attention from the association with their brand. We could immediately show national, and even worldwide, relevance through integration with Google's existing widely used products.

However, it's important not to conflate the identity of an open standard with the brand of a corporate partner. While we engaged other open source developers to build apps on the standard and created partnerships with industry vendors who supplied transit data services to provide standards-compliant export functionality for their customers, we received pushback: agencies didn't want to be perceived as giving their data to Google exclusively, and developers were reluctant to develop off of a standard that had Google in the name. We eventually changed the name from Google Transit Feed Specification to General Transit Feed Specification—and the effect was transformative. It greatly reduced resistance from software vendors; proponents of existing transit data standards; companies that assembled and resold public data; and transit agencies who were worried about losing control of their data.

In addition to a national partner, the involvement of other developers and partners (including civic hackers, other cities, and larger vendors) is crucial for scalability and neutrality of the standard. Be agile and evolve to support other entities and applications.

It's amazing that GTFS has since been adopted relatively quickly on a worldwide platform, but it's even more amazing to think it has been adopted worldwide voluntarily. Apparent and persuasive ROIs, its unpretentious and evolving nature, and its supporting community are all key growth factors.

Standards for Better Public Service

Why did we do all this? I believe it comes back to the core meaning of the term "public service." It is about providing the best experience possible to our citizens. At TriMet, we believe it should be just as easy for our customers to plan transit trips as it is to get driving instructions. Opening up this data to allow for wider use and integration with existing services is putting a new face on public transportation and reaching a much wider audience than we as a single local agency could ever hope to. Contrary to speculation that third-party transit applications are drawing attention away from transit agencies and their brand, TriMet is finding that many applications are reaching a broader audience. They direct potential customers to more comprehensive information on an agency's site that may otherwise be unknown.

We still offer our own TriMet trip planner, as we feel it is our responsibility to provide that service to our customers, but Google Transit, Bing Maps, and all the other apps that developers have built using this data, offer our customers another way to plan their trips with different options and features. GTFS lets us meets citizens where they already are and builds interoperability across municipalities as it expands to more cities.

The next logical step after GTFS was developing a specification for real-time transit data in addition to schedule data. TriMet, MBTA, BART, and MTS worked with Google on a new specification for real-time transit data, not just scheduled: the General Transit Feed Specification-realtime or GTFS-RT ("What is GTFS-realtime?" 2012). This information is very beneficial to our customers, and wide adoption is growing. We look forward to seeing the impact of civic data standards as they expand to other areas of transit and public service.

As Chris Harrelson has said:

> It's perhaps easy to jump to the conclusion that Google is the hero in this story, in the typical role of the innovator who overcomes the inefficiencies of the past, but this is really not true in this case. This is a success story about a new model of cooperation in order to solve a problem that cannot be addressed directly with either market forces or a classic government solution. Everyone had an equally important role to play, and without TriMet and other government advocates, this story would not be possible. (Harrelson, personal communication, 2013)

GTFS began with a single public agency and single private company working together to solve a common problem creatively. The extensive community of agencies and GTFS users continue to collaborate on evolving the standard to meet the requirements of many more applications. The end result is that it is now just as easy to get transit directions as it is to get driving directions from nearly anywhere in the world.

About the Author

Bibiana McHugh has worked in TriMet's Information Technology Department since 1997 and currently leads a team of innovative web developers and analysts as the IT Manager of Geographic Information Systems and Location-Based Services. She leads several open data and open source software initiatives including opentripplanner.org, maps.trimet.org, rtp.trimet.org, developer.trimet.org, and trimet.org/apps. After initiating collaboration with Google for the first release of Google Transit, she helped pioneer the now worldwide standard General Transit Feed Spec (GTFS). She received a degree in Geography from the University of Kansas.

References

Bay Area Rapid Transit. (2013). For Developers. Retrieved from http://www.bart.gov/schedules/developers/index.aspx

Faludi, J. (2005, June 5). A Call for Open-Source Public Transit Mapping. Retrieved from http://www.worldchanging.com/archives/002937.html

Garg, A. (2005, December 7). Public transit via Google. Retrieved from http://googleblog.blogspot.com/2005/12/public-transit-via-google.html

Google Developers. (2012, January 12). What is GTFS? Retrieved from https://developers.google.com/transit/gtfs/

Google Developers. (2012, July 26). What is GTFS-realtime? Retrieved from https://developers.google.com/transit/gtfs-realtime/

Google Maps. (2013). Transit: Cities Covered. Retrieved from http://www.google.com/landing/transit/cities/index.html

Hughes, J. (2007, May 18). General Transit Feed Spec Changes (Msg. 1). Message posted to (https://groups.google.com/forum/#!msg/gtfs-changes/C5dgsKGkpDA/kyxN1DCS-dQJ

KiZoom. (2006). The Google Transit Feed Specification — Capabilities & Limitations: A Short Analysis.

The White House. (n.d.). About Open Government. Retrieved from http://www.whitehouse.gov/open/about

TriMet. (2013). App Center: Transit Tools for the Web and Mobile Devices. Retrieved from http://trimet.org/apps/

TriMet. (2013). Developer Resources. Retrieved from http://developer.trimet.org/

PART III:
Understanding Open Data
Editor's Note

This section explores some of the larger scale implications of opening government data. Industry experts outline emergent impacts on our public sphere, democratic processes, and economy—while also articulating the enabling factors that are needed to bring about potential transformative benefits.

In Chapter 11, Eric Gordon and Jessica Baldwin-Philippi argue that the open data movement suggests more than just access to government data—it is the reframing of data from a government resource to a publicly owned asset to which every citizen has right. As a result of this reframing, many new tools have been developed that encourage citizens to place their personal data into service of collaboration and active citizenship. This chapter describes how this culture of open data has facilitated good civic habits, which point to active learning and sustainable civic engagement.

Building on that theme, in Chapter 12, User Experience expert Cyd Harrell explores design principles as applied to open data, and argues that a citizen-centric approach is key to fully realize the benefits of open data in civic life and engagement.

Next, we hear from Michael Chui, Diana Farrell, and Steve Van Kuiken from the McKinsey Global Institute, who examine how open data can generate economic value in Chapter 13. They offer a framework of enablers that open data leadership should take into account in order to unlock this potential value.

And in Chapter 14, Alissa Black and Rachel Burstein of the New America Foundation discuss the unique opportunities open data and innovation at the local scale to improve the lives of citizens and make government more responsive and adaptive to residents. They caution against excluding smaller, less-resourced cities from the open data movement, and outline several steps to ensure that advances in civic innovation are inclusive of all kinds of local governments.

CHAPTER 11

Making a Habit Out of Engagement: How the Culture of Open Data Is Reframing Civic Life

By Eric Gordon and Jessica Baldwin-Philippi

We live in data rich times. Digital tools, from Facebook to Fitbit, have made more and more thoughts and actions collectable. Thoughts and actions that were once understood as ephemeral and public can now be fixed and privatized. Indeed, many of the artifacts of public life have become sequestered into proprietary and isolated databases, from individual mobility patterns to reflections on current affairs. While this data does not have any obvious function, recent revelations about the National Security Agency monitoring Americans' metadata points to just how revealing this data can be. Still, the story has created surprisingly little concern because of a general lack of understanding about how metadata can be used. The majority of Americans are comfortable with the federal government accessing their metadata for the purpose of national security (Pew Research/Washington Post, 2013); likewise, they expect that corporations will preserve their privacy by enabling them to control who has access to their personally identifiable data. Both personally identifiable data and metadata are generally seen as passively generated, harmlessly owned and protected by corporations, and "rented" when needed.

Enter the open data movement—a loosely defined effort of technology and policy hackers seeking to reposition data and its uses into the public domain. From health records to geodata, people are creating standards and repositories that facilitate access to, interoperability across, and transformation of datasets, outside of corporate interests. While open data is proving disruptive to a myriad of domains, from music to news, it is particularly powerful in the areas of government and civic life. What we call civic data are any data that inform public life, from the location of fire hydrants and blighted properties to citizen reports of potholes. These are not private data; they are signals transmitted within the public realm that remain publicly accessible.

Over the last several years, governments have pushed to standardize and release large datasets. Technologists have created thousands of tools to aggregate, filter, and facilitate production of this data. Within this sphere of activity, users transition from being renters to co-owners and creators. When they access or contribute data to an open system, they expect not only a service, but also that the aggregate of the data they produce contributes to something larger. Indeed, open civic data is a public asset that can be reused and recombined toward a collective good. The net result is more than just access to standard datasets. The "culture" of open civic data is the reframing of data from a government resource to a publicly owned asset to which every citizen has a right.

While civic hackers and government employees continue to chip away at the technical and political problems of data accessibility and interoperability, there is a culture of use that is burgeoning in the civic realm that needs to be attended to. New tools enable citizens to access, share, and contribute to civic data repositories. Each time someone uses a tool to help them choose a public school, catch a bus, or report a pothole, they are interacting with and contributing to civic data. When they actively choose to share their own data or access public datasets, they are contributing to a culture of civic data that shapes and refines expectations of how information can and should be used in public life. These simple, yet powerful actions are habits. Civic habits—or any habitual practice of engaging in civic institutions or community life—are the foundation of the culture of open civic data. These actions become the raw material of civic life.

Why should the open civic data community be thinking about civic habits? Habits are what ultimately will sustain the culture of open civic data. Without habits, there is no demand for data and no foundation on which to build emergent civic actions. In this essay, we look at one kind of civic technology: Constituent Relationship Management (CRM) systems, or 311 reporting tools. CRM systems cultivate civic habits by making civic actions accessible and repeatable. By looking at three distinct generations of CRM systems, we demonstrate how habits, once established, can be reflected upon so as to generate more and different civic actions.

Making Civic Habits

A habit is a settled or regular tendency, especially one that's hard to give up. We tend to think of habits as bad: smoking, gambling, etc. "The fact is," as psychologist William James wrote in 1892, "our virtues are habits as much as our vices. All our life, so far as it has definite form, is but a mass of habits" (James, 1925).

When we talk of civic habits, we are talking about all the practices that form civic life, from bad habits like throwing trash on the street to good habits like picking up another person's trash; from posting a nasty comment about a neighbor on Facebook to tweeting about traffic. Civic habits are everyday repetitive practices that have a bearing on public life. As James put it, we are "mere bundles of habits, we are stereotyped creatures, imitators and copiers of our past selves" (James, 1925). The social context of a city, therefore, is a mere bundle of habits with tools and systems in place that reinforce or disrupt existing habits. Consider how an antiquated data management system in government can perpetuate bad civic habits as city workers produce incomplete or substandard data. Consider how poor placement of recycling bins can produce bad civic habits as people grow tired of carrying a plastic bottle around and just throw it in the nearest trashcan. Now consider how access to open data can produce good civic habits by providing opportunities for people to visualize and augment the world around them so as to make better, more informed decisions.

Habits are even more valuable than the sum of their parts. They are the building blocks that are necessary if a citizen is to move beyond individual or serial actions to be more aware and able to reflect about his or her role in civic life. The philosopher John Dewey argued that all learning is premised on habitual actions (Dewey, 2011). According to Dewey, it is only when something becomes habitual that one has the opportunity to reflect on it—like learning an instrument or a language. Learning happens when one becomes aware of the systems in which actions are taken. For example, when a child is learning to play the piano, she begins immediately to make music by pressing keys in no apparent order. She does not actually learn to play the piano until she understands that strings of notes compose melodies and groupings of notes compose chords. If she never has the opportunity to place her habits within larger systems, if there is no internal or external structure to her learning, there is a danger of getting stuck in a non-reflective habit loop that merely continues the same action without the possibility of growth. When people have the opportunity to place their habits into systems, habits become productive of other habits and emerging systems.

Civic habits are all the actions citizens take that interface with public institutions or communities, from voting to reporting to littering to checking in on an elderly neighbor. Civic habits are produced through formal systems and processes. They are also generated informally by ad hoc groups and networks. What are often missing from this "mass of habits" are opportunities for reflection. It should come as no surprise that government often fails at producing processes and systems that both cultivate habits and provide opportunities to reflect. It is too often the case that government makes productive habit formation difficult because barriers to participation are simply too high. But as the culture of open civic data intersects with government processes, there are examples of government fulfilling its role as a systems designer for civic habits.

One such example is the rapidly growing field of Constituent Relationship Management (CRM) systems. All big cities in the United States have some mechanism for citizens to report problems, from potholes to downed limbs or graffiti. These systems have undergone a series of iterations, from traditional hotlines (CRM 1.0) to mobile applications and interactive web pages (CRM 2.0) to mobile and web tools that frame interaction within a reflective context (CRM 3.0) (see Figure 1). As we will explain, these systems are progressively influenced by the culture of open data. The move from 1.0 to 3.0 reflects an emerging context where citizens can contextualize habits within clearly demarcated systems so as to introduce new actions, new habits, and a new understanding of civic life.

FEATURES	EXAMPLES	EFFECT ON CITIZENS
CRM 1.0 • Data is physically and temporally disconnected from act of providing information. • Raw data is made public for anyone to analyze or graphically represent. • Process of providing data is transactional, not interactive (i.e. filling out a form).	• Raw data files. • Databases. • Data visualizations of past information. • Phone hotlines and online forms.	• Information is public, but not translated in accessible language; use requires skill. • Citizens engage in transactions with government institutions. • Interaction with other citizens not possible.
CRM 2.0 • Capability to view or interact with other data while providing information. • Immediate updating of data. • Easy to offer extra information—geolocation, photos, etc. • Interaction generally enabled, but not a necessary part of tool.	• Lists or map-based representations of reports on separate page from reports. • Ability to comment on, mark-as-important, or "favorite" other existing actions.	• Information is accessible. • Interaction with others is a possible, but seldom-used, affordance. • Civic habits developed/ encouraged by ease of use, mobile capability, etc.
CRM 3.0 • Use necessarily involves interacting with other data/users by adding extra steps or representations to the process of reporting.	• Upon reporting, other actions are recommended, and other actions are automatically shown. • Leaderboards show others' actions. • Interactive features on home reporting screen, not other page.	• Information is accessible. • Interaction with other people or other civic habits accompanies any use. • Civic habits made more reflective and communal.

Civic Habits and CRM

While CRM systems were originally developed as part of the New Public Management approach that emphasized a customer-centered or citizen-centered government, they are also deeply connected to the open data movement as both suppliers of civic data and as tools by which to display and publicize civic data. Over the last several years, governments and non-profits have developed a variety of tools. While they all collect, organize, and publicize civic habits to some degree, these tools' ability to foster good civic habits differ dramatically. Early CRM enabled habits, but did little to encourage them. While the next major developments in CRM facilitated the development and recognition of habits, it was not designed for reflection as a necessary or even important component of habitual action. Currently, as CRM tools are being improved and added to, there are isolated examples of designing for better, reflective civic habits that deserve attention and continuation.

Although it has certainly impacted governments' approach to data, the open data movement's first major impacts on CRM systems did little to move the public toward a culture of open data. Before mobile applications ruled the reporting scene, phone-based hotlines (and later web portals) provided insight into civic habits. Active in over 130 cities, traditional phone-based reporting systems are still in widespread use and largely considered to be success stories in terms of efficiency. CRM 1.0 tools enable citizens to provide information that is relevant to a series of reporting categories. Citizens enter information into a set of forms or relay this information to an operator. While these tools allow citizens to file reports efficiently and effectively, they lack interactivity. They are good at enabling transactions: citizens need something fixed, they report it, and the government responds. Even when reports concern public issues—a broken sidewalk or graffiti on a wall—the hotline system frames the habit as a private action: citizens get their particular, specific needs met; they are not prompted to view their needs as one of many or as an issue shared with others within a community.

Whether phone-based or online, the open data movement has directly impacted these tools. The Open311 movement, for example, has encouraged cities to follow many protocols to ensure that their data is made public and also able to seamlessly integrate with other cities' data and future applications. As a result, a significant portion of the data collected in these systems is made available to the public. Still, they are disconnected from the actions themselves. While they contribute to a valuable store of data, they do not feedback to the user to cultivate reflection on habits and understand how those habits fit into the landscape of the community and the city.

Mobile reporting apps and web tools do more than merely replicate the experience offered by older technologies. As CRM systems go mobile and take better advantage of the web, non-governmental groups have developed tools that can be used across cities. An example of a system created by a non-government group is SeeClickFix. Governments themselves have developed tools, such as NYC311, Chicago Works, and Citizens Connect (Boston). Building upon the existing open data movement, now over 25,000 cities are using SeeClickFix and thirty-two cities are developing apps that support Open311's set of open data standards. These systems display data to more citizens, but more importantly, they allow citizens to see their own data in relation to larger community datasets. Within these apps, data is immediately available and ready at hand, and it serves as the foundation for subsequent actions.

In Boston's Citizens Connect, we can see how CRM 2.0 does more to civic actions than categorize and publicize them; it makes them immediately visible to citizens and connects them to the creation of public knowledge. Rather than simply being confronted by a form to fill out, users can look at other reports—deciding to view them according to most recent or by a specific geographical location. SeeClickFix allows users to see the profiles of "neighbors" using the system in a specific area. These maps are the traces of collective civic habits, and through them, users can visualize their own habits, as well as those of the community as a whole. This visualization of civic habits marks the first step toward reflection.

These tools are widely considered to be successful. Existing apps are scaling themselves to function seamlessly across multiple cities, as is the case with Massachusetts' Commonwealth Connect, an iteration of Boston's Citizens Connect, and the amount of participation via these apps is significant—SeeClickFix hit its 500,000th report in May of

2013. Geolocation and easy camera access in these apps make reporting easier, reports clearer, and as a result, government responsiveness and efficiency of service better. These tools are well positioned to turn individual actions into habitual practice and to expand the influence of such practices to populations not currently predisposed to them.

Enabling reflection, however, has proven to be quite difficult. While these tools can present an individual's civic habits within a larger public context, they do not always succeed at generating motivation for users to pay attention to that context. A survey of 217 of Boston's Citizens Connect users (a response rate of about forty-one percent, sampled from all currently active users) has shown that users are unlikely to engage with the map-based visualization of recent reports or even bother to look at other citizens' reports. Thirty-eight percent of users report that they have never used the mobile app to look at other users' reports, and forty-one percent report they use this feature "a minority of the time." With only slightly over nine percent of users reporting they "always" make use of this feature, it is clear that although possibilities for reflection are designed into the tool, the typical use context does not yet motivate these actions.

There are exceptional cases of citizens working together to solve problems before the city can get to them—fixing a damaged mural or overturning a neighbor's garbage can to free a possibly-dead possum—but these are not the norm. CRM tools have not fully taken advantage of the emerging culture of open civic data to cultivate reflection on civic habits. They still tend to default to the mere facilitation of habitual practice, but as more and more cities commit to using these tools or seek to develop their own, non-reflective habits should not be enough. These tools have the potential to cultivate reflection, where taking individual action leads to actionable public understanding.

CRM tools should be iterated, redesigned, and expanded to create environments that not only allow for reflection upon one's role in civic life, but also actually necessitate it. Some good examples include SeeClickFix's asking and answering feature and Civic Hero, a gamified version of reporting. While these examples are promising, they may not go far enough—how one interacts with CRM should be fundamentally reconfigured for reflection. In other words, when a user picks up Citizens Connect to report a pothole, that impulse should be immediately framed within a larger social context.

Built as an API that connects to multiple existing tools—Boston's Citizens Connect and Commonwealth Connect, SeeClickFix, and Foursquare—StreetCred is one such example. It is designed to improve civic habits and encourage reflection upon these habits at multiple points in the interaction. In StreetCred, players are prompted to take specific actions using already-existing tools, such as Citizens Connect, and are rewarded with badges, which contribute to larger campaigns and real-life rewards. Actions, badges, and campaigns all contribute to a social reputation system that lets players see their participation within the context of community data.

The significance of this intervention is three-fold. First, StreetCred contextualizes one-off moments of participation within greater civic goals and highlights big picture needs of a community or city. Fundamentally, the idea of campaigns is meant to order discrete transactions into legible accomplishments with clear objectives. This practice attempts to interrupt and supplement existing habits with moments of reflection by encouraging actions that citizens have not taken, but are related to either citizens' own interests, or major issues within the community. Second, through location-based interactions, StreetCred makes players aware of how their actions contribute to overall participation at a local, community, and city level. Campaigns are often related to local geographic areas, and users' actions and standing are always displayed within the map-based interfaces that highlight an individual's actions within their local community. As opposed to systems where the act of reporting can be a private interaction with a city, StreetCred allows users to take civic action alongside and in comparison to other citizens. By constructing APIs that connect data from a variety of aggregators, be they privately or publicly owned, StreetCred highlights the fact that open data is not limited to government-run programs.

Conclusion

Civic life is a mass of habits. By enabling moments of civic participation to be collected in ways that are accessible, interoperable, and visible, the open data movement has provided citizens with a way to easily understand these habits and opened up a bounty of new opportunities to simply and flexibly cultivate them. As more and more data is collected and collectable, it is government's responsibility to create and/or support the systems in which habits are formed and reflected upon.

As CRM systems and civic apps undergo further development and iteration, we must move beyond simply designing to make civic actions easy and sustainable. Instead, design choices that encourage reflective civic habits and collaborative and communal participation ought to be the norm. Not only can tools be designed to improve and deepen the civic experience, but their iterations can also set the stage for the development of a more robust culture of open data that extends beyond the civic realm.

About the Authors

Eric Gordon studies civic media, location-based media, and serious games. He is a fellow at the Berkman Center for Internet and Society at Harvard University and an associate professor in the department of Visual and Media Arts at Emerson College where he is the founding director of the Engagement Game Lab (http://engagementgamelab. org), which focuses on the design and research of digital games that foster civic engagement. He is the co-author of Net Locality: Why Location Matters in a Networked World (Blackwell Publishing, 2011) and The Urban Spectator: American Concept Cities From Kodak to Google (Dartmouth, 2010).

Jessica Baldwin-Philippi is a visiting assistant professor of civic media at Emerson College and a researcher in the Engagement Game Lab. Her work focuses on how engagement with new technologies can restructure forms of political participation and ideas about citizenship, and has covered a variety of political contexts, from political campaigns' use of social media, to games designed to increase participation, to tools that can mediate relationships between citizens and governmental institutions.

References

Dewey, J. (2011). *Democracy and Education.* New York: Simon and Brown.

James, W. (1925). *Talks to Teachers on Psychology; And to Students On Some of Life's Ideals.* New York: Henry Holt and Company.

Pew Research Center/Washington Post (2013). "Public Says Investigate Terrorism, Even If It Intrudes on Privacy: Majority Views NSA Phone Tracking as Acceptable Anti-Terror Tactic." Retrieved from http://www.people-press.org/files/legacy-pdf/06-10-13%20PRC%20WP%20Surveillance%20Release.pdf

The Beginning of a Beautiful Friendship: Data and Design in Innovative Citizen Experiences

By Cyd Harrell

The past decade has brought enormous and growing benefits to ordinary citizens through applications built on public data. Any release of data offers advantages to experts, such as developers and journalists, but there is a crucial common factor in the most successful open data applications for non-experts: excellent design. In fact, open data and citizen-centered design are natural partners, especially as the government 2.0 movement turns to improving service delivery and government interaction in tandem with transparency. It's nearly impossible to design innovative citizen experiences without data, but that data will not reach its full potential without careful choices about how to aggregate, present, and enable interaction with it.

Why Design Matters

Public data is rarely usable by ordinary citizens in the form in which it is first released. The release is a crucial early step, but it is only one step in the process of maximizing the usefulness of public resources for the people who own them. Because data carries important information about the parts of people's lives that are necessarily communal, it needs to be available and accessible to all. It needs to be presented in ways that illuminate the information it contains and that allow residents to interact with it and incorporate that information into their lives.

The real-time transit apps that are such a strong early example of useful open data do more than offer a raw feed of bus positions. The best of them allow riders to search arrivals on multiple lines of their choosing and adjust their commute plans accordingly. We can see the difference between great and merely adequate design in markets where multiple applications have been built based on the same data. Designs that more smoothly facilitate the tasks that people want to do are the most adopted. Conversely, valuable data that is presented in a way that is at odds with citizens' mental models or awkward to use often doesn't get the attention it deserves.

When internal systems or processes first become transparent to end-users via the internet, something profound happens. Assumptions that seemed rock solid can come into question, and the entire reason for running the systems and processes can be redefined. I had the privilege of working at a large financial company during the early days of online stock trading in the 1990s. Since it was founded, the company had employed brokers to interact with customers and accept their trade requests. If the back-end systems supporting trading happened to go down, the brokers covered for them with multiple layers of backup plans. As experts and daily users, they also covered for quirks in the system, odd error messages, etc. The company invested heavily in technology and had a track record of ninety-nine percent system uptime, of which it was justifiably proud.

However, once it opened its doors on the web and allowed customers to place trade orders online, things changed. Ninety-nine percent uptime meant potentially fifteen minutes of downtime in twenty-four hours, which was enough to inconvenience thousands of customers if it happened to fall during the market day. A metric that had been important to the company, and on which it thought it was winning, was no longer close to good enough. Error messages written for employees who received six months of training (and were, of course, being paid to be there) were not clear or friendly enough for customers who were becoming accustomed to online interaction through retail. The company had to rethink everything from how it measured its mainframe performance to how it designed its web pages in order to present errors gracefully. It had to intentionally write and design error messages for the first time. It had to consider the needs of people who were not being paid to be there (and indeed, who had plenty of options with the company's competitors) in making choices about its technology systems.

I'm happy to say that my old employer recognized and took on the challenge, and it continues to be a leader in modern, internet-enabled financial services today. I see an analogy between what happened in that industry in the 1990s and what is happening in government now in the 2010s. It was the opening of the systems to customer interaction that triggered a revolution in how the company approached designing for customers. This wasn't just a financial industry phenomenon. As retail stalwarts like Nordstrom attracted online customers, inventory systems designed for internal use became accessible—or at first inaccessible—to customers, creating a frustrating experience. What Nordstrom did in its 2010 redesign has some similarities to a municipal open data release: the company exposed its entire inventory to customers shopping online, enabling people to directly find what they were looking for, wherever it existed within the company's distribution and warehousing systems or its stores (Clifford, 2010). Again, the needs of customers now able to interact with Nordstrom's systems engendered a profound rethinking of what information (data) it provided and how (design) it provided it.

Open data has the potential to trigger a similar revolution in how governments think about providing services to citizens and how they measure their success. It's a huge opportunity, and to take advantage of it will require understanding citizen needs, behaviors, and mental models, and making choices about how to use data to support all of those. In other words, it will require design.

Where Does Design Come In?

Data science can be understood in terms of seven stages: acquire, parse, filter, mine, represent, refine, and interact (Fry, 2004). For the eagerly waiting civic hacker, the first step, acquire, is accomplished through an open data release. For the skilled civic hacker, or for many journalists, that step is the critical one—she can thank the agency that released the data and proceed with her project. The average city resident, however, finds him or herself dependent on others for six of those seven steps after data is released, and in particular, on the final three steps—represent, refine, and interact. These steps are strongly associated with the practice of citizen-centered design.

The difficult task of making data meaningful and useful to all the people who can benefit from it can draw on many methods and examples, but skipping these final steps or doing them poorly can lead to confusion and underutilization of the data that activists have worked hard to get released. Consider US Census data, to take a large example. Early versions of American FactFinder simply provided links to available datasets—a valuable service and a vast improvement on what was available before, via the internet. Still, it was very challenging for untrained people to wade through it.

The latest version of FactFinder, which was released with the 2010 census data in early 2013, has employed design in order to go much further (see http://factfinder2.census.gov). This has been a process of evolution, from the first online releases after the 1990 census to today. The latest version allows a search by ZIP code and returns a set of tabs, each of which highlights one critical piece of information, such as the total population of that ZIP code on the population tab. The Income tab highlights median household income. There are many more facts available in neatly arranged web tables via links, and there is even a Guided Search wizard that helps users find their way to tables that are likely to interest them. It's not Nordstrom.com (or any other large retailer with a design staff and design culture) in terms of ease of use, but it does a great deal to return this data, which is collected by the government and owned by the people, to the people in a form in which they can use it.

Examples From a Design Perspective

There's more to designing open data well than just making it searchable and presenting it attractively. In a recent study of US counties' official election department websites, my collaborators and I discovered a problem with election results released online (Chisnell, 2012). Counties, as everyone who follows elections knows, are the units that precincts roll up to, and for most of the US, they are the level of government that has officials who are responsible for ensuring fair elections and publishing results. All of the counties that we studied fulfilled their statutory obligation to provide vote totals within their county, but voters with whom we conducted usability sessions were dissatisfied with what they found. Why? The counties are releasing the same information they have released for decades, to newspapers in earlier days and to radio and television journalists as the twentieth century progressed. For hundreds of years, journalists (and state election officials) have performed the service of aggregating these county tallies for voters, so that they know who actually won. This is what voters have come to expect as the meaning of "election results"—"who" or "which side" prevailed in the contests they voted on. So, voters looking at county election websites were confused and disappointed by the results sections, which provided only local tallies and no "results."

There's nothing wrong with this public data, but there is a problem with information design. Voters look to these sites for what they think of as results, particularly on second and third rank contests that may not be well covered by the media. The sites currently don't provide voters' idea of results, but simple design changes would allow them to. Without complicating these sites' visual or interaction design, the counties could provide links to the overall outcomes of the contests they report on and satisfy everything citizens want. Design isn't necessarily about being fancy or even pretty—much of it is about the right information at the right time.

The government has collected the first names of children registered for Social Security since the program began. They've collected baby names from birth registrations for longer. In fact, births and names are a basic public record. In the 1990s, after the advent of the web, these records became much more interesting because the data was made available in a form that was easy to explore. We can thank an SSA employee named Michael Shackleford for writing the first search program and making first name data public (Graham, 2013). The agency has since evolved its own design and seen others build on top of its open data. One famous example is NameVoyager. NameVoyager offers a brilliant design on top of public data—the step of visualizing the popularity of names over time on a graph, with pink and blue bands representing girls' and boys' names, and the simple interface that constricts the bands as the user types each letter of a name turns a bureaucratic dataset into a game.

Mobile apps using transit data are one of the biggest citizen-facing open data success stories, but again, an app that simply provides a feed of GPS coordinates for buses isn't a winner. Those that provide the most features aren't necessarily the best ones either.

Weather data has seen some interesting developments in 2012 and 2013 in terms of design. Government weather data has been considered a public good since the government gained the capability to collect meaningful weather data. However, until very recently, it has been offered to the public through basically a single information model. This model was regional (because information was distributed by broadcast), focused on large events and weather patterns, both because those make sense in the regional model and because the entities with the most pressing need for weather data were agricultural and industrial.

Now, consider three recent weather apps, all for mobile phones, that take public weather data a step further: Dark Sky, Swackett, and Yahoo! Weather. All use essentially the same public data, and each offers a different experience. Swackett (released in January 2012) proposes that the main reason individuals need weather data is to understand what kind of clothes to put on or whether or not to bring a jacket. Its interface shows a whimsical figure, which the user can customize through different editions, dressed appropriately for that day's predicted weather in the user's location. More traditional weather information is available through navigation.

Dark Sky (released in April 2012) doesn't show a person, but it also assumes that an individual's reason for looking up the weather is both hyper-local and immediate-future. Dark Sky's default screen shows expected rainfall over the next sixty minutes for the user's current location. It answers the question "do I need to take an umbrella if I go out right now," and it sends notifications like "light rain starting in five minutes." (All of this is only useful because the data is excellent.)

Yahoo! Weather's new app, released in April 2013, combines government data with Yahoo's repository of photos shared by its users to provide a simple temperature with a photographic background that gives a sense of what that weather feels like in the current location. Its designers chose radical simplicity—there are no radar maps, no extended forecasts, and no extras. Different people might choose differently among these three apps—none of them is clearly "better" than the others—but they all employ design in combination with open data to deliver an experience that far exceeds anything that existed prior to the 2010s.

Even our work in open data standards can be supported by good design choices. I don't mean colors and fonts, but choices about where and how to display information that takes account of how people use it. I've been guilty of being a killjoy in the past when I've heard about restaurant health inspection score data being released and civic hackers building apps on it. As a UX designer, I've never observed anyone paying attention to the required public posting of scores in restaurant windows, and it's hard for me to imagine that anyone would actually use such an app in the course of ordinary restaurant going. That said, when Code for America collaborated with the city of San Francisco and Yelp to place restaurants' latest scores within their Yelp profiles using the LIVES standard, I predicted that this would be a useful and successful design.

Why? Yelp is one of the key places where people make decisions about restaurants already. Having one more piece of information available within that interface supports established behaviors that would be difficult to change, whereas having to download and install a separate app specific to health inspections would complicate the process of evaluating restaurants. While this may seem like just an implementation choice, it's a design choice that makes an enormous difference to the user experience.

Much of the work that we are proudest of at Code for America involves strong design, as well as clever technology. BlightStatus, built for the city of New Orleans by Alex Pandel, Amir Reavis-Bey, and Eddie Tejeda in 2012, is celebrated for its success in integrating data from seven disparate city departments. It employs plain language, simple and familiar web affordances, and clear information hierarchies.

DiscoverBPS, the Boston Public Schools search app created by Joel Mahoney in 2011, succeeds because it looks at the process of school choice from a parent's perspective. Rather than listing data school by school, it allows comparison across factors that are likely to be important to families (based on the creators' user research). In reducing the burden required to extract meaning (i.e. the specific information categories they care about) from public data, it uses design to make the information more accessible to everyone.

How Do Successful Collaborations Between Officials, Data Geeks, and Designers Work?

Design is a less familiar field to some members of the open data community, but it shouldn't be intimidating. Designers, in particular designers who practice user-centered design, interaction design, or other disciplines from the broad user experience field, are accustomed to working in cross-disciplinary teams and being transparent about their processes. Much like geeks in other fields, they are often idealistic and unable to resist working on interesting problems.

At Code for America, we include a fellow with a design background on every team, in collaboration with coders and data scientists. The designer's first role is to understand the problem from a citizen perspective. They may review analytics, conduct interviews or end-user observations, or facilitate more formal research. From here, they go on to propose experiences or interactions that would improve the audience's life, without immediate reference to what's technically feasible. This is one starting point for collaboration. Many designers sketch at the stage where developers begin hacking around. Inspiration is equally possible from this direction or from what a developer may dig up in understanding the dataset; a free-ranging conversation between the two disciplines is often magical.

We also ask designers to set goals for the end-user experience of anything we build and to work with their city partners and developer colleagues to align around what qualities the experience should have. Some of these are general—it's always a goal for an application to be simple, beautiful, and easy to use—but many are specific to the problem and audience. A 311 dashboard for a busy city official and a Parks & Recreation app for neighborhood residents will have very different design goals. Once these goals are known, a good designer can guide a team in arranging information and choosing interface elements to support them. Designers are also expert in identifying barriers to adoption or use based on their knowledge of the audience.

To be clear, design training isn't required to do any of this, although an experienced designer can be a great asset to a team and designers are starting to join the open data and civic hacking movements in greater numbers. Many of the core design and user research techniques are well documented and require less time to learn than a new programming language. So, design can play a role as an activity, as well as a team member.

What Could Open Design Look Like?

Whenever I write about design in government systems or open data, I run up against the question of whether design, too, can be open. While the answer is an unqualified yes, the processes and culture aren't as mature as they are for open data or open source software. One interesting example is the Gov.UK design principles, which attempt to open a successful design process ("Design Principles," 2012). Organizations adopting these principles would follow many of the techniques described above.

Traditionally, design has been among the most copyable disciplines— there is no reverse-engineering required to make a Submit button that looks like someone else's excellent button. There have been lawsuits over the years that have attempted to protect designs (witness Apple suing Microsoft over early versions of Windows), but most have been unsuccessful. It's understood that compelling designs will be imitated. At the same time, there's something important about a willingness to be imitated and to have a two-way dialogue with others working to improve experiences in the same space. The city of Buenos Aires has committed to open-sourcing the design of its open data catalog, and the Gov.UK website publishes critical elements of its design, in addition to the process principles. Both of these designs are strong, and hopefully, their openness encourages more people to start from strong foundations.

How else can we share? We can share examples of useful design goals that contributed to successful applications. We can share learning experiences about particular audiences and tasks. While there may be reasons why a Chicago transit rider is different from a Seattle rider, it's highly likely that they have many needs in common. If a member of our community interviewed fifteen commuters in Seattle and proposed a set of design goals for a transit app based on those experiences, those goals could be a useful starting point for a team working on a transit app anywhere. We need to develop better mechanisms for this level of sharing as we develop a culture of open civic design.

Conclusion

Design is a critical practice for enabling open data to reach its full transformative potential. Without citizens being able to interact with government data directly, we are unlikely to trigger a revolution in how services are provided. We all know how much we need that revolution, for reasons of cost, fairness, and human dignity.

Methods drawn from the user experience field are the easiest way to translate open data into a format that's usable and accessible for the average (or non-average) citizen. The most successful and broadly used open data projects have always relied on design, whether or not people formally trained in design were part of the teams. Our task now is to bring our best design ideas into our shared movement and take advantage of everything the discipline has to offer. With design, we can give the public back its data in real use, as well as in name.

About the Author

Cyd Harrell is a user experience expert with over fifteen years of experience improving online and software products. As Code for America's UX Evangelist she works with fellows and staff to help create inventive and cost-effective civic technology that serves the needs of real users. Previously she has been a Board Member at Brightworks School and the VP of UX Research at Bolt Peters.

References

Chisnell, D. (2012, December 6). What I'm working on now. (Web log). Retrieved from http://civicdesigning.org/featured-story/what-im-working-on-now/

Clifford, S. (2010, August 23). Nordstrom Links Online Inventory to Real World. The *New York Times*. Retrieved from http://www.nytimes.com/2010/08/24/business/24shop.html?_r=0

Fry, B.J. (2004). Computational Information Design. (Doctoral dissertation). Retrieved from http://benfry.com/phd/dissertation-110323c.pdf

Government Digital Service. (2012). Design Principles. Retrieved from https://www.gov.uk/designprinciples

Graham, R. (2013, April 14). What baby names say about everything else. The *Boston Globe*. Retrieved from http://www.bostonglobe.com/ideas/2013/04/13/what-baby-names-say-about-everything-else/Ln9kVOl9haGhFoHwQv9h7I/story.html

CHAPTER 13

Generating Economic Value through Open Data

By Michael Chui, Diana Farrell, and Steve Van Kuiken

The private and public sectors have begun to embrace "big data" and analytics to improve productivity and enable innovation. We have documented the tremendous economic potential that can be unlocked by using the increasing volumes and diversity of real-time data (e.g., social media, road traffic flows) to make better decisions in a wide variety of sectors, from healthcare to manufacturing to retail to public administration (Manyika et al., 2011).

Open data—governments and other institutions making their data freely available—plays an important role in maximizing the benefits of big data. Open data enables third parties to create innovative products and services using datasets such as transportation data, or data about medical treatments and their outcomes, that are generated in the course of providing public services or conducting research. This is a trend that is both global—in less than two years, the number of national governments that have become members of the Open Government Partnership has increased from a founding eight to more than fifty—and local; state/provincial, and municipal governments, including New York, Chicago, and Boston, have begun to "liberate" their data through open data initiatives.

Some of the key motivations for open data initiatives are to promote transparency of decision-making, create accountability for elected and appointed officials, and spur greater citizen engagement. In addition, however, it is increasingly clear that open data can also enable the creation of economic value beyond the walls of the governments and institutions that share their data. This data can not only be used to help increase the productivity of existing companies and institutions, it also can spur the creation of entrepreneurial businesses and improve the welfare of individual consumers and citizens.

McKinsey & Company is engaged in ongoing research to identify the potential economic impact of open data, the findings from which will be published in the fall of 2013. In this piece, we would like to share some of our preliminary hypotheses from this work, including examples from our research into open data in healthcare (See "The 'Big Data' revolution in healthcare," McKinsey Center for US Healthcare Reform and Business Technology).

Definitions

It's helpful to first clarify what we mean by open data. We use four criteria to define open data:

- Accessible to all. This is the key criterion—the data becomes accessible outside of the organization that generated or collected it.

- Machine-readable. Data must be useable, which means it must be made available in formats that are easily used in third-party applications.

- Free. Zero or low costs for data access aid openness.

- Unrestricted rights to use. Data that is unencumbered by contractual or other restrictions leads to the maximum potential of innovation.

However, we also recognize that these are the ideals of "openness" and there is still significant value in making data more widely available, even if its use is not completely unrestricted. For example, the US Centers for Medicare & Medicaid Services (CMS) has released some health-care claims data, but only for use by qualified medical researchers, and with strict rules about how the data can be used. Nevertheless, providing this data outside of CMS multiplies the amount of value it can create. Similarly, there is great variation in the degree to which data can be considered machine-readable. Data in proprietary formats is machine-readable, but is less useful than data in open-standard formats, which do not require licenses to use and are not subject to change with format updates decided by a single vendor. And while a strict definition of open data requires zero cost for data access, some institutions have chosen to charge a fee for accessing data, still providing considerable value.

Very closely related to this definition of open data is the concept of "my data," which involves supplying data about individuals or organizations that has been collected about them. In the United States, the "Blue Button" encourages healthcare providers to give patients access to their health information (see www.bluebuttondata.org). Similarly, the "Green Button" program encourages energy providers to give consumers access to energy usage information such as data collected by smart meters (see www.greenbuttondata.org). In "my data" applications, information is not made accessible to all, but only to the person or organization whose activities generated the data. These users can opt in to make their data available to other service providers (e.g., a service that analyzes energy consumption and suggests ways in which to improve energy efficiency).

Why Now?

It's also worth considering why the open data movement is gathering momentum. First, the amount and variety of valuable data that is being generated and collected by institutions has exploded: transaction data produced by government, sensor data collected from the physical world, and regulatory data collected from third parties such as transportation carriers or financial institutions. Secondly, the ability to process large, real-time, diverse streams of data has been improving at an exponential rate, thanks to advances in computing power. Today, a smartphone has sufficient processing power to beat a grandmaster at chess.

Equally important, there are institutional forces accelerating the adoption of open data initiatives. Both within and especially outside of government, decision makers are demanding more precise and timely insights, supported by data and experimentation (e.g., running controlled experiments on the web or in the real world to determine how people will actually behave). At the same time, governments are under pressure to become more transparent, while simultaneously doing more with less due to fiscal constraints. The financial pressure also compels governments to look for economic growth and innovation, which could be catalyzed by new businesses based on open data.

Finally, there is a social benefit: open data can democratize information, as more individuals gain access to their own data through my data initiatives, and people with programming skills gain access to more datasets. Individuals can develop applications that use open data, reflecting their interests, rather than relying on data services provided by large organizations.

How Open Data Creates Economic Value

Our emerging hypothesis is that the effective use of open data can unlock significant amounts of economic value. For example, in US healthcare, we found that more than $300 billion a year in value potentially could be created through the use of more open data, e.g., through the analysis of open data to determine which therapies are both medically effective and cost-efficient. We also recognize that access to data alone does not unlock value. In healthcare, many systemic reforms need to be in place before data-enabled innovations such as large-scale analyses of comparative effectiveness and genetically tailored therapies can achieve their maximum potential. Yet, if reforms are in place, truly transformative changes in the healthcare system can result. We believe similar changes can occur in many other domains.

So what are some of the archetypes for value creation that we discovered? Building on our big data research, we see five common ways in which the use of open data can unlock value.

Transparency

In many cases, we find that decisions are made without access to relevant data. Simply providing data to the right decision maker at the right moment can be a huge win. For example, most patients and primary care physicians have limited knowledge about how well different hospitals do in various types of surgery or how much different providers charge for a particular procedure. When such data exists—and is provided in a usable format—the resulting transparency can lead to better decisions. In our study of US healthcare, we estimate that ensuring that patients go to the right care setting (e.g., the one with the best record of outcomes and the best costs) could unlock $50 to $70 billion in annual value.

Exposing Variability and Enabling Experimentation

Closely related to transparency is the concept of exposing variability in processes and outcomes, then using experimentation to identify the drivers of that variability. For example, open data can be used to expose the variability in improving student achievement across various schools or school districts. When this information is made transparent, it creates incentives to improve educational outcomes. In addition to simply exposing differences in performance, open data can be used to design and analyze the outcomes of purposeful experimentation to determine which organizational or teaching techniques raise student achievement.

Segmenting Populations to Tailor Actions

Open data can also be used to ensure that individuals and organizations receive the products and services that best meet their needs. There is an old saying in marketing that we know that half of marketing spending is wasted, but we don't know which half. Open data can sometimes help marketers find the additional insights that can make their efforts more effective. For example, a provider of rooftop solar panels could narrow its targeted offers to customers who both have sufficient roof area, and sufficient solar exposure by using aerial imagery and weather data available from public sources.

Augmenting and/or Automating Human Decision-Making

Open data can be used to augment the data that is being analyzed to improve or automate decision-making. We know from research in behavioral economics and other fields that human decision-making is often influenced by cognitive biases. Furthermore, our minds are limited in the number of data points we can process. Advanced analytical techniques can help overcome these limitations. For example, researchers only identified the cardiovascular risks of COX-2 inhibitors (a class of anti-inflammatory drugs) after analyzing data on millions of individual doses. In some cases, data can be used to make real-time decisions automatically. For example, by combining data from embedded sensors with open data traffic information, it is possible to create systems that automatically adjust the timing of traffic signals to relieve congestion.

Creating New Products, Services and Business Models

Some of the most exciting applications of open data come about when it is used to create new products and services by existing companies, or to create entirely new businesses. For example, in 2012, more than two hundred new applications of open health-care data were submitted to the US Health Data Initiative Forum. One submission, from a startup called Asthmapolis, combines usage data from sensors on asthma medicine inhalers with open environmental data (e.g., pollen counts and data on other allergens) to develop personalized treatment plans for patients with asthma.

Enablers to Create Economic Value

Successful open data initiatives have many elements and the open data community is beginning to share practices and stories to make success more likely. Based on our ongoing research, we suggest that the following elements are needed for a successful open data initiative.

Prioritize Open Data Efforts According to Potential Value

Too often, open data initiatives seem to prioritize releasing data based on the ease of implementation (i.e., making available the data that is easiest to release). We believe the prioritization process should also take value creation potential into account. For instance, datasets collected for regulatory or compliance purposes that enable companies to benchmark their performance against other players in the marketplace (e.g., energy efficiency data, purchasing data) can drive significant increases in economic performance for companies and consumers, even if the release of this data doesn't directly benefit the public sector agency. Of course, it isn't possible to predict all of the ways in which open data can be used to create value, so it's still important to release open data to the large community of potential outside innovators, even if it's not clear how it will be used. But in the near term, considering potential value creation along with ease of implementation should be part of the prioritization process.

Activate a Thriving Ecosystem of Developers to Use Open Data

To a certain extent, open data is a "platform play," i.e., a foundation on which third parties can build innovative products and services. Tim O'Reilly, founder of O'Reilly Media, has famously described the concept of "Government as a Platform" (O'Reilly, 2011). To have a successful platform, you need to have a thriving ecosystem of contributors that build on your platform. For a successful open data initiative, it is important to activate a thriving ecosystem of developers that will build applications that use open data. This requires activities akin to marketing, including raising awareness of the availability of open data, convincing developers to try using open data (potentially through special offers, perhaps contests), supporting their experience, and even encouraging them to return to use other open data. The "Datapaloozas" that the United States Government has sponsored are an example of activating an ecosystem of developers to consume open data, as they convene developers at common events, celebrating successes and raising the visibility of and excitement around open data.

Build the Infrastructure to Manage Data

Clearly, a scalable and reliable data infrastructure has to be put in place. Ideally, an institution's internal data infrastructure will be designed in such a way that makes it easy to open data to external connections when the decision is made to do so. One guiding principle that can help make this possible is to build internal interfaces as if they were external interfaces. Amazon.com requires all of its internal IT services to have standard application program interfaces. Then, when it wants to expose a new service that it has developed internally to the outside world, the process is relatively straightforward.

Identify Channels to Release Data

Thoughtful consideration must also be given to the channels through which open data is distributed. These decisions can greatly affect the uptake and continuing use of open data. Are you releasing data in open data formats that make it easy for third party developers to use? Do you provide appropriate metadata to help guide the users to the data? Do you provide means through which users of the data are alerted automatically when data has been updated?

Protect Data That Needs to be Protected

Some institutions have decided to make "open" the default for their data. However, there are often good reasons not to release all of an organization's data or to restrict openness along one of more of the open data dimensions (e.g., with fees or restrictions on use). Thoughtfully identifying the criteria for such restrictions will be important; they could include safety, security, privacy, liability, intellectual property, and confidentiality.

Provide Leadership to the Open Data Community

Last but not least, a successful open data program needs real leadership and a commitment to supporting an open data culture. In some cases, the benefits of releasing data could be outweighed by the perceived risks to managers, who might see an open data initiative as adding more work (e.g., dealing with outside stakeholders), while simultaneously making it more likely that facts in the data might be misrepresented, or even reveal issues about their operations. Leaders will have to set a tone from the top that the overall benefits make an open data initiative worth the investments and risks. Furthermore, leaders will also have to engage with the external community of data consumers, learning to treat them as "data customers," and being responsive to their concerns and suggestions.

Particularly for smaller municipalities, it can be a challenge to find the resources, both financial as well as human, to invest in open data initiatives. One point that can help the investment case for open data is that much of the infrastructure for open data, e.g. building internal IT service interfaces as if they were external interfaces, actually improves the efficiency and scalability of the institution itself. Secondly, technology innovations, such as cloud services, are making the level of required investment more manageable. And more generally, taking advantage of external resources, from open source software to innovation fellowships and civic hackathons, can also unlock additional capabilities. Ultimately, institutions will have to determine the relative priority of creating value through open data to support their missions in the context of the other priorities.

Overall, open data can generate value for multiple stakeholders, including governments themselves, established companies, entrepreneurs, and individual citizens. Understanding the scope and scale of this value potential, particularly for stakeholders outside of the organization opening its data, and how to effectively create an ecosystem of data users, will be essential in order to generate this value.

About the Authors

Dr. Michael Chui is a principal of the McKinsey Global Institute (MGI), McKinsey's business and economics research arm, where he leads research on the impact of information technologies and innovation on business, the economy, and society. Prior to joining McKinsey, Michael served as the first chief information officer of the city of Bloomington, Indiana, where he also founded a cooperative Internet Service Provider. He is based in San Francisco, CA.

Diana Farrell is a director in McKinsey & Company's Public Sector Practice, and the global leader and a co-founder of the McKinsey Center for Government (MCG). Diana rejoined McKinsey in 2011, after two years as Deputy Director of the National Economic Council and Deputy Assistant on Economic Policy to President Obama. She is based in Washington, DC.

Steve Van Kuiken is a director in McKinsey & Company's Business Technology Office, and leads McKinsey's Healthcare Information

Technology work, serving a wide variety of healthcare organizations in developing and executing technology strategies, including payors and providers, pharmaceutical and medical products companies, and IT providers to the industry. He is based in McKinsey's New Jersey office.

The authors wish to thank their colleague Peter Groves, a principal at McKinsey & Company based in New Jersey, for his substantial contributions to this article.

References

Manyika, J., Chui, M., Brown, B., Bughin, J., Dobbs, R., Roxburgh, C., & Hung Byers, A. (2011). Big Data: The next frontier for innovation, competitiveness and productivity. McKinsey Global Institute, May 2011. Available at http://www.mckinsey.com/insights/business_technology/big_data_the_next_frontier_for_innovation

O'Reilly, Tim (2011). Government as a Platform. Innovations, Winter 2011, Vol. 6, No. 1, Pages 13-40.

CHAPTER 14

Local Scale and Local Data

By Alissa Black and Rachel Burstein

Today, the town hall meeting conjures visions of televised, invitation-only debates in which candidates for national office respond in scripted paragraphs to the prepared questions of selected constituents. But in the eighteenth and nineteenth centuries, town hall meetings were a space in which citizens came to debate the issues of the day, and to vote on appropriate action. For Henry David Thoreau (1854), town hall meetings in which each man was afforded a voice on questions as morally significant and politically complex as Massachusetts' enforcement of the Fugitive Slave Act were the "true Congress, and the most respectable one that is ever assembled in the United States." Thoreau was fundamentally distrustful of the big cities of New York and Boston, where the press, politicians, and special interest groups obscured citizens' voices.

Of course, Thoreau's assessment of the town meeting was steeped in romanticism. Non-citizens were largely excluded from the proceedings, and the homogenous population of the rural towns so loved by Thoreau allowed a purity of conscience more difficult to sustain in nearby Boston, in which a complex economy, population density, and diversity made the inclusion of individual residents' voices more complicated, and policy decisions less tied to moral certitude alone. But still, in the town meetings of his beloved Concord, Massachusetts, Thoreau saw the promise of American democracy most fully realized. The ideal of residents contributing directly to the governance of their communities through the town hall meeting is one that persists to this day.

As in the town hall meeting system in which residents co-governed with elected officials, true engagement in the twenty-first century involves not only listening, but also collaboration and action. The full potential of the twenty-first century virtual commons is dependent not just on the voicing of ideas by residents, but on the incorporation of these ideas and concerns into innovative and constructive public policies by cities, and the ability of cities to address difficult issues of access, digital literacy, language barriers, and awareness that often interfere with the ability of the virtual commons to reach and empower all populations.

Such exchanges need not rely on new technologies. Participatory budgeting, in which residents submit proposals for and vote on funding allocations for city-funded projects is one example of a non-technology driven approach to establishing a new civic commons. But new technologies and approaches developed or engaged by local government—including the sensible release and adequate guidance in the use of open data—can offer a path toward developing a new and vibrant public square.

Towards a Twenty-First Century Town Hall

The local level provides an unparalleled space for government to harness the power of community groups, neighborhood associations, other supporting organizations, and residents themselves to convene citizens, share knowledge, and identify and develop better ways of responding to community needs. Close proximity and the potential for developing personal relationships allow organizing to have a broader impact. Local government has the ability to serve and respond to the needs of diverse populations through engaging residents and community groups directly in a way that is not possible at the state or federal level.

In fact, innovation at the local level of government looks very different than innovation pursued by federal agencies. With more direct contact with the public than their colleagues in Washington, local government innovation can be more directly responsive to an existing community need as articulated by community groups and ordinary citizens. The smaller scale of local government means that soliciting and incorporating feedback directly from the community is much more feasible. Innovation at the local level can change the relationship between residents and their government, rather than focusing on the transactional elements of government alone.

Service delivery is at the heart of most residents' engagement with municipal government, regardless of city size. Without the services offered by cities—as varied as schools, libraries, garbage pickup, public safety, and public transit—many residents would be in tough shape. Before ten o'clock in the morning, the average person might wake up, take his city-owned trash can to the curb for pickup, wave to the street cleaner funded by city coffers, and return his books to the city-supported library before hopping on a bus whose route has been set by city planners. His level of engagement with local services is far more tangible, personal, and expansive than his everyday experience of state or federal services.

Because of this immediate relevance of municipal services to the average citizen's life, the local level is a promising point of entry into establishing a modern day public sphere.

From Data to Engagement

Any conversation about relationships between government and citizens at the local level necessitates a consideration of data. Our cities are prolific generators of data that directly impacts our daily lives—everything from train schedules to trash pickup days. They're also collectors of data, like enrollment in social services or parking meter usage. Local community groups also often serve as stewards and curators of important data about their own communities. Both city- and community-generated data can be powerful fuel for meaningful civic dialogue and action.

For example, in the Tenderloin, a low-income and predominantly minority neighborhood in San Francisco, the City failed to respond to noise complaints because there were no data to support the claim that the noise level was beyond an acceptable limit. So, the Gray Area Foundation for the Arts (GAFFTA), a non-profit digital arts and technology organization located in the Tenderloin, joined with residents and local civic hackers, to place noise sensors around the district to collect data on noise levels throughout the day (see http://tendernoise.movity.com/). Armed with data from the noise sensors, GAFFTA was able to prove that the noise levels in the Tenderloin exceeded the allowable levels because, for example, most of the city's fire and emergency vehicles used streets in the Tenderloin to travel across town, and the City permitted more emergency construction permits that allowed crews to begin and end loud construction work late in the day.

This story illustrates how community groups and other nonprofits can use data to improve the lives of those living and working around them. Residents, community groups, non-profit organizations, and businesses already play important roles in local governance as knowledge disseminators, identifiers of community needs, and as advocates for the implementation of governmental policies and programs—and data can be a tool to further this engagement. Empowered with the data proving that noise levels were above those acceptable in other parts of San Francisco, GAFFTA and Tenderloin residents were able to make a case for rerouting emergency vehicles and reducing construction in the noise polluted district.

When civic data held by the government is made open for diverse populations to use and remix, it expands the possibilities for data to facilitate civic engagement and enable citizens to collaborate with their city to co-create better public services. Open data has the potential to empower citizens to identify community needs, propose and develop new approaches, and engage new constituencies.

This is exemplified by a number of cities that publish crime data and the neighborhood groups that emerge to deter crime in the city. Equipped with data, the neighborhood groups are better able to identify trends in crime and take proactive measure to prevent crime. In this way, citizens' use of datasets—such as transportation and crime—have the potential to reshape the way that local governments deploy public safety or public transit services, making them more efficient and equitable systems. When approached in the right way, these open datasets can serve as catalysts for meaningful exchange about community priorities—in some ways a modern-day public square for multiple constituencies.

But to realize the full potential requires more than simply declaring a dataset open and putting a PDF version on a website. First of all, the data must be not only open and available, but also in a useful (and preferably machine-readable) format. When civic data is conducive to being repurposed and interpreted by government and citizens, new value and meaning can be unlocked. For example, a list of crime reports in an Excel format is not that helpful for a parent trying to understand whether the route her child takes to school every day is safe. But when that list of crime incidents is mapped, the information becomes much more consumable. The data become even more useful when the parent can input his child's route to school and a system displays only the crimes reported within a five-block radius of that route. This shows the power of data to improve citizens' lives when those data are made accessible to the average citizen.

It can also be made more powerful when multiple datasets are used to tell a more comprehensive story. For example, in charting the location of abandoned vehicles, it is possible to tell a larger story about crime. In neighborhoods where more vehicles are abandoned, more crime generally occurs, and understanding the correlation between the two allows local governments to take crime prevention measures in areas where vehicles are being dumped, providing a better way of assessing community need than simply responding to the loudest voices.

Standardization can help scale the impact of open civic data to millions of people when government and private companies partner to create a consistent way of formatting data and making it available to the public. In 2005, Google and Portland's Tri-Met transit agency made it possible to plan a trip in Google using public transportation, and then published their standard specification. Called the General Transit Feed Specification (GTFS), this created a standard way of presenting transit information from any transit agency, like fares and schedules, which could be used by Google's Transit Trip planner. This standard allowed millions of people in cities throughout the world to plan their public transportation trips more effectively. This seemingly small action changed the public's expectation for transit planning and transit data sharing.

The Challenge of Inclusive Engagement

Open data that powers inclusive citizen engagement requires a level of co-governance that goes beyond simply publishing data for transparency's sake. This next step from transparency to engagement is not always easy, but promising examples show that when done right, the impact can be significant.

For instance, an app developed by Sam Ramon's Fire Department is used to leverage bystander performance and active citizenship to improve cardiac arrest survival rates. The City makes 911 emergency call information publicly available via the app, PulsePoint, in which residents trained in CPR are alerted if a person in a location near to them has gone into cardiac arrest. The tool goes beyond the mere presentation of data by promoting "active citizenship" so that residents are supporting their neighbors and public safety agencies. PulsePoint demonstrates the potential to move beyond openness to forming the cornerstone of a new public square in which government, citizens, and other groups work together to improve their communities.

In order for open data to fulfill the mission of inclusivity, open data platforms must speak to multiple publics. By making data more accessible to those without technological know-how, open data can democratize the conversation leading to a better understanding of community needs and resulting in more responsive government. Ordinary citizens can serve as important sources of data and can help to analyze those data if information is presented in understandable ways. Coupling the release of open data with digital literacy training and increased government-supported access to internet for underserved populations can make open data more inclusive. Putting open data in service to the public's priorities and interests can also assist in this process.

An obstacle is that many cities still don't see pursuing an open data policy and developing accompanying resources to make those data meaningful as within their reach. This is more than just a perception problem. San Francisco, Philadelphia, Boston, and Chicago grab headlines when it comes to technological innovation, but most cities do not have the resources of these major urban areas. There are fewer than three hundred cities in the United States with populations of 100,000 or more, yet there are over 7,500 municipalities with populations above 2,500 nationwide (International City/County Management Association, 2012). The vast majority of the nation's cities have populations of 25,000 or fewer residents. And over 3,500 cities have council-manager systems of governance, rather than the strong mayor systems predominant in the country's largest cities.

The size and form of government have implications for the resources available and the method through which change happens in local government. According to one recent survey, while seventy-nine percent of cities of populations of 300,000 or more have open data portals, just thirty-six percent of cities with populations under 50,000 do (see Hillenbrand, 2013). And an approach in which a charismatic mayor greenlights civic technology projects, as has been the pattern in Boston and Philadelphia, is not open to most locales where a council-manager system predominates.

With budget shortfalls and increasing demands for service, most local government employees have other priorities besides open data. In a recent survey of city managers and county administrators in California, thirty-five percent of respondents identified a service delivery project as the most important new approach instituted by their locale in the last five years (Burstein, 2013). Twenty-eight percent of cited projects involved some element of regional collaboration. Projects that fell into two areas that commentators often hail as the holy grail of local government innovation—civic engagement and e-government—each accounted for only eleven percent of responses. While elements of both of these areas were certainly features of other kinds of projects, civic engagement and e-government were not the end goals. Instead, improving service delivery to residents was the primary objective. This shows the deep disconnect between the potential of open data and perceptions and abilities to create sound open data policies and practices in city governments across the country.

With the advent of open source and low cost tools that can help streamline the process of opening up data, and the increasingly open attitudes towards collaborative approaches like city-sponsored hackathons, it's more feasible for even small cities to pursue open data policies. But in order for open data to emerge as a powerful civic commons in which diverse residents are engaged and involved in the process of collaborative co-governance in cities throughout the nation, open data advocates need to do a better job of connecting the open data movement with the service delivery goals at the forefront of the minds of most city administrators. We need better ways of illustrating the value of open data to residents, and we need better ways of talking about open data as a strategy for supporting existing policy goals.

Cities also need more resources. The open data community of hackers, businesses, non-profits, community groups, residents, philanthropic foundations, and local government employees who have implemented open data initiatives elsewhere need to play a bigger role in developing resources for smaller, less well resourced communities. We can make valuable contributions—including building and maintaining open source civic software—to help transform the meaning of civic innovation beyond service delivery and toward collaborative, co-governance.

Open data has the ability to reshape the public's relationship with government, reinvigorating the long dormant space of the public square in the increasingly digitized but equally fragmented cityscape of the twenty-first century. Open data is a piece of a larger movement toward civic innovation capitalizing on the advantages of a smaller scale that holds enormous promise for our nation's cities and for twenty-first century democracy. But that will only occur if the open data community moves forward with sensitivity and wisdom to the realities of our cities' ecosystems and needs.

About the Authors

Alissa Black directs the New America Foundation's California Civic Innovation Project. Based in the Bay area, Ms. Black is exploring the use of innovative technologies, policies, and practices that engage disadvantaged communities in public decision-making throughout California. Prior to joining New America, Ms. Black was the Government Relations Director at Code for America, a non-profit organization that helps governments work better through the use of technology and new practices. She also has extensive experience as a leader in local government, having worked in the New York City Mayor's Office and the City of San Francisco's Emerging Technologies team, where she led the development and deployment of Open311, the leading national standard for citizen reporting.

Rachel Burstein is a research associate at the California Civic Innovation Project at the New America Foundation.

References

Burstein, Rachel (2013). The Case for Strengthening Personal Networks in California Local Government: Understanding local government innovation and how it spreads. Retrieved from http://newamerica.net/sites/newamerica.net/files/policydocs/The_Case%20for%20Strengthening_Personal_Networks_in_CA_Local%20Government.pdf

Hillenbrand, Katherine (2013). From Hieroglyphs to Hadoop: The Development of Civic Data. Retrieved from http://datasmart.ash.harvard.edu/news/article/from-hieroglyphs-to-hadoop-192

International City/County Management Association (2012). Form of Government Statistics - Cities (2012). Retrieved from http://icma.org/en/icma/knowledge_network/documents/kn/Document/303818/Form_of_Government_Statistics__Cities_2012

Thoreau, Henry David (1854). Slavery in Massachusetts. Retrieved from http://www.africa.upenn.edu/Articles_Gen/Slavery_Massachusetts.html

PART IV:
Driving Decisions with Data

Editor's Note

What happens when local governments focus on open data as a tool for making better decisions—moving beyond transparency to become data-driven entities themselves? In this section, we hear from practitioners who share the rationale and results behind their efforts to help government not only open data for public use, but to internally leverage data to continuously improve business processes, policy, and resource allocation.

In Chapter 15, Mike Flowers, the first-ever Chief Analytics Officer for New York City, describes New York City's success of applying predictive data analytics to create efficiencies in government leading to real service delivery improvements. From their bootstrap beginnings based on leveraging existing open datasets, he traces the arc of their program's successes and expansion.

Next, Beth Blauer shares her experience building the first statewide performance improvement program with Maryland Governor Martin O'Malley in Chapter 16. She documents the key success factors she learned while building that program, and shares how she is now using her work in the private sector at open data provider Socrata to help make performance management programs easier for other local governments to implement.

Chapter 17 provides of a case study of Louisville's evolution of the StateStat approach. Louisville's Theresa Reno-Weber (Chief of Performance Management) and Beth Niblock (Chief Information Officer) describe the tangible successes of open data for performance management through the LouieStat program—including reducing the amount spent on unscheduled overtime by $3 million annually. Focusing on Louisville's adoption of the lean startup "minimum viable product" model, they extrapolate lessons that can help cities across the country better use open data to build capacity to do more with less.

Ken Wolf and John Fry, who have extensive experience at working with local governments to implement their performance management software, build upon the case studies of data-driven performance management in other cities with an outline of the long term vision for collaborative benchmarking and sharing of best practices in comparative advantages between cities. In Chapter 18, they share the early indications that this opportunity exists, and what's needed to take it further.

CHAPTER 15

Beyond Open Data: The Data-Driven City

By Michael Flowers

Being a data-driven city is about more efficiently and effectively delivering the core services of the city. Being data-driven is not primarily a challenge of technology; it is a challenge of direction and organizational leadership.

College seminars, management consultants, and whole sections of the *Wall Street Journal* have all started to focus on something called "big data." The general definition of big data that's evolving is that it's an exponentially larger set of information than we're accustomed to analyzing, generated by machines, produced frequently, and often tagged with geo-location. The applications of big data are often an afterthought, while the conversation focuses on the quantity of data, how we'll warehouse it, and assumptions along the general ethos of "more is better." The reality is that big data holds promise, but it should not be confused with being data-driven.

A focus on outcomes is often lost in the discussion of big data because it is so frequently an afterthought. We have a huge fire hose of information, but even a fire hose is only valuable when it's pointed at a fire. Data by itself is not inherently valuable. Collecting information about traffic patterns in a CSV file is not in itself helpful; the data becomes more valuable when it is used to form traffic-enabled maps and when city planners use the information to redesign traffic patterns. However, what really matters is not the CSV file, the map, or the traffic patterns, but the outcomes: using data to improve traffic and cut down on commute time, reduce automobile traffic and improve our air quality in the city, create crosswalks and bike lanes that decrease the incidents of car and truck accidents with pedestrians and cyclists, and allow us to live faster, cleaner, and safer lives.

If you're looking for well-managed, focused, and data-driven institutions, look no further than the major American cities. City governments provide the services that are the backbone of modern life: the water we use when we brush our teeth in the morning; the roads, buses, and subways that take us to work; the teams that keep our streets clean and our parks green; the schools where are children are educated; and the police and fire forces that keep us safe. Increasingly, we see that Americans are choosing to live in cities. Attracted by the economic and cultural opportunities, Americans and immigrants are pursuing their dreams right alongside hundreds of thousands, if not millions, of fellow citizens. They're not drawn to spacious apartments or luxurious commutes—in fact, they're often making trade-offs on housing and transportation. They're moving because they are committed to an urban life.

This great urban migration is placing even higher levels of demand on basic city infrastructure: water, sewer, fire, police, housing, healthcare, education, parks, and so on are all in higher demand. Meanwhile, cities have even fewer resources to meet those needs. In response to economic conditions of the last decade, cities have witnessed tax revenues that are lower on a per-capita basis, which means that mayors and city leadership are forced to do more with less. In practice, that means finding new ways to get even better outcomes out of our current systems and processes.

A data-driven city is a city that intelligently uses data to better deliver critical services. Transparency, open data, and innovation are all important parts of the modern civic identity, especially in a city like New York, which is focused on strengthening its position as a tech leader. However, being a data-driven city is really about more efficiently and effectively delivering the core services of the city: smarter, risk-based resource allocation, better sharing of information agency-to-agency to facilitate smart decision-making, and using the data in a way that integrates in the established day-to-day patterns of city agency front line workers. Being data-driven is not primarily a challenge of technology; it is a challenge of direction and organizational leadership.

For New York, a series of 2011 apartment fires helped galvanize our focus on the ability of data—in this case, the data that we already had—to save lives.

Apartment Fires in the Bronx and Brooklyn

In the spring of 2011, a pair of house fires in apartment buildings in the Bronx and Brooklyn killed five people as a result of unsafe living conditions. This sort of fire is not an isolated incident. When many people crowd into unsafe apartment conditions, with portable cooking devices, questionable electrical wiring, and inadequate fire escape access, catastrophic fires will take lives. The occurrence is all too common in a densely populated city like New York. The City receives over 20,000 citizen complaints a year from buildings suspected of being unsafe boarding houses.

New York collects an immense amount of information about every single one of our buildings. We know when and how buildings were built; we know if the building is receiving water service and is, therefore, inhabited; and we know if buildings are in good order based upon the location's history of ECB (environmental complaint board) violations on quality of life issues. Every day, we receive over 30,000 service requests (complaints) through 311 from New Yorkers, which gives us more location-specific intelligence. We know even more about the neighborhood where the building is located: we know how often 911 runs are made to that block-face, if road construction is being done, if there are accidents in the intersections, and what kinds of businesses are on the block.

In the case of the fire in the two buildings, by the time they occurred, the City had information on tax liens, building complaints, sanitation violations, and building wall violations. Did we know enough about these buildings before the fire that should have raised a red flag? Could we determine which pieces of information are the most valuable predictors of catastrophic outcomes? Our team, the Mayor's Office of Data Analytics, set to work to answer those questions.

Analyzing the Illegal Conversion Problem

Providing safe, abundant, and affordable housing is a priority for the leader of every community, from the mayor of a town of 25,000 to the mayor of New York City. Every year, more people move to New York City, and as they do, housing demand increases, the price of rent grows, and individuals are often in a bind as they search for affordable housing.

Because of this strain, the City continues to invest in constructing new affordable housing and maintaining our large system of affordable housing buildings. However, unscrupulous landlords often take advantage of the high demand by providing substandard apartments. They create these apartments by subdividing existing space, with disregard to fire exit access. They put deadbolts on bedroom doors in single-family houses and rent them out as hotel rooms. They put a half bath into a garage, seal the door with tape, and rent out the space. They put beds next to boilers in basements, which is an area that is prone to carbon monoxide poisoning and boiler explosions. In general, they allow for gross over-occupation of small spaces without sanitary conditions. The City classifies these substandard apartments as "illegal conversions."

The New York City Building Code has one primary goal: safety. That code wasn't created out of thin air; it has been created and refined with hundreds of years of civil enforcement in the city, often in response to catastrophic accidents. Rules around fire escape access, size of space, inhabitation of basements, etc., are all designed to prevent New Yorkers from dying in building accidents. The City enforces that building code with a team of building inspectors, who always examine buildings in the construction process and continue to monitor buildings as they mature. These inspectors are trained professionals. When they find an illegal conversion, they do a great job of enforcing the code by either ensuring that the space is immediately configured for safe living or vacating the space to get the residents out of the path of harm. With new residents moving to the city every day, though, and landlords willing to take advantage of them, especially those who are most vulnerable to exploitation, the City must address a constantly growing and changing stock of illegally converted living spaces.

The City's single largest source of intelligence on illegal conversions is New Yorkers who phone in (or use the web or mobile app) to 311 with tips. We have millions of eyes and ears on the street, and every day, we get over 30,000 new pieces of intelligence. Often, that intelligence has immediate, direct value; when a New Yorker calls in a street light that's gone out, we're able to send a truck and replace the bulb. Almost every single one of those street light complaints is founded, meaning that the light is actually out. That makes sense because you can look at the lamppost and see if it's shining or not. Seeing an illegal conversion is much more complex. The individual who makes the complaint often has no direct access to the space, and instead, they're forming their hypothesis based on what they see on the outside of the building in terms of population flow in and out of the building, the number of cars parked on the street, the amount of trash generated by the building, etc. Unfortunately, only eight percent of the specific 311 illegal conversion complaints from the citizenry are actually high-risk illegal conversions.

Illegally converted housing spaces are the worst of the worst because they are the places where we're most likely to lose lives. When we send out a building inspector to look at an illegal conversion complaint, ninety-two percent of the time, they get there and there's nothing serious in terms of safety risk. That's not to say that those ninety-two percent of complaints are worthless. They often send inspectors to places where less serious violations are found, and the very act of sharing intelligence on a location helps us build up the profile of the space. Still, we have a limited number of inspectors, and they have a limited amount of time. What we really want to do is sift through that pile of 311 illegal conversion complaints and find the eight percent of complaints that are the most serious. That's where we should be sending inspectors immediately.

Thanks to twelve years of leadership by Mayor Bloomberg, the nation's most data-driven mayor, we have no shortage of data from which to build a catastrophic risk model. By conducting an analysis of historic outcomes (past illegal conversion violations) and identifying similar characteristics in those locations, we were able to create a risk model that takes each inbound 311 illegal conversion complaint, pairs it with existing information we know about that building, and predicts whether or not the complaint is most likely to be founded, meaning there are severely bad living conditions.

It is important to note that while our team has evolved to use sophisticated tools and data, we started this project out with a couple old desktops and versions of Microsoft Excel that broke down after 36,000 rows of data. Using the rudimentary tools that are found on virtually every business machine, a talented young analyst was able to conduct the correlative analysis that told us what to look for in the 311 complaints.

By prioritizing the complaints that are most likely to be dangerous, we are remediating dangerous conditions faster, without any additional inspector manpower. That is a safety-based resource allocation plan.

Collecting Information That Drives Analytics

The experience of the Department of Buildings' illegal conversions risk filter demonstrated firsthand for us how difficult it could be to gain access to agency datasets and make sense of them, especially in the context of simultaneously analyzing datasets from different city agencies.

Large organizations are often stove-piped, and few organizations exemplify that problem more than cities. New York City, for instance, has over forty different agencies and over 290,000 employees. Traditionally, these agencies have focused on their chartered responsibilities (policing, fire prevention and response, health, etc.) often independently and kept data within their walls. Even on special projects, where analysts from multiple agencies conducted a cross-functional analysis, the data sharing was one-off and only allowed for a moment-in-time analysis. There was no ongoing data cooperation that allowed for performance measurement and solution iteration. Half of the effort to becoming data-driven is connecting the data, and that is an organizational challenge, not a technological one.

There is an important distinction between collecting and connecting data. Data collection is based upon the actual operation of services in the field. Our analytics team gets very tactical data, for instance, on the numbers of trees that fall down during a storm. It's our job to work with the data that is currently collected. For instance, the Parks Department decides how to respond to a tree and how to record that information, and we take it, but we do not let data collection get in the way of critical operations. Using analytics as a reason to change data collection can become a political problem, and at the very least, it is an organizational problem of retraining the front line. Instead of constantly pushing for new data, we rely upon what is already being collected and consult the agencies over time as they change and modernize their practices. Fortunately, cities have moved toward business reporting metrics in the last decade, and there is already a lot of data available. Led by Mayor Bloomberg, all city agencies measure their performance against annual goals and report that performance directly to New Yorkers. Those goals are important, but what we're really interested in is the underlying data that tracks performance.

Data connection is different. In the past, when the Parks Department removed a tree that fell down on a sidewalk on a Wednesday and the Transportation Department went to repair the sidewalk on a Thursday, we had no way of connecting those two pieces of data. The first problem is that they are not housed together. The second problem is that even if we had them together, we wouldn't have had a clear way to connect them. Each agency has its own ontology of terms and data that have all been created through reasonable, rational evolution of service, but which sometimes make it nearly impossible to connect that data. One department may use a GIS identifier for the location of the downed tree, whereas another may refer to it by its cross streets.

For us, we found that BBL/BIN (borough block lot/building identification number), along with a specialty geocoding software program one of our analysts wrote, was the Rosetta Stone to connecting the city's operational intelligence. For most city agencies, BBL and BIN are the standard way of identifying a location; however, they're not used by all agencies, nor are they universally appropriate. However, we can take whatever geo data we have (an address, an intersection, etc.) and geocode it to the nearest BIN/BBL. By focusing on the common denominator, which is structures in specific locations in this case, we're able to tie together datasets that have previously never been linked.

Having integrated data is important because of its application in stronger problem solving. The more information we have through which to run correlative analyses, the better we can form risk filters. In the case of the illegal conversion filter, two of the most important pieces of input are whether the building is current on its property taxes and whether banks have filed any mortgage foreclosures. Those two pieces of information come from two different sources—the New York City Department of Finance and the Office of Court Administration (mortgage default records), and their continued access is necessary to the ongoing effectiveness of the filter.

The capacity to connect data and analyze it is powerful, but it's still dependent upon the agencies playing ball by giving us their data to examine. One way to get the data is to demand compliance with our project. Anyone who has ever worked on a team or in a business knows that demanding compliance is rarely the best solution. Instead, we have to sell our service to the agencies. The agencies deliver city services, and because what we really do is help them deliver city services more efficiently, we treat them as our clients. We work toward solutions to their problems in order to make their lives easier. It's all about them, just as it should be. They are the ones who are actually keeping this city clean and safe every day, and if we can demonstrate that we'll help them do their jobs better with very little effort and a very small footprint, they'll want to partner with us. As a result, and without exception, we have never failed to get what we need in order to deliver this service back to them.

It's important to note that even in our office, we still have lots of city data that is outside of our walls. We don't yet have granular information from the New York City Department of Education or from internal employee management systems. We also don't have data on particulate matter at the sewage treatment plants, the pollen counts on a given street, etc. Keep in mind that you don't need everything to get started, and, conversely, you need a reason to collect and connect the information you ask for. When we have a project that requires particulate matter at the sewage treatment plants, we'll reach out to the Department of Environmental Protection and collect it, but until then, we'll work with what we have. A rational, project-based approach to data collection and connection is the best way to build success over time.

Agencies Are Our Clients

When we collect information from agencies, we're asking for them to give us access to their legacy IT systems and share all of their information. They don't have to say yes, but they do, for two reasons. First, by participating in the data exchange, they have access to the information of other agencies as well. They're able to avoid picking up the phone every first Tuesday of the month and calling the IT department of another city agency and asking for a one-off query of information because they're able to automatically access the information through our data sharing platform. Second, and more importantly, agencies like sharing their data with us because we help them.

Just as data is not valuable without a specific outcome in mind, neither is a centralized analytics team. Intelligently applied, an analytics team does not look for new problems to solve, but works with the teams in the field to solve existing problems in a way that makes their jobs more effective without burdening their work.

It is the agencies, and specifically, the employees at the agencies, who are on the ground and who understand all of the details of the service of delivery. These are the teams that can give us the best-observed information on what's going on and how we can work to fix problems. Moreover, these are the teams that are going to implement whatever solution we find through our analysis. Having them on board is fundamentally important to actually delivering more valuable service. The best way to have them on board is to work on a problem that actually impacts their day-to-day lives.

In the case of the building inspectors, that was an intelligent way to automate complaint priority. The building inspectors have an enormous amount of professional experience, and when they are able to read complaints and compare it with their own experience, they're able to identify those that are often the worst. With fewer and fewer inspectors, more and more illegally occupied buildings, and more and more 311 complaints, devoting the time to successfully risk assess those complaints one-by-one by hand has become an onerous challenge. When we use a filter to prioritize tickets, we're not ignoring the experience level of those inspectors. Instead, we're giving them a leg up by doing an automated first pass on the inspection priority, essentially applying their accumulated institutional knowledge in an automated fashion. They can still read and reorder based on their knowledge set, but we're starting them off with an intelligent list.

With these agencies, we can talk about the benefits of an analytics approach all day, but what they really care about are the results. We have a ROI-driven mayor, a ROI-driven budget office, and leaders at all of the agencies that are ROI-driven. If we ask them for their time and their data to improve their delivery of service, we should deliver improved service, and at the very minimum, we should be measuring the change in levels of service in order to understand the impact.

Measuring results may require new ways to think about the metrics. The goal of the Department of Buildings illegal conversion risk filter is to reduce the number of deaths through fires and structural collapses. However, the reality is that due to the professional excellence of our agencies, those events are so rare, even in a city as large as New York, that it can be difficult to accurately measure the performance improvement from such a small dataset. Instead, we had to think about the leading indicators of outcomes.

In the case of catastrophic building incidents, "vacate orders" are a leading indicator. In the case of illegal conversions, remember, our building inspectors go out to all of the 311 complaints. Sooner or later, they are going to find all of the illegal conversions that have been reported and remediate that condition. When we re-prioritize the tickets, we are not altering the total number of illegal conversions that will be found. However, the important part is actually the "sooner" rather than "later" piece. In the case of illegally converted structures, which incidentally are at risk of fire, it makes a huge difference to the residents if we inspect the building three days after a complaint comes in or thirty days later. When we increase the speed of finding the worst of the worst by prioritizing the complaint list, we are reducing our time to respond to the most dangerous places, and we are in effect reducing the number of days that residents are living at risk. We calculated that as a reduction in fire-risk days.

As a result of the success of the program, in our next management report, the Department of Buildings will add two risk-based, outcome-based metrics as their critical indicators of performance measurement. This fundamental shift in how we measure performance is directly attributable to focusing on what is most important in this analytics project: we are reducing the amount of time that people are at increased risk of burning to death and that reduction in time is what we're tracking.

Routinizing and Operationalizing the Insight

The greatest challenge for the analytics team is moving from insight to action. Insight is powerful, but it's worthless if the behavior in the field doesn't change. Getting the analytics into the field is dependent upon creating the lightest footprint possible, so that the intervention doesn't cause a headache to the worker in the field.

To understand what will or won't be disruptive, the analytics team needs to get a firm grasp on the way that operations are handled by the front line. When we work with an agency on a project, we shadow them to understand how they actually do their job. Seeing the way that the work is actually done is often very different from how it's described on paper or in a meeting and is an important step in the process.

Immediately, we discount any intervention that changes the way that the front line works. New training and processes are non-starters because of the immense organizational difficulty in effectively turning battleships and reorienting them around new processes. Even new forms are frowned upon, as they get in the way, or at least change the way, the fieldwork is done.

Our concept is simple—a light footprint means that the solution must be delivered upstream of the front line. If our task is to re-prioritize inspections, we build that automatically into the inspection assignment generation system, so that the assignment is already delineated with a priority level by the time it reaches the inspectors. If our solution is a technological fix that connects two formerly disparate pieces of information and delivers a new piece of information, we make sure that piece of information is being delivered right alongside currently reported data, not in a different, detached method. It sounds simple, but it's so easy to go wrong. Don't change the front line process; change the outcome.

Keep Focused on What Will Work

While the buzz around big data seems to have been generated out of thin air, the outcomes associated with it will only come from hard work, with years and years of effort. Just as with any other business or government process, the steps are incremental in nature.

Analytics is not magic, and it's not necessarily complicated. Analytics really means intelligence, and intelligence is better information that helps us make better decisions. To the extent that we can automate that information gathering and analysis, for instance, in automatically sorting the priority level of work orders, we're streamlining the efficacy of the approach. The most important thing to remember, however, is that we are not changing the approach.

An effective analytics project is one that gets in and gets out sight unseen. Let the results speak for the project.

Lessons Learned

When I first joined the Bloomberg Administration at the end of 2009, it was just me at a cubicle, making phone calls, studying organizational charts and data schematics, surfing our open data page to see what was available, and visiting every office I could in my on and off time to see what was going on. It was six months before I hired my first analyst, a fresh-from-college economics major who had won his rotisserie baseball league three years in a row and was preternaturally affable. We tried a few different projects that didn't end up going anywhere, but taught us extremely valuable lessons about how to make disparate pieces of city data work moderately harmoniously together to tell us the stories we needed to hear. It wasn't until spring 2011—almost a year and a half after I started this project—that we delivered our first actionable insight. In the two years since then, we have become a central component of the administration's approach to government, implementing citywide analytics-based systems for structural safety, emergency response, disaster response and recovery, economic development, and tax enforcement—and we've only just started to scale out.

This isn't triumphalism. Moreover, it was far from easy. Tacked up over my desk since my first day is a quote from Teddy Roosevelt, and more days than not, early on, I found myself reading it over and over again.

> It is not the critic who counts; not the man who points out how the strong man stumbles, or where the doer of deeds could have done them better. The credit belongs to the man who is actually in the arena, whose face is marred by dust and sweat and blood; who strives valiantly; who errs, who comes short again and again, because there is no effort without error and shortcoming; but who does actually strive to do the deeds; who knows great enthusiasms, the great devotions; who spends himself in a worthy cause; who at the best knows in the end the triumph of high achievement, and who at the worst, if he fails, at least fails while daring greatly, so that his place shall never be with those cold and timid souls who neither know victory nor defeat. (Roosevelt, 1910)

What I'm trying to stress is you have to start somewhere, while bearing in mind the following lessons we've learned:

- You don't need a lot of specialized personnel.

- You don't need a lot of high-end technology.

- You don't need "perfect" data (but you do need the entire set).

- You must have strong executive support.

- You must talk to the people behind the data, and see what they see and experience what they experience.

- You must focus on generating actionable insight for your clients that they can immediately use with minimal disruption to existing logistics chains.

Above all else, you need to be relentless in terms of delivering a quality product, while remaining flexible in terms of how you do it. For New York City's analytics program, pragmatic, inventive problem solvers are always welcome, but ideologues need not apply. Finally, you need to remember at all times that the point of all this effort is to help your city and its people thrive. Keep all this in mind. Just dive in and do it. You may be amazed at what you find.

About the Author

Michael Flowers is Chief Analytics Officer and Chief Open Platform Officer for the City of New York. Prior to joining the Bloomberg Administration, Mr. Flowers was Counsel to the US Senate Permanent Subcommittee on Investigations for the 110th and 111th Congress, where he led bipartisan investigations into off-shore tax haven abuses; failures in the mortgage-backed securitization market by US investment and commercial banks and government agencies; and deceptive financial transactions by the North Korean government. From March 2005 to December 2006, Mr. Flowers was Deputy Director of DOJ's Regime Crimes Liaison's Office in Baghdad, Iraq, supporting the investigations and trials of Saddam Hussein and other high-ranking members of his regime. Mr. Flowers is a magna cum laude graduate of Temple University School of Law in Philadelphia.

References

Roosevelt, Theodore (1910). "Citizenship in a Republic." [Speech] Retrieved from http://www.theodore-roosevelt.com/trsorbonnespeech.html

CHAPTER 16

Why Data Must Drive Decisions in Government

By Beth Blauer

The Dawn of the Data-Driven Government

The government landscape in 2013 includes a host of challenges and opportunities. The economy is uncertain, politics are highly polarized, and many more people are relying on government services compared to just a decade ago. We're also living in a time of unprecedented digital openness, convenience, and transparency in everyday life.

It's this landscape, where eighty-five percent of American adults have internet access and fifty-six percent own a smartphone, which has turned "google" into a verb and made everyone a restaurant critic (Fox, 2013). Citizens expect to find the answers to almost any question online and are demanding more answers from government. Yet, in large part, government-related accessibility has lagged, until now.

By adopting cutting-edge technologies, such as cloud data storage and application programming interfaces (APIs), to unlock and share their treasure troves of data, some government agencies are not only catching up with the private sector in terms of innovation, but also accelerating beyond it. Data has long been recognized as a government asset, but now it can more easily be shared and utilized both inside government and among citizens, entrepreneurs, and researchers, to find solutions to persistent civic problems.

A new era of data-driven government and civic innovation is taking shape, and the results are amazing so far. They provide only a hint of what is possible in the future. It's not a matter of whether data-driven government can create the best solutions to society's problems; it's a matter of how soon different governments will embrace the idea and reap the benefits.

As the former leader of one of the earliest and most successful data-driven programs in government, Maryland StateStat, I want to share my story of how I arrived at that role, what we accomplished during my tenure, and why I have now chosen to move to the private sector to create a platform for data-driven governance.

How I Joined Data-Driven Government

For most people, government is an ancillary part of everyday life; that is certainly how I saw it before I decided to attend law school. I had a general goal to help people with my law degree, but getting into government had never been of interest.

A day that changed so many people's lives, September 11, 2001, ended up moving me toward a career as a public servant.

At the time, I was fresh out of law school, newly married, and working at a New York City hedge fund. A painful slip in a pothole on September 10, 2001 sent me to the doctor's office on the morning of September 11, rather than heading to work in the World Trade Center Complex.

The experience prompted a lot of reflection and a shift in priorities. My husband and I decided to move back home to Baltimore. And, I remembered why I went to law school in the first place: to help people.

I changed my career trajectory to pursue a job as a public defender. While studying for the Bar, I worked as a juvenile probation officer to get court experience. The more time I spent at the Maryland Department of Juvenile Services, the more my appreciation grew for the process, as opposed to the practice, of law.

At this time, Mayor Martin O'Malley of Baltimore was undertaking some inspiring work. While leading Baltimore's government, he began taking cues from New York City's success with the CompStat program.

For example, the CompStat team in NYC had cross-referenced crime maps with police department resource maps and uncovered a glaring disparity: crime-fighting resources were evenly distributed, but crime wasn't. By being smarter about dispatching departmental resources, NYC's leadership was able to clean up the city significantly. When crime disappears, something else usually moves in. In New York City's case, it was industry, business, tourism, and more vibrant neighborhoods. The data-driven approach proved powerful.

Mayor O'Malley wanted to use this approach to clean up Baltimore, but in a much broader capacity. He was focused on reducing crime, but he also wanted to impact and improve the city as a whole. He wanted the suburbanites who had abandoned their city to return. He wanted a vibrant downtown full of safe and happy visitors. He wanted all of Baltimore's children to have the best education, and he wanted a cleaner, more efficient city.

As a result, he led a team to create his version of CompStat—called CitiStat. It was a game-changer. The shift to a data-driven approach not only impacted crime, but also provided a data-based decision-making platform for all city agencies. It gave birth to services that benefited citizens, like 311 non-emergency issue reporting and a forty-eight-hour pothole response guarantee.

I observed the success of CitiStat from my role in the juvenile justice system and was naturally drawn to the data-based analysis of problems.

The Birth of Maryland StateStat

When Baltimore's Mayor O'Malley became Maryland's Governor O'Malley in 2006, it was clear that CitiStat would be rolled out statewide. After his election, he named me Chief of Staff of the Department of Juvenile Services. Then, based upon my work in the juvenile justice system (and my tendency to disregard the status quo and naysayers), Governor O'Malley invited me to be the Director of StateStat.

In my following five years heading up the program, I was able to play a key role in a fundamental change in the way the Maryland State government operated. The goal from the beginning was to make data-driven decisions and welcome innovation.

We initially focused on the larger agencies within the state government. Governor O'Malley's vision for Maryland was ambitious and bold. His goals included ending childhood hunger in Maryland by 2015, achieving a twenty percent decrease in crime statewide by 2018, and getting Chesapeake Bay to the "Healthy Bay Tipping Point" by 2025. He knew from his experience with CitiStat that data from multiple agencies would be essential to solving these complicated issues. He purposefully pulled together people from different departments, and their data, to find solutions.

Stories of Success with StateStat

Childhood Hunger

Take, for instance, Governor O'Malley's goal of ending childhood hunger. It's a pretty weighty goal. Plus, it's hard to quantify success in ending hunger. Do you measure the number of free lunches delivered? How else can hunger be measured?

To make things more complicated, the government services that address hunger are disparate and separated by agency walls. Reducing the number of hungry kids is on the radar of schools, non-profits, and social service agencies. Until O'Malley's StateStat program began in 2006, these stakeholders had never truly focused on pooling their data resources and working together to find solutions, even though they were all trying to accomplish the same end. Add to that the stigma of using food stamps or getting free lunches, and it was obvious that the State did not really have a handle on how many children were "hungry."

Once we were able to gather all these stakeholders in the same room and compile the data we did have, it became obvious that school meals were the lynchpin. We determined that if we could feed more kids more meals at school, we had the best chance of improving their situation. We worked together to extend free meal services geographically where needed.

Free lunch turned into free breakfast, then dinner, then summer programs with free meals, too. What were the results of our efforts? In addition to no longer being hungry, these well-fed children performed better at school. We saw dramatic improvements in academic results and significant decreases in behavioral issues. While we couldn't draw a direct correlation between the free meals and the improved academic performance, most leaders in Maryland agree that without the expanded free meals programs, Maryland wouldn't have been awarded the designation of best schools in the country by Education Week five years in a row: 2008, 2009, 2010, 2011, and 2012 ("Quality Counts 2012," 2012).

Safety for Foster Children

In another dramatic story of impact, we worked with the Department of Human Resources to find out how foster children in Maryland were faring. Were they safe and well cared for? As part of our analysis, we wanted to overlay a map of foster kids' addresses with a map of the locations of the state's most violent criminals and all registered sex offenders.

This location information had never been compared because it was separated in different departments. Also, because of legal barriers, it was not brought together as part of the screening process for foster parents.

Once we gathered together and visualized the data, we found that some of our most vulnerable children were living near some of our most dangerous criminals. We were able to dispatch safety assessments to the most worrisome situations. This effort is still one of my proudest accomplishments as the Director of StateStat.

Financial Stability

In 2007, Governor O'Malley decided to raise taxes. We saw the economic meltdown as an impending reality so we first sought to identify waste and eliminate it. In 2006, the O'Malley administration began the process of eliminating nearly six thousand State positions (O'Malley, 2013). In addition, while most states were cutting taxes like crazy, we made the very unpopular decision to raise taxes—and not insignificantly. Applying data helped us with this process.

Raising taxes, in hindsight, allowed Maryland to weather the recession better than most states. We weren't immune to widespread, to-the-bone funding cuts, but by making data-driven decisions about revenue increases and service reductions, the state was one of only nine states to retain an AAA bond rating during the recession.

StateStat's Results

The data-driven approach has made a significant impact in Maryland, from determining the right approach to better air quality to getting unemployed workers back on the job. Compiling information from different agencies has given us new insight and proved the power of data.

All told, StateStat's success was nothing short of staggering. In its first three years, the state saved $20 million in overtime in our public safety agency alone. We cut costs by consolidating our print shops and state car fleets and reducing duplication in projects.

O'Malley also made good on his commitment to reduce crime. Violent crimes in the state decreased by twenty-five percent from 2007 to 2012. In fact, homicides were down twenty-seven percent in 2011 compared to 2006. The city of Baltimore, in particular, saw a historic reduction in crime.

In addition, the O'Malley administration managed a massive $8.3 billion in spending cuts in its first seven years, while recovering eighty-one percent of jobs lost during the recession—that's the eighth fastest rate in the nation. Meanwhile, O'Malley's team helped to expand health-care coverage to more than 360,000 residents, most of them children.

In 2012, Maryland had the fifteenth lowest foreclosure rate in the nation. Eighty-seven percent of high school seniors graduated from high school, and fifty-six percent more students took Advanced Placement exams in science, technology, engineering, and math-related topics in 2012 than they had in 2006.

The list of achievements goes on and on.

How was such widespread success possible? I believe that it is our commitment to the philosophy of governing by data. It can't be overemphasized. The data-driven approach wasn't a side project. The StateStat program oversaw eighty percent of all budgets and personnel in the state. Agencies checked in with StateStat monthly, if not weekly, and StateStat was reviewed quarterly against Governor O'Malley's fifteen stated goals.

In many ways, the timing of StateStat's beginning was ideal. Data-driven decision-making is always useful, but in the midst of the Great Recession, we absolutely had to do more with less. In order to drive efficiency and make the right decisions for citizens, we needed to understand which services were the most valuable. The answers were in the data.

The Shift to Open Data

Our biggest challenge with early StateStat was that the data was coming from multiple places. Without secure databases, we didn't have a central place to gather and store information. Instead, we were manually compiling spreadsheets. We needed a way to give a curated view of data from multiple sources to the public or internal teams.

We looked at business intelligence and database solutions, but in the end, open data won. Our open data portal centralized and standardized the data so any department could see another department's information—and so could citizens.

We used the portal as the basis for public dashboards. We constructed a framework for setting goals that the public could appreciate and displayed the data related to our goals. By making the StateStat process more public, we helped citizens understand how the government was working for them.

Being open about our efforts helped us engage constituents. When we released public data and contextualized problems, citizens rallied and responded. When they saw the Recovery Act dollars we received, they started to point out projects needed in their communities. We created a website for them to make comments and give feedback on where we planned to spend the money.

Our efforts toward transparency through open data sparked a citizen-led, quality-of-life movement in the state.

Essentials of Data-Driven Government Success

After five years at StateStat, I felt like we had a good method for using data to make better decisions and engage the community. The three basic guidelines I developed were to:

- Curate data and inform people about the government conversation.

- Let developers access the data and allow the ecosystem to flourish.

- Nurture a collaborative environment where data analysts talk with the government and developers, and everyone understands the big picture and feels empowered to take risks and set ambitious goals.

Meanwhile, Governor O'Malley defined the leadership style needed to be successful. He bred this technology-based accountability into every level of Maryland's government, and then supported it by putting the right people in positions to make data-driven decisions. He had the vision of how StateStat would become a repeatable, scalable machine that, armed with the right data, would be able to tackle practically any challenge the state faced.

This vision from the top and unwavering commitment to make it work is essential to creating the success we had in Maryland. In terms of transferability and scalability, this is the biggest hurdle to seeing a StateStat-style approach reproduced by governments worldwide. A strong leader is the key to ensuring widespread, long-term adoption within an organization.

Why I Moved to the Private Sector

While working on the open data architecture within the StateStat model, I collaborated with our open data platform provider, Socrata, to implement and optimize our open data portal. I recognized that Socrata had the scalable technology necessary to expand open data and data-driven governance to a much larger audience. This idea inspired me.

What if I could take what I learned in Maryland and design a product that would jump-start any government in the world to become data-driven?

Socrata invited me to their team to build that product. We named it GovStat, and its creation has been a career-defining project for me. It takes the best practices that decades of previous "stat" models had experimented with, and that Maryland's StateStat relied on, and creates a platform that any state, city, or county can use to implement data-driven decision-making. I wanted to make the move to data-driven governance quick and easy and give other agencies a high likelihood of success.

For governments just starting with a data-driven approach, I wanted this tool to guide them through the best practices for setting goals, applying metrics, and tracking performance. For more seasoned organizations that have experience using open data, this platform can be used to elevate their performance tracking and reporting capabilities quickly and efficiently.

For those instances, and in every one in between, built-in citizen communication is key. With GovStat, goals, metrics, timelines, and tracking are reported to citizens through dashboards that give the data context and exposure. This is the completion of the loop, so that citizens can be involved in efforts to improve their quality of life.

People often ask why I left Governor O'Malley's team to work in the private sector. I think that what we created with StateStat was transformative. I also think that government as a whole—locally, nationally, globally—needs to change. We can't afford not to adopt a data-driven approach and miss out on the benefits of greater creativity and collaboration in decision-making.

Working with Socrata was the fastest way to move the needle in that direction. In all honesty, once you work for Governor O'Malley, you never really stop. I can now evangelize his message of the importance of this approach and spread the word that the often-difficult task of running government can absolutely work and bring amazing results for all.

The Future of Data-Driven Performance Management in Government

The success we have had in Maryland has drawn attention from other states and cities. During my time as Director of StateStat, many government officials came in to observe and talk to us about transferability. In the six short years since StateStat was born, many states, counties, and cities across the United States have adopted a data-driven approach to leadership. President Obama's Executive Order on Open Data signed on May 9, 2013, signals a bold new commitment to a data-driven federal government.

Every "stat" program is slightly different, but they all operate based on the four tenets born out of NYC's CompStat initiative:

1. Accurate and timely intelligence: Know what is happening.

2. Effective tactics: Have a plan.

3. Rapid deployment: Do it quickly.

4. Relentless follow-up and assessment: If it works, do more. If not, do something else. (Godown, 2009)

Data-driven governance is more than the open data it's fueled by. The traditional view of open data's greatest impact is that it creates a development engine to get data out into the open where it can stimulate economic activity in the private sector. There are plenty of real-life examples of this in the app development arena alone—from getting restaurant reviews alongside health code violation reports on your mobile device, to receiving a text when the city tows your car. These are the types of tangible quality-of-life improvements open data advocates have prophesied.

I believe, however, that the most transformative products of open data come when government is given efficient, low-cost access to tools that allow them to use data to drive progress toward things that are important to them and their citizens. Then, open data affects not only the people who rely on government services, but also extends to everyone who interacts with government in their day-to-day lives. We all have to interact with government, whether it's getting a driver's license or requesting a permit to build a home.

All these interactions influence our happiness index. Each of those interactions is impacted by the way government services its citizens. Open data has the power to be transformative in service delivery and influence the expectations that people have. It has the power to turn the tide on the idea that government can't work.

One of my favorite sayings is that "the rising tide raises all ships." There are examples of government working, even during the harshest austerity. The more people we have in government using open data, the better all governments will be. The more opportunities we have to proliferate best practices, figure out ways to build efficiencies into the enterprise of government, propel good behavior, and cultivate entrepreneurial spirit, the more we will see it come to fruition in reality.

This is all possible when governments are data-driven and align their resources to those outcomes that are supported by the tracking of data.

This is my vision. The creation of GovStat is a step toward engaging as many people as possible, as quickly as possible. The faster we can standardize the measurement of common problems, like crime, blight, and poverty, the sooner we'll be able to replicate and scale what is working in small pockets on a broader scale. If New Orleans has a program that's wildly successful at combating blight, let's standardize that and create a platform for sharing that thought leadership. Why should Philadelphia recreate the wheel when much of the problem has already been solved?

We're at a nexus of open data and performance insight, and the most explosive, ripe, and exciting opportunities lie in a data-driven governance approach. It's not a matter of whether or not this approach can be adopted on a wide scale, but when. We must use data and be more agile in government in order to solve the problems we are facing locally, nationally, and globally. The tighter we weave together open data and performance, the faster we can realize the results and the richer the data will be.

About the Author

Beth Blauer is director of GovStat for Seattle-based Socrata, an open data platform provider. She served from 2008 to 2012 as director of Maryland's StateStat and the Governor's Delivery Unit for Maryland Governor Martin O'Malley.

References

Education Week. (2012). Quality Counts 2012: The Global Challenge. Education Week, 31 (16). Retrieved from http://www.edweek.org/ew/qc/2012/16src.h31.html

Godown, J. (2009, August). The CompStat Process: Four Principles for Managing Crime Reduction. The Police Chief, vol. LXXVI (no. 8).

Fox, S. (2013, July 1). Pew Internet: Health. Retrieved from http://www.pewinternet.org/Commentary/2011/November/Pew-Internet-Health.aspx

O'Malley, Martin, State of Maryland. (2013, January 30). State of the State: Better Choice; Better Results. Retrieved from http://www.governor.maryland.gov/documents/2013StateoftheState.pdf

Beyond Transparency: Louisville's Strategic Use of Data to Drive Continuous Improvement

By Theresa Reno-Weber and Beth Niblock

Government embodies our highest aspirations and our lowest expectations.

We have high expectations for all that we want our government to do and all of the services we ask it to provide, regardless of politics or fiscal constraints. We expect government to collect our trash, inspect our restaurants, maintain our roads, protect our property, and provide services to our most vulnerable citizens. These are just a few of the myriad tasks. Most governments perform these functions with a level of resource and reporting constraints that would challenge any well-run organization. Many of us have experienced, in one way or another, the reality that the majority of cities do not operate like well-run organizations.

Much has been written about the principles and practices of creating great organizations. In Louisville, we've focused on how to implement those principles and practices in the government context, using open data to drive a culture of continuous improvement.

Government Is Not Special

Whether it's getting a driver's license, ordering a new recycling or trash bin, or reporting a pothole in the road, all too often, citizens experience an overwhelming inefficiency in the process. The whole encounter is too long, overly cumbersome, or unnecessarily redundant. The customer (citizens, businesses, academics, etc.) frequently leaves, frustrated and potentially angry about his or her experience. These experiences are too often excused by everyone, customer and government employee alike, as "that's just government for you."

As a society, we are stuck in the mindset that government is somehow different and unique from private or social sector counterparts. We assume that any of the practices they employ to address complex challenges couldn't work or wouldn't apply at a city government level. This is simply not the case.

We've been inspired by contemporary books like James C. Collins' *Good to Great* (2001), Ken Miller's *We Don't Make Widgets* (2006), and more recently, Eric Ries' *The Lean Startup* (2011). They've taught us that government can be more like the best parts of a successful business or new startup—innovative, proactive, fast moving, and responsive to the needs of its customers. Government can perform on par with the best-run organizations in the world, and in Louisville, we are working hard to prove it.

Over the last year, Louisville Metro Government has:

- Removed more than two hundred days from key administrative processes, like hiring.

- Reduced unscheduled overtime and workers' compensation expenditures by more than $2 million.

- Certified more than one hundred employees in proven performance improvement methods for measuring, tracking, and improving results in an organization that are widely used in the private sector, such as Lean, Six Sigma, and Project Management.

- Better aligned the budgeting process with city and departmental strategic objectives.

- Continually evaluated the performance of multiple, unique departments and shared the results of those evaluations with citizens in a comprehensible, online format.

And, the Louisville Metro Government's Office of Performance Improvement (OPI) helped make all this happen with a full-time staff of just three people and a budget of no more than $300,000. These accomplishments have been possible because of the use of open data and some basic startup and business innovation principles.

For cities that have begun to use data and best-in-class management and performance improvement practices, these results are not unusual. The City of Baltimore implemented CitiStat, a comprehensive data tracking and performance management tool, in 2000. The program was designed to maximize accountability by requiring city agencies to provide CitiStat analysts with metrics representing performance. During monthly and bimonthly meetings with the Office of the Mayor, each agency must examine sub-standard performance and propose solutions that can be carried out in an efficient manner. By 2007, they had used data to strategically reduce and control worker's overtime to save more than $30.9 million. The program has been so effective that it has been sustained through three different administrations and supported by both sides of the political aisle. After leaving city office, former Baltimore Mayor (now Maryland Governor) O'Malley applied the CitiStat principles to create Maryland's StateStat performance improvement program with equal success.

In Iowa, the state government has used Lean process improvement methods in the last three administrations. It's not about politics, but about "doing government better," says Teresa Hay-McMahon, president of the Iowa Lean Consortium, a group of Iowa businesses and governments that employ Lean to drive improvements in time, cost, and quality.

While many cities succeed with management practices (like Lean, Six Sigma, and Performance Management) and measurement systems (like CitiStat or StateStat), many other cities have attempted these improvements and given up. So, the questions become: How do you successfully apply these concepts to the work of city government? What does it take to make change stick? How do you get the buy-in you need to sustain it and really make an impact for citizens and your bottom line? How do you get beyond data for the sake of data and use it to inform decisions and drive culture change? We're tackling these questions in Louisville and learning some lessons along the way.

Open Data is the Foundation

In January 2003, the City of Louisville and the surrounding Jefferson County merged to form a consolidated city-county government. Today, the Mayor and a twenty-six-member city legislature called the Metro Council govern Louisville Metro.

While the city population is approximately 750,000 people, the combined city and county population includes close to 1.3 million people, making Louisville the thirteenth largest city in the country. Nearly 5,500 dedicated employees work across more than twenty departments and agencies to service the city and county. The workforce is largely unionized, with approximately seventy-six percent of all employees in a union. The city's general fund budget is approximately $530 million, and the total operating budget is just over $650 million.

The Start of Our Journey: Financial Transparency

Louisville's journey from transparency to truly open data started in 2009, when the Metro Council passed a financial transparency ordinance. The ordinance established the guidelines that the transparency site was to meet. It established that the Metro Council would begin to publish detailed expenditure information for the various programs in the Metro Government.

The first iteration of the website featured information including employee names and salaries, annual budget and funding sources, quarterly revenue estimates, and annual audits. We also published all metro payments for supplies, personnel, equipment, etc., including a description of expenditures with links to actual grants or contracts, and all contracts valued at $50,000 or more.

One of the discussions surrounding transparency during the previous administration was how to help citizens interpret the data. There was some concern that just putting information on the transparency site without context would lead to misinterpretation.

What we feared most happened. The transparency site went live, and the next day, there was an article in the blogosphere about how Metro Government had spent $28,000 on alcohol. Those who worked on the site were scrambling to explain the expenditure. The reason was simple: Metro Government licenses liquor establishments, and the amount showing in the checkbook was the license refunds for the year. But releasing that data without context or explaining the license refunds created a needless media headache.

Making Open Data Serve the Citizen

We learned two lessons from that experience: the data needs user-friendly names, and it needs to be released in context to avoid misinterpretation. Louisville's Open Data Portal has come a long way from that initial launch, and we've made efforts to present the data in a way that puts citizens' needs first. As of 2013, the new and improved site provides anytime access and views into the latest city data in an easy-to-use format. It now features the most popular datasets for download in an easy-to-interpret interface, with more options to view, sort, and filter—great for anyone wanting to see city data and for IT developers wanting to build apps or online tools in creative new ways using city data.

We offer raw datasets for city expenditures, employee salaries, board members, park locations and amenities, animal services population results, news and calendar events, and links to other sites with useful data and maps. Accurate data is automatically uploaded, eliminating resource- and time-intensive manual processes. Most importantly, published data sources are exposed via API with metadata and filtering views, giving software developers more flexibility in how they can use the data.

Even with all those improvements, however, there was still more to be done to leverage data better internally in order to provide transparency into city operations, give citizens access to use that data to build new tools, and create a more efficient city that delivers better services and more effectively allocates taxpayer dollars.

Moving Beyond Open Data to Continuous Improvement

Louisville's early open data efforts had already been underway for several years when Mayor Greg Fischer took office in January 2011. The mayor put forth a Citizen's Bill of Rights that underscored the importance of the city's ongoing focus on transparency and open data. Transparency was one of six main priorities. The mayor recognized that it could be the key to delivering on other commitments.

Mayor Fischer is the driving force behind the continuous improvement movement now taking root across Metro Government. He is a former entrepreneur and successful businessman who helped launch a Center for Quality of Management (CQM) chapter in Louisville for business owners in the 1990s. He came into office on the promise to run the city government more like a successful business. He started by asking questions that are elementary in successful businesses: What are we trying to accomplish? What do our customers (citizens) expect and need from us? Where are we doing well and where is there room for improvement?

Mayor Fischer was familiar with Baltimore's CitiStat program and wanted to launch a similar program in Louisville. To run this program, he created a new role titled Chief of Performance Improvement. The role is one that many for-profit companies have also created, though it's more often called CPO or Chief Performance Officer.

The Chief of Performance Improvement began with the mandate of helping departments answer the question "What are you trying to accomplish and how would you know if you've done so successfully?" Once that question was answered, the city could focus on being sure that each department had the skills and resources to accomplish its mission. This led to the three key areas of focus: planning (what is the city government doing today and what does it want to do tomorrow?), performance management (how well are we doing it?), and continuous improvement (how do we do the work and how can we do it better?).

Alongside the new Chief of Performance Improvement position, the mayor launched Louisville's Office of Performance Improvement in January 2012. That same month, with the support of the Technology Department, the first Louisville Statistics (LouieStat) forum was held with the Department of Public Works & Assets.

The premise of LouieStat is that each participating department identifies and tracks a series of success metrics specific to its work against its own history, goals, and relevant benchmarks. Additionally, the entire city is tracking certain enterprise metrics: unscheduled overtime, workers' compensation claims, complaints into MetroCall 311, and the amount of sick leave used by employees. Every six to eight weeks, the department meets with the city's entire senior leadership team, including the mayor, to go through these numbers, identify issues, and address key problems.

As Mayor Fischer admitted, getting started wasn't easy:

> The first forum with Public Works and Assets was pretty rough... The department came with twenty-six pages of data and metrics, and the senior leadership team had no way of interpreting the data as good, bad, or indifferent. (G. Fischer, personal communication, 2013)

The forum, however, proved to be a critical first step in improving the way the government works. First, it sent the message that we weren't going to wait to develop something perfect, but that we were going to get started and improve as we went along—"Sixty percent and go," as Mayor Fischer would say. For an entrepreneur, this is known as the MVP or "minimum viable product" concept (Ries, 2011). Once you have an MVP—the most bare bones version of what you're trying to build—you launch it, test it, and immediately set to work improving it incrementally, rather than making big upfront investments to perfect something that may or may not work.

The forum also made it clear that the focus was not just on data. It was about converting data into useful information to drive issue identification, problem solving, decision-making, resource allocation, and, ultimately, performance improvement. Data in a vacuum is never useful, so while we had a good amount of data in raw form, we needed to start using the data to identify ways to continually improve what we were delivering to citizens and how.

Implementation Is Messy

In that first year, OPI brought nine departments into the LouieStat program: Public Works & Assets, Fire & Rescue, Corrections, Parks, Public Health & Wellness, Animal Services, Codes & Regulations, EMS, and Economic Growth & Innovation. Departments were prioritized based on criteria including size of department, citizen impact, performance readiness, and span of control.

As part of integrating LouieStat, departments began working with OPI analysts to develop the right operational metrics for their specific functional area and to put together historical data and relevant benchmarks. This was complicated, since some departments, like Fire & Rescue, had a wealth of operational data, and others, like Parks, had very little data—most of which was captured in handwritten paper logs.

As we began to track, analyze, and share the data with departments, all of the issues one might anticipate began to surface. Many departments did not have a strategic planning process, and as a result, had never clearly articulated their goals externally or internally. For those who had or were able to create goals, there was still a great deal of resistance to creating and evaluating metrics. Many complained that the data was not good; that it didn't represent the true situation; that it was misinterpreted; or that there were inappropriate entries or people being counted "against them" in the system. All of these complaints were valid.

As we had learned in our initial open data work, though, the data will never be perfect, at least in the beginning. The minute you start tracking and analyzing it, you will begin the process of improving it—so don't wait for the data to be perfect to start.

Still, we quickly realized we needed a way to focus in on the data that mattered most to the mission success of each department.

Strategic Planning in Performance Management

Strategic planning needed to be a part of our approach if we were going to focus our analysis on what truly mattered. At that time, Metro did not have a comprehensive or coordinated strategic planning process. While some departments had their own planning processes in place, many did not, and strategic and operational planning were lumped into and driven by the annual budget process. OPI helped establish a new planning process. The goal was to translate the mayor's multi-year vision and objectives into a comprehensive strategic plan that cascaded throughout Metro Government. OPI also helped align the strategic goals and initiatives of all Metro departments and agencies with the current administration's goals.

The process culminated in the mayor's six-year strategic plan for Louisville Metro Government and more than twenty individual six-year strategic plans at the department or agency level. Contained within each plan are measurable targets we are trying to achieve as a city and as individual departments, so we can check our progress as we go and focus our attention on what matters.

We are now in the process of designing a type of "budgeting for outcomes" process that should align the city's spending with its priorities. This design process is already raising important questions about the role of government in achieving the city's priorities. At the very least, connecting strategy to budget is forcing departments to question the value of some entrenched programs with unclear outcomes.

Performance Management: How Are We Doing?

The strategic plans gave us a good understanding of what we were trying to do at a strategic level, and to some extent, at an operational level. Yet, we were still faced with a wealth of potential metrics for any given department. Public Works & Assets, which has five major divisions, including Solid Waste Management, Fleet, Facilities, Engineering, and Operations & Maintenance, has hundreds of operational metrics we could evaluate. The challenge is finding the vital few "Key Performance Indicators" (KPIs). OPI worked with departments to establish the best

KPIs for their work, focusing on answering two critical questions:

1. What results (informed by strategic plans) are we trying to achieve?

2. How would we know if we were achieving them?

For example, we established three KPIs for the Louisville Fire Department: amount of property damage (in dollars), number of civilian fire injuries, and number of home fire inspections. We set goals for each KPI informed by past performance and where we want to be—$7,717,608 in property damage, zero civilian fire injuries, and 1,032 home fire inspections completed—and track and report progress related to those goals.

The departments in LouieStat come before the mayor and his senior leadership team (which consists of the heads of Finance, HR, Technology, Legal, Policy, Performance Improvement, and Communication) every six to eight weeks. Through consistent tracking and data analysis of their KPIs, the team works to identify and discuss what the department (and Metro Government) can do to continually improve the services it delivers to the citizens of Louisville. This also means ways we can better meet the strategic goals we've committed to. In between LouieStat forums, OPI supports the departments through measurement identification, data analysis, performance reporting, training, and coaching. All KPIs are then posted on the public LouieStat website (www.louiestat.louisvilleky.gov) for citizens to view.

The LouieStat process faced much resentment and skepticism at the beginning, but once departments got going, attitudes started to change. While the focus is on where the department is underperforming—and identification of the root causes impacting performance can be quite targeted—the mayor frames the interaction with each department as ultimately asking the question "how can we help?" This has been a refreshing surprise to many department directors. Because of LouieStat, department leaders gain important insights that offer them a clearer direction in managing employees and a quantifiable measure of their successes.

This experience led to a realization of how important it is to celebrate success. For many, simply being able to present the work of their departments in a meaningful and clear way to the city's senior leadership team and the mayor was a powerful incentive.

Mark Bolton, Director of Corrections, explained:

> As you go down a path of something new, there's always trepidation. What is this about? What are we getting into now? But it truly is all about how can we be the best at what we do...that's what Mayor Fischer is all about and that's what this department is all about. (Bolton, personal communication, 2013)

For those departments not yet participating in LouieStat, Louisville Metro Government created a "Day of Celebration" during which teams nominated from across city government were recognized for their innovations and successes. The inaugural Day of Celebration in 2012 was hosted as a part of Louisville's internationally recognized IdeaFestival and celebrated both performance improvement and innovations in government. More than a hundred nominations were submitted, and recognition was given to employees at all levels of the organization for contributions to "daily, continuous improvement and breakthrough work." In addition to recognition of success, the annual Day of Celebration includes a training and education focus with breakout sessions providing an introduction to performance management tools.

Capability Building and Continuous Improvement: How Do We Go From Here to There?

> Don't just give me your hands, give me your hearts and minds.

—Louisville Mayor Greg Fischer

Many transparency initiatives and data programs stop short of their true potential, equating putting the data out there with success. OPI even started with the mantra "What gets measured, gets improved." However, we realized that this is an oversimplification. It is not sufficient to simply evaluate current performance, set a target for where you want the department or organization to go, and trust that it will get there on its own.

As recent literature in behavioral economics makes clear, most people inherently want to be good, if not great, at what they do. However, many people, especially in municipal government, have not been supported with the training or resources to do so. The culture has not been set up to support continuous improvement. Many municipal employees are operating with legacy systems, and in some cases, legacy mindsets. To be successful, a performance management program must focus on embedding the skills and capabilities required to improve performance and truly close the gap between baseline data and the targets or goals established for each KPI within departments. Transforming to a high performing, continuous improvement-focused government is no easy task.

What it really comes down to is changing the mindsets and behaviors of those in government to recognize the opportunities around them and have the know-how and ability to then capitalize on those opportunities to deliver positive change. Of course, this is much easier said than done. Employees need to change their habits and behaviors, and the organization needs to adopt new processes.

Many people come to work every day and are completely occupied with "fighting fires"—rushing to battle crises as they come up. They work straight through, get to the end of the day, and aren't really sure what they have to show for it. They know they've been busy, but they don't feel like they've made any progress. Others come to work and do the same thing day in and day out. They do the work given to them or asked of them without really enjoying it or taking pride in it. We have their hands, but not their hearts and minds.

We want to help people get out of the business of fighting fires (as much as we can, given the nature of city services and municipal government) and only using their hands. We want to get them into the habit of using their hearts and minds to challenge the status quo and continually improve what they deliver to citizens and how they deliver it.

Over the course of our effort, we've identified three general categories of the way that people react to change. There are those who relish it, those who are skeptical of it, and those who truly dislike it:

- Those who relish change find it motivating and exciting, are always open to it, and are often the first to "buy in."

- Those who are skeptical of change are not convinced of the value of the change being made or they have seen many unsuccessful attempts at change. They want to be sure the effort will be successful before they "buy in."

- Those who truly dislike change only see it as extra work and are happy with the status quo. They will be the last to come around and may never truly "buy in" to the change.

Our focus at the start of our journey has been to engage those who relish change. We see them as the early adopters or "first followers," if you are familiar with the "Dancing Guy" YouTube video on how to start a movement (if not, we highly recommend you check it out). Not surprisingly, the proportion of people in the different groups follows the normal distribution of the bell curve, with those who embrace change first equal to about twenty percent of people in the organization. They can then be used to help bring along the approximately sixty percent who are skeptical of change. The twenty percent remaining who truly dislike change will either eventually join in or perhaps leave the organization.

Those skeptical of change often have a good reason to be. Many change efforts or transformations fail. They come in with a new administration and are gone when the administration leaves or, worse, before they ever get off the ground. One of the better explanations of complex change management defines five key elements for successful change management: vision, skills, incentive, resources, and an action plan (Villa and Thousand, 1995). The absence of any one of those core elements yields something less than successful change. In Louisville, we've distilled the above components into three principles and added a fourth to anchor our efforts to continually improve government:

- Communication, Vision, and Action Plans: "I know what is expected of me, I agree with it, and it is meaningful."

- Building Reinforcement Mechanisms and Incentives: "The structures, processes, and systems reinforce the change in behavior I am being asked to make."

- Developing Skills and Offering Resources: "I have the skills, capabilities, and opportunities to perform in the new way."

- Driving Culture Change through Role Models: "I see leaders, peers, and others behaving in line with the changes requested of me."

With these four key principles in mind, we began engaging the group of first followers by communicating. Within a month of launching OPI, we sent an email out to all Metro employees about the work of OPI and asked if anyone was interested in being involved, sharing thoughts, and learning more about Performance Improvement. In the first couple of months, we had over one hundred responses. This was not a huge number of people for an organization of nearly six thousand, but enough to get started and help scale the impact of an office of three people. For these individuals, as well as Metro leadership and department management, OPI offered training in Lean, Six Sigma, Project Management, and overall management best practices. Many of these individuals were then assigned to cross-functional teams.

OPI facilitates the work of cross-functional teams who are asked to solve known problems that span multiple departments or stakeholders within Metro Government. Their job is to come up with plans to directly support a strategic objective or goal. In the first year, teams addressed issues impacting our structural budget imbalance, like high unscheduled overtime, long hiring processes, and inappropriate cost recoupment for special events.

This Stuff Really Works: Tangible Results

Since the launch of OPI in 2012, Louisville Metro Government and the various departments and employees involved in the continuous improvement work have reached a number of accomplishments.

Public Works & Assets: Missed Trash Pickup

Public Works & Assets was the first department in the LouieStat program. Citizen calls for service through the MetroCall 311 system was one of the initial enterprise metrics evaluated. The most prevalent calls into our 311 system (approximately six hundred calls a month) were about missed trash pickups. PW&A came to an early LouieStat forum with an "analysis" of their data and a plan to improve their performance. The department's proposed solution was threefold: to buy another truck, hire more people, and reassess their routes. Each of these represented a significant cost. While the department was basing their recommendation on data, it brought up some vital questions:

- Did six hundred missed trash pickups equal poor performance?

- Were the missed pickups due to resource constraints, poor routes, or something else?

- If we made the recommended changes, what level of improvement could we expect?

As OPI worked with the department to answer these questions, the six hundred missed trash pickups per month shifted from being perceived as a poor result to actually a successful result. PW&A conducts over 800,000 trash pickups a month. Six hundred missed pickups is a miss (or error) rate of less than one percent! Statistically, this is quite good. When we compared the "success" of this metric with some of the other issues competing for resources in PW&A, we could not justify the investment it would take to close the gap on a small rate of error—not when we had roads to pave, sidewalks to fix, and other issues to address. Understanding the data underlying the perceived problem helped us better allocate resources where they were needed most.

Corrections: Fingerprinting Errors

At any one time, Louisville Metro Corrections department may have anywhere from 1,700 to 2,200 inmates in its facility. There are numerous processes that support the safe intake, housing, and release of these inmates. Fingerprinting is one of the most important processes. Completed at the time of an inmate's booking, fingerprints help identify the inmates in our custody. Fingerprints are sent to the state for verification, and any incomplete or improperly taken prints are sent back to Louisville to be retaken and resubmitted.

Each month, corrections would get anywhere from two to three hundred fingerprints sent back from the state for reprocessing. This required the inmate to be pulled from housing, taken back to the booking area, and reprinted. This level of rework was inefficient and added an unnecessary level of risk. Applying a reactive problem solving process, the corrections leadership team began by identifying the problem and analyzing the root causes. As they looked into the data, they found that the fingerprints coming back were all taken by a handful of officers who had never been formally trained on how to fingerprint. When they evaluated the booking process, they found that no single officer was assigned to fingerprinting. Instead, whoever was in the area when an inmate came in took the fingerprints. With this information in hand, the department began a training program for booking officers on how to properly administer fingerprints. The department assigned two trained officers each watch to administer fingerprints. Within one month, the number of fingerprints sent back from the state dropped from an average of 250 per month to 10.

Louisville Metro Government: High Cost of Unscheduled Overtime

In January 2012, Louisville's Chief Financial Officer and Director of Human Resources produced a report that revealed that more than one in five city employees increase their base pay each year by at least fifteen percent with overtime—and some city employees were doubling their salaries. In total, the city was spending $23 million on overtime each year. Scheduled overtime, which is either contained in collective bargaining agreements or through state laws, accounts for about thirty-two percent of overtime, or $7.2 million.

Unscheduled overtime accounted for nearly $14 million and was spread across most city departments. We used LouieStat to track the amount of unscheduled overtime a department pays out and formed a cross-functional team to work on the problem. Through the reactive problem-solving process, the team identified the largest drivers of unscheduled overtime and targeted solutions within departments, as well as across Metro, to reduce the amount. Solutions included using a redesigned tracking and approval process within departments and changing some of the language in union contracts. We also generated a new monthly report for department directors that shows just how much overtime is being paid out in their department. It identifies the supervisors approving overtime, the departments' current totals compared to previous year totals, and estimated overtime budgets. With these changes, Metro has seen a reduction in unscheduled overtime by more than $1.4 million, or fourteen percent, in the last fiscal year.

Louisville Metro Government: Lengthy Hiring Process Cycle Time

Complaints over the time it took to fill vacancies were high in January 2012. The hiring process could take anywhere from two to six months—if you were lucky. This length of time was attributed as one of the driving factors of unscheduled overtime costs. As the cross-functional team applied PDCA and Lean to the issue, they quickly mapped out a process that could take anywhere from twenty-eight to more than three hundred business days to fill a vacancy—over a year for some positions.

By analyzing the steps in the process for the department, Human Resources, Finance, and the Mayor's office, Metro discovered opportunities to streamline and improve it. For example, departments were required to get OMB's approval to refill a position if someone resigned or was fired during the year, even if the position had already been approved and budgeted for. By cutting redundant steps in the process, multiple signatures from the same office, unnecessary approvals, and idle wait time between steps, and instituting more structure to the process (i.e., standardizing the process across departments, placing time limits on how long any one step can take, etc.) the team was able to reduce the hiring process from a maximum of three hundred days to a maximum of seventy-five days.

Looking to the Horizon: Where Are We Headed Next?

Building on our progress in developing a culture of continuous improvement within city government, our next steps are to roll out those same processes into the community. Even as we continue to work to make government better, we recognize that one of government's most important roles has to do with convening other actors to address community problems that reach far beyond government's capacity to address alone. To that end, we see the future of Louisville's Performance Improvement journey as having three parts.

Taking Open Data to the Next Level

- Benchmarking to meaningfully compare Louisville's performance to other cities or organizations.

- Creating geospatial tools to provide more accurate locational information to make data more useful and relevant.

- Releasing underlying data supporting LouieStat KPIs to allow citizens, developers, etc., to access "raw data" to apply their own analyses and unlock additional insight.

- Instituting a more deliberate feedback loop for allowing outside parties to help "audit" (update/refine) the data and information that government holds.

Leveraging Data to Optimize Internal Government Processes

- Using Predictive Analytics to marshal resources for proactive action by departments.

- Cascading improvement efforts throughout city government, including participation in LouieStat by every department

Convening Community Partners, Using a Common Set of Metrics to Drive Coordination

- Creating issue-based Stat Programs to take the principles of LouieStat beyond department-centric challenges & metrics to include community partners

Louisville's First Issue-based "Stat" Program

A great example of where we are heading and how we hope to deploy these advances is the pilot of Vacant & Abandoned Properties Statistics (VAPSTAT), our first issue-based stat program. Similar to LouieStat, which evaluates metrics to assess performance and identify opportunities for improvement specific to individual departments, VAPSTAT will analyze progress against key vacant and abandoned property metrics that cross multiple departments and involve multiple community stakeholders.

The community stakeholders will be engaged to determine the most relevant data points (like the number of code enforcement service requests, foreclosures, demolitions, and the amount of liens collected). With this information, the mayor, his senior management team, and key community players will track trend data to assess the impact of current initiatives and identify new tactics or operational changes that must be made to ensure we reach our goals—with the ultimate objective of eradicating vacant and abandoned properties from our community. This information will be presented and discussed in an open forum, where individual citizens, neighborhood groups, and non- and for-profit organizations can bring their data and resources to the table to provide a comprehensive community approach to the complex problem.

VAPSTAT will build on the city's open data resources in several ways.

Benchmarking Against Peers

VAPSTAT will benchmark Louisville's data against BlightStatus in

New Orleans and other cities with high levels of vacant properties, like Detroit and Philadelphia, to understand the scope of the problem and progress relative to other cities.

Creating Geospatial Tools

VAPSTAT will overlay vacant and abandoned lots/structures with fire, type of crime, and property violations through our code enforcement database, using site addresses to help understand how vacant and abandoned properties correlate with other issues.

Putting Raw Data in Exportable Formats

Our open data portal currently contains datasets for property maintenance, vacant and abandoned property listings, and crime data.

Using Predictive Analytics

VAPSTAT will combine water and electrical connectivity, postal service data, and property maintenance data to anticipate and better plan for resources needed to address problems through proactive outreach and prevention work in more targeted areas.

These tools will enable government and community partners to meaningfully engage in a dialogue that is focused on measurable results, not just words. Effective interventions will be immediately seen and highlighted, enabling the community to replicate what has worked. Most importantly, any organization seeking to get engaged in resolving the issue will have a clear way to engage with other community players—catalyzing partnerships, reducing duplication of efforts, and leveraging existing resources.

Conclusion

Along our journey in Louisville, four major takeaways have helped us get started and build momentum. First, recognize that data will never be perfect—start with the data you have now (in startup speak, a "minimum viable product") and improve as you go. Second, use data to open a conversation about strategy and prioritization. Third, engage and support your "first followers"—they become your ambassadors and cheerleaders. And finally, celebrate success. It doesn't have to be about financial rewards; recognition and praise go a long way.

Data for transparency's sake is a great starting point for driving change. But that's all it is: a starting point. The trick is to convert the data into useful information that can be used to identify ways to continually improve performance. Once that becomes the focus, then you will be surprised at how many "intra-preneurs" will spring up to help make government better.

With the right support, data enables meaningful conversations about strategy and planning, which, when aligned with the right incentives and skill-building opportunities, can create a culture of continuous improvement. That is the true goal of government reform and the driving mission of our work in Louisville.

About the Authors

A native of Connecticut, Theresa Reno-Weber moved to Louisville in 2010 with her husband, who was born and raised there. She most recently worked with McKinsey & Company, a top-tier management consultant firm that works with businesses and governments across the globe. She has worked with fortune 100 companies, government agencies, and non-profits across the US, Europe, and the Middle East. Theresa is a former Lieutenant in the US Coast Guard, where she served for ten years before earning a Master of Public Policy from Harvard University's Kennedy School of Government.

Beth Niblock was appointed to be the first CIO for Kentucky's newly merged Louisville-Jefferson County Metro Government in 2003. She was recognized as one of *Government Technology's* Top 25 Doers, Dreamers, and Drivers in 2011.

References

Collins, J. (2001). *Good to Great.* New York, NY: HarperBusiness.

Miller, K. (2006). *We Don't Make Widgets.* Washington, DC: Governing Books.

Ries, E. (2011). *The Lean Startup.* New York, NY: Crown Business.

Thousand, J. S. & Villa, R. A. (1995). Managing Complex Change Toward Inclusive Schooling. In R. A. Villa & J. S. Thousand (Eds.) Creating an Inclusive School. Alexandria, VA: Association for Supervision and Curriculum Development.

CHAPTER 18

Benchmarking Performance Data

By Ken Wolf and John Fry

Come senators, congressmen, please heed the call

Don't stand in the doorway, don't block up the hall...

It'll soon shake your windows and rattle your walls

For the times they are a-changin'.

—*Bob Dylan, 1964*

Fifty years later, and the times they are still a-changin'. Back in the 1960s, the battle being fought was about freedom, individuality, and expression. Today's battle is about openness, transparency, and engagement. Citizens are demanding more from their public servants than ever before—and at all levels of government. Not only do we expect our governments to provide ever-increasing levels of service to us at ever-decreasing costs, but we also want to be part of that process. The cry to rid government of waste, fraud, and abuse has been encouraged by sound-bite politics. We need to understand how our government agencies are performing, where they could be doing better, and how they can improve. We want to help influence that conversation and know that action-oriented decisions are being executed. We expect to see measurable results and want to feel the effects of those improvements in our everyday lives. We're like the shareholders of a public corporation that want to hold our executive leadership accountable for achieving our corporate goals.

We are experiencing a radical transformation in the volume of public data available today and the velocity and means at which it is delivered to citizens. For example, the International Open Government Dataset Search web page (Tetherless World Constellation International, 2013) lists 1,028,054 datasets in forty-three countries, containing 192 catalogs and 2,460 categories of datasets. How are local government leaders responding to this phenomenon as it relates to measuring and improving operational performance? What benefits do they hope to achieve from this transparency? What does the future of local government leadership look like in terms of managing better and driving improved performance? And, how does collaboration of performance results and sharing of best practices across cities support that future vision?

This essay explores how transparency and collaboration in the municipal performance management process leads to increased engagement, better-run government, and improved outcomes for citizens. First, we'll provide some background on what performance management in the public sector is and why we do it. Second, we'll discuss accountability and transparency to the public and share insights from real cities doing this today. Finally, we'll talk about how open data can be leveraged across and among cities to provide context and insight that inform the performance improvement agenda. We'll learn how, despite our preconceived notions, cities large and small are openly collaborating to help each other improve.

Let's start by getting a baseline understanding of what performance management is and why we do it.

What Is Performance Management?

Performance management, specifically as it relates to the public sector, is a management system to improve the delivery of services using quantified measurements that are collected and reported to focus attention and action on areas of organizational performance in need of improvement.

Performance management is, first of all, a management system. While this statement may appear obvious, another commonly used term, "performance measurement," obscures the focus of performance management. Performance management is action-oriented, although quantitative measurement to monitor the effectiveness of the delivery of public services remains a core component. It is the periodic and routine management review of these ongoing measures that leads to new initiates, reallocation of resources, modification of service processes and policies, and anything else that improves the service delivery of our government.

A key first step to a successful performance management process is to make sure we are measuring the right things—the issues that matter to citizens. We call these "outcomes." Outcomes typically come in two forms—outcomes of effectiveness (doing things better) and outcomes of efficiency (being more cost-effective at doing so). One advantage of measuring outcomes is that, unlike department operations or business processes that may change over time, the outcomes that citizens desire do not. This allows us to define a long-term vision for improvement and develop a roadmap that gets us there.

There is a growing emphasis on asking citizens what is important to them, and in doing so, we often learn that our initial assumptions are off. San Francisco learned from citizen surveys that perceptions of street and sidewalk cleanliness were affected by foul odors. Bellevue, Washington, developed a set of sixteen "vital signs," then used focus groups to validate those vital signs. Bellevue's departments thought that the things they do most frequently were most important, but the public felt that the most severe outcomes were most important. For example, the police department focused on less severe crimes that occur more often, but the public apparently cared more about the most serious, though less frequent, crimes.

Measuring outcomes of effectiveness and efficiency is much more meaningful than simply measuring activity. Counting how many potholes we filled last month doesn't tell us very much. It tells us how busy we are, but not whether we are particularly good at pothole repair. How long that three-foot pothole has been sitting in the middle of her street is something that might matter to Jane Q. Citizen. Two days? Two weeks? Two months? Longer? A measure of effectiveness that matters to her might be the average amount of time that elapses between the reporting of a pothole by a citizen and its repair. We'll also want to know the average cost to repair a pothole so that we can determine whether or not we have an efficient pothole repair operation.

Once we decide what we'll need to measure, we need to begin capturing, reviewing, and analyzing the data. Naturally, we'll need the right technology to do so. We need a tool that can interoperate with the myriad of other systems within our operations. Furthermore, we need the ability to visualize the data in ways that tell a clear story. This tool needs to help us see patterns and relationships, correlate data across departments and agencies, and be intelligent enough to present us with the most important and relevant information, so that even our ongoing performance management process is as efficient as it can be. It should alert us when performance is moving in a negative direction so we can respond accordingly, and it should highlight positive trends so that we know that our actions are keeping us on the right course.

Why Bother?

Having an effective, ongoing performance management process in place is the key to running a successful government. Through these processes, management gains increased visibility into operational performance and results. Operational improvements can be realized through optimized resource allocations. It can even spur policy review and modifications.

Even more important is the fact that introducing these approaches as part of the way of doing business inside local government can establish a high-performance culture within the organization. This creates greater internal alignment by better communicating organizational priorities to the team.

By introducing open data into performance management processes, we can make great leaps forward in increasing accountability and data-driven communication with stakeholders. That means knowing the stakeholders of local government and monitoring how a good performance management process can properly engage them through the data.

Accountability and Communication

Government accountability is about setting expectations and reporting to stakeholders what has been accomplished relative to those expectations. It is more about the communication of actions and results, rather than the actions and results themselves. Accountability rests on an assumption of responsibility by elected and appointed officials in government to protect and serve citizens and act as stewards of the public's resources.

The four major stakeholders of local government are:

- Department heads, who oversee the operations within each service area.

- Municipal management, who coordinate the different service areas and are responsible for the implementation of policies.

- Elected officials, who set policy, may have a management role, and are one step from the public.

- The public, either through individuals or stakeholder groups.

The benefit of a good performance management system is that objective data about the accomplishments of government can be seen by anyone, even if it is packaged in different ways and in different levels of detail. This integrated accountability promotes rational decision-making because of the commonality of the facts. Staff, management, and the public see these facts through their individual lenses:

- Staff: are we getting the job done?

- Management: is the job getting done efficiently and effectively?

- Public: are we getting the results we pay for?

To that last point, we are seeing two interesting trends emerge that support open data with respect to operational performance.

Public Participation

First, citizens, in part thanks to technological developments, are taking a more active role in wanting to understand and contribute to the performance of their cities and towns. Products like SeeClickFix, which capture input directly from citizens through their mobile devices, are informing city agencies of service needs in real time and with greater volume than ever before. They allow citizens to report everything, from graffiti to potholes to streetlights in need of repair. However, these new capabilities are also setting expectations in the minds of citizens that these incidents will be addressed on a timely basis. They expect results and feedback. City managers need to track overall performance and response times and report how well they're doing back to the public, both individually and in the aggregate.

The use of citizens or non-government organizations to help deliver public services is known as "co-production." Co-production can be provided by individuals or by organized volunteer groups. Originally, it was represented by low technology involvement, such as the Neighborhood Watch, an organized group of volunteers trained to reduce crime and vandalism in their neighborhoods. Technology is increasing the potential for citizens to produce services in conjunction with their local governments.

High Performance Cultures

At the same time as it is becoming easier for citizens to identify problems for their governments, forward-thinking government officials, some of whom have been influenced by private sector experience, are realizing the benefits of holding themselves and their organizations accountable to the public. A mayor or city manager instills a high performance culture within his organization when he establishes an ongoing process of tracking operational metrics across departments and agencies—and publishes those metrics to the public in conjunction with the objectives and strategies they are intended to measure. By giving each of his department heads direct responsibility for establishing those objectives, strategies, and metrics, he is driving accountability and strengthening the relationship between citizens and their government leaders.

How Cities Are Communicating Performance Results With Their Public

To date, only a small percentage of cities have gone so far as to publish their performance strategies and results publicly on their websites. These pioneers realize the value of continuously monitoring performance, striving to improve results, and sharing those results with their citizen stakeholders. Although the processes used to collect, review, and publish performance data and the content and format of the information that is presented vary widely across cities, they all have certain common characteristics:

- These initiatives are driven from the very top of the organization, often by the mayor or city manager.

- Performance data is collected, reviewed, and published on a routine basis.

- Department managers are integral to the process.

- There is a specific part of the organization dedicated to the performance management program. In smaller cities, this might be all or part of the responsibilities of a single individual. In larger cities, there is often a department or office of performance management that involves a larger team.

In reviewing websites of many of the cities that engage in performance reporting, we found a great deal of diversity in the manner in which these municipalities went about their reporting:

- The population sizes range from towns that may have less than 50,000 residents to the largest of cities throughout the nation, including New York City.

- The frequency of the data reporting varies, including monthly, bi-monthly, quarterly, semi-annually, and annually.

- Some report performance against targets and discuss the goals and objectives of their departments, while others do not.

- The most commonly used source of data is operational measures, which are collected by the departments, but some of the cities use citizen satisfaction surveys and outcomes based on inspections or other ways of determining results of the operations.

- Several of the cities have found ways to have the public determine what measures are important to them, including focus groups, citizen surveys, and individual suggestions.

- There are no apparent correlations between these diverse factors, such as a tendency for the larger municipalities to report more (or less) frequently.

We spoke to officials who manage performance programs from four cities that are widely known for their performance initiatives. The following are highlights of their programs:

San Francisco, California

San Francisco's performance program is called "San Francisco Performs." It is primarily focused on supporting the mayor's proposed budget and helping to provide context to citizens. Annually, San Francisco issues the "Controller's Annual Performance Report," a comprehensive report with over one thousand performance metrics across the city's forty-eight departments (e.g. Airport, Fire, and Human Services). That amounts to approximately twenty metrics per department. San Francisco also issues a smaller, bi-monthly "Performance Barometer" report on a subset of key measures. This report is approximately seven pages in length and includes a rotating "highlighted measure" and a few of the key performance indicators for various activities, such as Public Safety, Streets and Public Works, and Customer Service.

Kyle Burns, Performance Analyst & Program Lead in the San Francisco Controller's Office stated in an interview:

> The benefits of reporting performance data to the citizens are all about accountability. Why? Because it's important. The mayor's office uses the performance metrics to make decisions on resource allocation in the budget process… Transparency and the idea of having the data published allow citizens to understand how the city is performing and delivering services. (Burns, personal communication, 2013.)

Bellevue, Washington

The City of Bellevue, Washington, has been, "Managing for Results" since 1997, when the city manager started a performance management program based on two key goals: creating an evidenced-based government and sharing that information with the public via their website. The title they selected for their program, Managing for Results, indicates their orientation to outcomes, or results that matter to citizens. They describe their philosophy with the question "So what?" This indicates their interest in determining why a measure ultimately matters to citizens.

A cornerstone of Bellevue's program is to investigate and utilize diverse methods that reach and engage citizens. In addition to using their website for their performance program, in City Hall, there is a board posted which displays the city's Vital Signs—a set of sixteen key metrics. Bellevue produces an annual performance report following reporting guidelines from the Association of Government Accountants' (AGA) and shares this with citizens on their website. They also conduct and report on the results of citizen surveys about satisfaction with public services to complement the operational metrics they collect. Their use of community indicators, which are measures that get close to the ultimate concerns of citizens but may not be totally under the control of any single department or even the city as a whole, is evidence of their sincere belief in communicating to citizens. According to Rich Siegel, Performance & Outreach Coordinator, "We need to let citizens know if we are doing better, the same, or worse. We are likely to get support for projects when they know how well we are doing."

Austin, Texas

Austin, Texas started "Managing for Results" in 1992. "The core focus of the performance program is to focus on the customer," said Shannon Szymczak, Corporate Budget Manager. Szymczak continued, "It's an old saying, but you have to measure what matters." With over twenty years of experience measuring performance, its performance system has evolved. Austin started with over four thousand metrics, but is now down to one thousand. In 2011, they began to report on twenty-one dashboard measures that were chosen by focus groups of citizens.

Much of the focus of the performance program is aimed at the budget process. Each department is responsible for developing departmental goals to inform the budget process. Since 2005, everything reported to the budget office is made available publicly. Austin emphasizes results by distinguishing performance measures from operational measures, which assess activities. A forward-thinking approach is demonstrated in displaying the results for the past three years in the context of targets for the current and upcoming year. According to Szymczak, "goals must be measurable."

Baltimore, Maryland

Baltimore, Maryland, is appropriately credited as a pioneer of the CitiStat model. CitiStat and all the management methods known as the Stat models share an emphasis on relentless follow-through. Officials accomplish this through periodic meetings in which they review performance and determine action plans to resolve issues. These meetings occur about once per month—or even more frequently in some implementations. The updated results are reviewed in order to evaluate actions taken based on the decisions reached in prior meetings.

The Baltimore Office of CitiStat is a small performance-based management group responsible for continually improving the quality of services provided to the citizens of the city. Staff analysts examine data and perform investigations in order to identify areas in need of improvement. The mayor or members of her cabinet attend the CitiStat meetings, which are held every four weeks, and ask the presenting agency questions about its performance. As a result of its success, local governments have adapted the CitiStat model across the US and around the world.

Through the CitiStat program, Baltimore had been tracking metrics internally for many years prior to sharing them with citizens. Initially, department managers had concerns that it might be hard for citizens to digest the information or that it would be taken out of context. Although the CitiStat process emphasized internal management and improvement in delivering services to citizens, the data was no longer being released publicly. The mayor signed an executive order in August 2012 to promote increased transparency. Chad Kenney, Director of Baltimore CitiStat says, "The key is to not overwhelm citizens with a lot of data and to put the data into context so it's understood." Department managers understand the detailed data because they understand the service processes. Citizens do not have the advantage of this context.

Baltimore's public-facing reports include month-to-month and year-to-year comparisons in order to provide a baseline for citizens to evaluate performance. Some of their current initiatives include making this data more understandable by providing neighborhood-based information and working with local groups who help citizens understand the data.

Lessons Learned

What takeaway points did these four cities, as a group, suggest? How have they addressed the challenges of publicly reporting data?

Address Department Concerns of Misinterpretation

It is common for department managers to be concerned that the public will be critical and misinterpret data because they do not have knowledge of the operations of the city. In addition to providing the public with more summarized information about results and outcomes in order to reduce the misinterpretation, other responses have included:

- Emphasize performance exceeding expectations, as well as performance not meeting expectations.

- Ignore individual data points and emphasize stable trends.

- Emphasize results, rather than activities, to allow the same metrics to be reported, even when business processes change.

- Partner with non-government organizations to present the data to the public to increase their understanding.

The balancing act is ongoing: transparency to the public and other stakeholders versus the validity of the interpretation of the data. Perhaps even more important is the perception by department managers that others (including their own elected and appointed officials) do not understand their service area. Hence, some of the responses above show support for the managers' concerns.

Our company, Revelstone, has experienced these concerns with some of its customers. Our practical experience is that leadership needs to support the importance of the data and responsibility of the service area to make its value proposition to all stakeholders. We also found evidence in the four cities we talked to that appropriate data for stakeholders will be different than that used for an internal review of operations in the service area. Baltimore, which built its CitiStat program around a model to promote frequent operational review, has the shortest program of reporting to external stakeholders. More time is needed to see if the partnership with non-governmental organizations will help public use and interpretation of the data or whether it will still need further summarization and a results orientation in the public-facing data reporting.

Public Use Is Not Always Extensive

Most of the cities felt that the use of the data by the public was not extensive. Almost all of them recognized the challenge of presenting the data at a level of detail that would encourage use by the public. To accomplish this, they used dashboards, barometers, vital signs, and community indicators that were a small set of the detailed measures that were used for internal management. Each of these mechanisms focuses on metrics that are most important to the public. These cities are increasingly concerned with presenting the appropriate data to the public—both what they think is important and the level that will encourage the public to spend time learning about how their city is performing.

One of the major challenges is to convert greater accessibility to data to greater participation and engagement by citizens. The maxim "Build it and they will come" does not apply here. The cities that we engaged with, which are among the most progressive in the arena of publicly accessible data about their municipal performance, recognize the work that needs to be done.

In addition to the efforts in these cities to increase public use of their data, there is support from a number of non-government organizations that are stakeholders in the increase in public transparency. Some of these organizations include the Governmental Accounting Standards Board (GASB), the Association of Government Accountants (AGA), and the Government Finance Officers Association (GFOA). Their work helps move best practices in public reporting more quickly to other cities and towns.

The interest in performance reporting to citizens has grown in the last decade. Several of the aforementioned organizations provide guidelines to help local governments provide effective public reporting. In June 2010, GASB issued "Suggested Guidelines for Voluntary Reporting." These guidelines are termed SEA (Service Efforts and Accomplishments) Performance Reporting. According to GASB, the primary purpose of a government is to help maintain and improve the well being of its citizens by providing services.

Other organizations promote similar guidelines for public reporting and make awards to local governments that effectively follow those guidelines. AGA does this through their Citizen-Centric Reporting Program. The National Center for Civic Innovation recognizes local governments that engage citizens in the performance reporting process. GFOA has put an increasing emphasis on performance management in its publications and recognizes it in its Awards for Excellence.

Benefits of Public Performance Reporting

The cities we talked to cite increased transparency as a benefit of public reporting. Bellevue believes it is the fact that they are transparent and a high-performing city that accounts for the light public use of the data.

Most of the cities believe that performance data broadens the perspective of the citizen beyond anecdotes and what a citizen observed on a single occasion. Most of these cities also tie the performance data to the budget and state that doing so has enabled them to get public support for capital programs and increases in revenue generation when they were needed.

The Multiplier Effect: Inter-City Collaboration

Open data is about sharing and exposing information for the good of all. In the context of local government, this can be about more than just the relationship between cities and their citizens. There are over 39,000 counties, cities, and towns in the United States, along with another 37,000 special districts that run discrete operations, such as water and sewer, fire protection, airports, mass transit, business improvement, etc. Each of these entities working independently to establish goals and strategies, measure and review performance, and share their results with the public are certainly on the right track to managing better. Yet, imagine if they were able to harness their collective knowledge to help each other improve. What kinds of benefits could be achieved in a world where cities shared performance data and collaborated with each other to get better? We call it the "power of the network."

A good performance management system allows us to answer three basic questions:

- How are we doing?

- What could we be doing better?

- How can we learn from our peers to improve?

Up until this point, we have been primarily concerned with the process of local governments managing performance from an internal perspective. We've also discussed the requirements of any technology solution that enables the capture and reporting of performance data to occur. All of this helps us answer the first question, "How are we doing?" We can also begin answering the second question, "What could we be doing better?" by examining trends in our data—are we getting better or worse? So, how do we gain even better insight into the "what" question and follow that by answering the third question, so that we don't have to reinvent the wheel ourselves? The answer lies in the two inter-jurisdictional collaborative facets of performance management—compare and learn.

Compare

By comparing our measures, we gain actionable information. In providing a context through comparison, we can assess whether we are doing well or not as well as we would like. There are a multitude of contexts and many ways to compare any measure. If we filled ten potholes, cleared ten crimes, or confined ten fires to the room of origin, are we doing well?

Temporal Comparisons

The most common context for comparison is to what we normally do, whether normal is defined as last month, the same time last year, or a seasonally adjusted index. All of these are known as temporal comparisons or comparisons over time. These comparisons are available to any government that routinely collects the same data and uses it to monitor its performance. It provides powerful information to see if you are doing better or not.

Peer Comparisons

An enhancement to simply seeing if you are doing better is seeing if you are doing as well as others. "Benchmarking" is the comparison of our own measures to the same measures in other jurisdictions and falls under the term inter-jurisdictional comparisons. Benchmarks can tell us whether our performance is better than most others who are doing the same thing or whether it needs improvement just to get in the game.

It is important to compare to like peers, that is, other cities that share characteristics related to what you are measuring. These characteristics can be demographic, such as population, land area, or median household income. We look for like demographics because they are correlated with the workload that is encountered when delivering a particular service. In some cases, we can also find like peers by considering service characteristics, which are more directly related to the workload to deliver the service. An example is the number of collection stops for solid waste collection. Service characteristics that reflect the level of service provided also help find like peers. Providers of twice-a-week solid waste collection would not typically be compared to once-a-week collectors.

Comparisons to Targets

Proactive management does more than just comparing current performance after the fact. It motivates better performance and sets goals (through performance targets). By comparing performance to targets defined beforehand, management is acting by making a statement about the performance level that is desired. Targets, if they are reported publicly, are a commitment to your citizens.

Both temporal and inter-jurisdictional comparisons inform the setting of targets. Anticipated changes in your workload, changes in resources available for the service, and your managerial initiatives, do this as well. To complete the performance improvement cycle, the performance measures are compared to these managerial targets, and the differences are analyzed and reviewed to initiate the third step of the performance management process, which is learning what can be done.

Learn

The next step is discovering what you can do, based on your measures and comparisons, in order to achieve improvement. If you have set managerial targets, the stage is set to learn, particularly in areas (and for measures) where the targets have not been achieved. The management team for each service area learns through internal discussions of the expectations versus the actual performance. Were the expectations inappropriate? Were expected resources not available? Did conditions change unexpectedly? Is something else required that has not been accounted for?

The review by a management team is very important and can keep performance on track, accessing just the knowledge of that team, but if you are benchmarking against other jurisdictions, you may be able to learn techniques and approaches that the internal team cannot envision. Technology has started to improve the effectiveness of this external learning, but there is even greater potential. We have seen the acceleration of the ability to spread improved techniques through email listservs of a community of colleagues, but the potential offered by combining context-specific data with social networking technologies offers the promise of practical and efficient capabilities to learn from others.

Towards Performance-Based Collaboration

At Revelstone, we built an online performance platform, Compass, with these three elements of the performance management challenge in mind—measure, compare, and learn. We think tools like this, which allow cities to collaborate through performance benchmarking and peer-to-peer learning, are the future of the government-to-government movement. When we first embarked on this journey of performance-based collaboration, we expected that municipal leaders would want to see how well they were doing in comparison to others. However, we assumed they'd be reticent to expose themselves and, therefore, would want to participate in the process anonymously.

To the contrary, we discovered a specific desire for people to identify themselves on the platform, so that they could identify like peers, initiate connections, and build learning-based relationships with each other. So, we built a feature in our product that allowed each participating entity to opt out and remain anonymous. Much to our surprise, to date, not a single user of Compass has chosen to participate anonymously; they all want to be part of the collaborative community. Clearly, our skepticism about the willingness of government leaders to share their performance results—at least with each other—was largely unfounded. Is it possible we are seeing this phenomenon only among early adopters of this technology and approach (i.e. selection bias)? Sure, but we are hopeful they will set the trend for the rest of the mainstream market that is sure to follow.

Will the need for improved performance drive local government leaders to expose their data to the public, or will the open data movement influence the culture of government to be more transparent and engage with the public to its benefit? Perhaps both. Either way, change is coming. It already has been demonstrated in larger cities, in some cases for decades. Now, advancements in technology are enabling smaller cities and towns to participate in the open data movement as well. These trends are also fostering a virtual community of municipalities that are the forerunners of the gov-to-gov movement. They are collaborating with peers to gain valuable context with respect to their performance and learn from each other to improve. We should expect to see accelerated participation as the viral effect begins to surface: "Hey, you should be doing this too, so I can learn from you and you can learn from me."

It is time for cities to embrace openness, transparency, and engagement, create a closer relationship with their citizens, and help improve their quality of life. In order to maximize impact, they should leverage each other in the process, taking advantage of the power of the network to drive learning, collaboration, and improved outcomes for all. The open data movement is here. "It'll shake your windows and rattle your halls."

About the Authors

As President and CEO of Revelstone, Ken Wolf is the guiding force behind Revelstone's vision to bring a low cost and easy-to-use performance management platform to local governments. With nearly 20 years in the technology industry, Ken has a solid track record of building market-leading businesses and high performing teams. Prior to launching Revelstone, Ken conceived and established Revelwood, a performance management consultancy, more than 15 years ago. Ken is a Certified Public Accountant and received a Bachelor of Science degree in Economics with a specialization in Accounting from the Wharton School of the University of Pennsylvania.

John Fry is the Program Director for Government Solutions at Revelstone and utilizes his experience of over twenty years in local government to guide the development of content focused on the needs of government. His diverse career includes being a municipal administrator and consulting on municipal efficiency, emphasizing the techniques of performance management and shared services. His education in data, research and computing led to his work in at the Fund for the City of New York, where he implemented the first performance management system in New York City, Project Scorecard.

References

Governmental Accounting Standards Board. (2010). *Suggested Guidelines for Voluntary Reporting of SEA Performance Information.* Washington, DC.

Tetherless World Constellation International (2013). *Open Government Dataset Search.* Retrieved from http://logd.tw.rpi.edu/iogds_data_analytics

PART V:
Looking Ahead

What is needed to take the open data movement even further? What obstacles, challenges, and concerns remain to be addressed? This section is devoted to identifying those issues, and envisioning a future of civic innovation powered by open data.

First, Greg Bloom, a long-time advocate for better social services data in Washington, D.C., explores the idea of open data as a common good. In Chapter 19, he outlines a vision for a future of "data cooperatives" to ensure better management and maintenance of this public resource.

In Chapter 20, we take a step back with John Bracken, Director of Media and Innovation for the Knight Foundation, one of the biggest philanthropic funders of open government initiatives. Based on his experience running the Knight News Challenge, he shares observations of ten key lessons the community needs to embrace to take the open government movement to the next level and better enable the potential of open data to be fully realized.

Next, Mark Headd, the first Chief Data Officer for Philadelphia, proposes that open data is an important first step to spurring new approaches to government service delivery in Chapter 21. He outlines why changing the way government procures technology is needed to enable more far-reaching change—both cultural and operational—within city hall.

And finally, in Chapter 22, open government advocate Tim O'Reilly concludes by outlining his vision of algorithmic regulation. How can government take advantage of innovations like advances in sensor technology and the emergence of the sharing economy to inform more effective regulation and governance? He argues that open data—when combined with clear desired outcomes and smart analysis—can be a key enabler to ensure accountability and continuous improvement in twenty-first century government.

CHAPTER 19

Towards a Community Data Commons

By Greg Bloom

The Front Line

Bread for the City is one of Washington D.C.'s largest and most comprehensive providers of human services: an institution nearly four decades old, with four departments offering dozens of services—health care, legal counsel, food provisions, social workers, and the "Bread Boutique" clothing room to boot—in two facilities on opposite sides of the city. About thirty-two thousand people walk through Bread for the City's doors each year, but out of all of these "walk-ins," only around twelve thousand people actually become "clients." The rest may need services that are provided elsewhere, at other non-profits or public agencies, and Bread for the City's social workers redirect them accordingly.

Finding accurate referral information—specifically, what services are provided where, when, and for whom—takes up hours of these social workers' time each week. In any given week, somewhere in the city, a new program is launching, or changing its hours or its eligibility requirements, or moving, or shutting down. There aren't any common channels through which this information is shared with the public—if it's shared publicly at all. So Bread for the City's social workers built a Microsoft Access database to track hundreds of organizations and over 1,500 services. People trust Bread for the City, and many come to the organization to get these referrals, as they wouldn't know where else to find reliable information.

Occasionally, outside parties have asked Bread for the City for a copy of its data to use in some kind of directory databasing initiative. The organization is unusually willing to share. After all, if someone else can make use of their data, then perhaps more people will find more direct routes to the help they need, saving them time and achieving better outcomes, making it that much easier for social workers to provide direct assistance to those whom they can help.

For nearly five years, I led communications for Bread for the City. During that time, I blogged occasionally about these directory initiatives. Once I started looking, I found them all over the place. A typical project would collect some data, put up a website or a Google Maps layer or a printable PDF, then stall out. New ones would keep coming. Even the D.C. government has more than a dozen different resource directories scattered across its many agencies, often in Excel or Microsoft Word and hopelessly out of date.

Eventually, I started gathering participants from these initiatives together to discuss what we came to call "the community resource directory data problem." In these conversations, my guiding questions were: how can we actually work together to solve this problem? How could Bread for the City's knowledge be pooled with knowledge from other sectors? What would be in the best interests of the struggling D.C. residents who might benefit from this information?

The Long Fail

We were far from the first to ask these questions.

Indeed, the "community resource directory problem" has been around nearly as long as there have been professionalized services that one might call "community resources." Before the digital era, in most communities you'd likely find at least one organization (such as an agency like Bread for the City, or a church, or a library) in which someone would labor to compile, print, and circulate such a directory every year or so. As the sector grew, the number of directories proliferated, and as early as the 1970s, the field of "information and referral" (I&R) formally emerged (Williams and Durrance, 2010).

In our "D.C. community resource directory" conversations, one of the regular participants had helped launch a citywide I&R initiative back in the mid-90s. Their plan was to build a "master directory" that would be accessible through computer kiosks in agencies and community centers throughout the city. Technologically, their plan may have been overly ambitious, but it was politics that ultimately brought this initiative down. Another large local organization had received funding to produce a resource directory, and it moved aggressively to protect its turf. The resulting struggle over who would own this data sapped the will of the coalition. The database was handed over to the local government, which did not really commit to sustaining it. So the D.C. public I&R system never became widely used, and the quality of its data decayed rapidly. Eventually, it was more or less forgotten.

A decade later, we would ask for this data back. In 2012 and 2013, with the help of the local Code for America Brigade (and no small amount of arm-wrestling among community partners), we managed to consolidate I&R data from the D.C. government, Bread for the City, and several other resource directory datasets into one master directory. We assigned a unique identifier to each organization in this directory, by which every contributing system can now recognize the data from the other systems. And we hosted it in a cloud catalog as open data, freely available for any application to query via an Application Programming Interface (API).

Technologically, this was actually pretty easy to accomplish—and it would not have been possible fifteen years ago, maybe not even five. We've reached a level of technical interoperability that makes it unnecessary to struggle over questions like whose server will host the data, and how the data will be delivered to which users. The answer can be "openly."

But this answer only gets us so far. It really only makes it possible for us to ask new kinds of questions, starting with: what should a twenty-first century "information and referral system" look like?

The 211 Legacy

Today, most official I&R systems still look like they did in the late twentieth century. Specifically, they look like 211—the nationally designated solution to the community resource directory problem. In most places in the country, you should be able to pick up a phone, dial 211, and request a referral from a call center specialist who supposedly has at their fingertips all the relevant information about local health, human, and social services.

211, however, is not one single system. It is actually a federated, decentralized network. More than two hundred 211s operate independently across the United States and Canada. Each 211 is shaped by the institutional landscape of its particular area. Some are run by local governments, most are independent 501(c)(3)s, and many are run (or funded) by the local United Way.

The United Way was the driving force behind 211's initial development. As a non-profit clearinghouse for charitable donations and volunteers, the United Way was one of the sector's best sources of directory information. It moved aggressively to "add value" to this data by securing contracts for the operation of 211 services around the country.

Today, many 211s appear to possess the best I&R data available in their communities. They dedicate considerable human resources to maintaining that data, and to maintaining the associated contracts (from government, local foundations, etc.) to deliver the data. But these 211 systems emerged just in time for the technologies they were built upon to start to slide into obsolescence, and they haven't changed much since. 211 systems are basically pre-Web 2.0. The network is only recently starting to consider the prospects of smart mobile applications. These are very much "closed" platforms, and there isn't any one governing body that can make the decision to open them up.

This was where we found an odd local advantage at our table in D.C. The city's 211 system, which is operated by the local government, had long been one of the least active systems around. The D.C. government had never invested in it, and the initiative languished. Eventually, we asked the city to hand the data over, and they readily complied. Despite the lousy quality of D.C.'s 211 data, we hoped that "opening" it would yield a clear path toward the development of an innovative, "community-based" I&R system. In retrospect, we were naïve about how big of a challenge this would be.

The Civic Technologists

To understand the particularly elusive nature of this problem, consider the contrast between Open211 and its more successful and popular cousin, Open311.

311 is a municipally-run calling system through which residents can both request information about public services and also report non-emergency problems that a city deals with, such as filling potholes or cleaning up vermin infestations.

Open311 is a set of protocols that standardizes the data types and flows of 311 systems, and "opens" them up via an API. This enables external applications to read from and even write to a city's 311 system. The resulting flurry of Open311-related innovation hasn't just expanded the number of ways in which you can use 311—it has actually shifted the paradigm around that use, from private interaction between individual and agency to public participatory engagement.

But Open311 had a clear path to success: municipal agencies may be siloed and sluggish, but because they are still part of one big system, a single point of leverage (say, the Mayor's office) can actually bring them all in line. An attempt to replicate this success with Open211 faced the more elusive challenge of "opening" data produced about and by non-governmental organizations.

Open211 launched in 2011, during the inaugural round of Code for America (CfA) fellowships. Having decided to take on the community resource directory data problem, a Bay Area-based CfA team discovered that their region's 211 had neither an API, nor an interest in building an API, or really sharing its data in any way. So their Open211 project (originally called "the Redirectory") actually bypassed the challenge of "opening" 211, and instead started from scratch. The team exported and scraped directory data from every source they could find, including government agencies, community directories, and Google. Then they imported this hodgepodge of data into a lightweight application that could display results on a simple mapping interface, print out referrals, send geo-targeted referrals via text messages, and receive user-submitted data that would expand and organize its listings.

This last part was key: Open211 not only enabled users to create and improve their community's resource directory data themselves, it was counting on them to do so. But the crowd didn't come. The team tried to recruit and train non-profits to use it, without much success. If people's hands weren't held through the process, the app just didn't get used. At the end of the yearlong fellowship program, the source code for the Open211 project was posted publicly on GitHub, a website for collaborative software development, but otherwise abandoned.

During interviews with several 211 administrators, I heard them predict precisely this outcome. The most effective 211s hire a team of researchers who spend their time calling agencies to solicit and verify their information. They might also send emails and letters to agencies requesting that they update their data themselves, but this doesn't yield great results. Someone at an agency will probably answer a phone call, but relatively few will log in or print and mail a form. There are lots of reasons for this. Requests get lost in the incoming flood. The task may not fall under any given staffer's responsibilities, or within their technical abilities. Many organizations will only respond to someone they trust. And for some organizations, making their service information more widely known just isn't a priority.

This all points to a question that the civic technology movement must consider: whose responsibility is it to produce and share knowledge about a community?

The Startups

Many social service agencies (especially ones that are smaller and less resourced than Bread for the City) still rely on analog referral systems such as binders full of handwritten lists of nearby services. A slew of startups have recently emerged to offer more efficient technology solutions that address this this need.

For instance, the Austin-based Aunt Bertha offers software that streamlines and digitizes the process of intake, relieving social workers and clients of great headaches of paperwork. In doing so, Aunt Bertha collects and publishes information about which organizations do what for whom. Another organization, Idealistics, produced software that helps case managers manage their cases, analyzes the data that they input, and suggests possible services to which their clients might be referred, much like ads in Gmail. A third entrant is Purple Binder (based in Chicago, the only major metropolitan area in the country to lack a 211 system of any kind), which offers social workers an appealing interface for the organization of their referral options.

These are for-profit companies that charge for their products, but even a cash-strapped non-profit will pay for software if it actually helps its social workers do their jobs better. And if the software helps social workers do their jobs better, the social workers will produce quality referral data. In this way, these startups are not only demonstrating that there is a market for new I&R solutions—they are also pointing toward a new paradigm for I&R, one that blurs the line between the producers and users of community resource data.

It's worth noting the irony that this wave of innovation has produced three separate solutions to the three different links in the social service pipeline—intake, case management, and referral—each with its own approach, which may be incompatible with the others. When I remarked upon this fragmentation to one of the entrepreneurs, he answered that this is how the market works: the best solutions will bubble up and scale. But it's worth considering that the market sometimes yields outcomes that are efficient for elites and institutions, yet not actually effective for most people or their ecosystems.

In a brief span of time, these startups have developed the kinds of sophisticated software for that have long been overdue in this sector. But are they truly solving the community resource directory data problem, or merely building business models around the problem's symptomatic pain points? If these startups evolve into yet another class of intermediaries, institutionally committed to protect their hold on data about our communities, the real problem—which is that communities lack effective means to produce and share their own information—may only be recreated and entrenched.

Given that the social sector itself grows around the miseries of cascading market failures, a truly transformative solution may require us to forge new patterns of social organization and resource allocation—in which, for instance, the competitive advantages of entrepreneurs are complementary values balanced against that of the common good.

The Vision

Before seeking a path forward, let's first imagine a world in which the "community resource directory data problem" has been truly solved:

A social worker doing intakes on a tablet is able to reference the same data that is displayed on a single mother's phone as she scans through emergency shelter options; this same data is queried by a directory application for which area librarians are trained to offer hands-on technical assistance for their patrons; a journalist sees this same data while researching city contracts; FEMA accesses this data during a crisis; a community planning consortium sees the data in its mapping tools. All of these instances involve different applications, and each of these applications might solicit its own kind of feedback, which can update, qualify, and expand the common data pool. And this shared knowledge about the services available in a community is combined with other shared knowledge bases—about the money flowing into and out of these services, about the personal and social outcomes produced by the services, etc.—to be understood and applied by different people in different ways throughout this ecosystem as a collective wisdom about the "State of Our Community."

When only considering the data and technology involved, this vision is not so far from reality. Given the technical interoperability made possible by APIs and the cloud, and gradual developments toward data interoperability in the social sectors, it is quite technologically feasible. But actually achieving it would require vast improvements in what Palfrey and Gasser (2012) refer to as the other half of the "layer cake" of interoperability: institutional interoperability, by which data can be exchanged across organizational boundaries, past barriers of law, policy, and culture; and human interoperability, by which people can understand and act upon this data. To really make progress toward human interoperability, we have to traverse the terrain of institutional interoperability—and there we encounter a messy case of the tragedy of the commons.

The Commons

A "commons" is a resource that is shared—and because it can be hard for people to share things, a commons is inherently subject to various social dilemmas.

Community resource directory data itself is a commons. It's public information, freely available, but unaggregated in its natural state. This data is abundant, and it can be used in many different ways, yet it is also nonrivalrous—meaning my use of it does not diminish your ability to use it. But when aggregated, it also decays, and it is costly to maintain. So the data is usually collected by organizations that organize it to narrowly serve their specific objective or earn a return on investment. This tends to render their data inaccessible or uninteroperable with other kinds of data.

To some extent, we can start to solve these problems by opening data, standardizing it, and developing free and open source software that can use it. But those steps alone do not address the various misalignments between costs and incentives, institutions and people, private agendas and the common good.

Consider our consolidated D.C. community resource database and the code for Open211. Both of these are publicly available on GitHub. They are "free" as in speech (anyone can see, use, and adapt the source code, and likewise the data). They are also, as the saying commonly goes, "free" as in beer (you will not be charged to use them, and that's nice), but it would be more apt to invoke the less common saying—that they are "free" as in puppies: someone will have to feed them, train them, and deal with the mess. The tragedy of the commons includes a multitude of these "abandoned puppies."

The tragedy of the commons, however, is far from inevitable. So far, we have considered commons that are unowned and ungoverned—"libertarian commons," Peter Levine (2003; 2007) calls them, in which anyone is free to do anything they want with an open resource. Yet this is not the only possible kind of commons. We have many well-established precedents for commons that are effectively owned, managed, and governed by those who benefit from them and collectively agree to act in ways that protect and sustain them over time. Successful arrangements of commons management take many forms, each shaped according to the unique properties of the resource, its users, and its place. Such strategies are often demonstrably superior to privatization or government regulation, because shared, localized control can better manage complexity and ensure accountability (New America Foundation, 2001; Ostrom & Hess, 2007).

In the specific context of understanding knowledge as a commons, Levine (2007) counters his description of the oft-tragic "libertarian commons" by proposing the development of "associational commons," through which an organizational mechanism can align diverse perspectives and interests, and establish various kinds of shared responsibilities. An associational commons consists not just of the resource itself (the open field of grass, or the open set of data) but also the synthesis of that resource with the web of social relationships that form around it. Wikipedia, for instance, contains both informal and formal layers of commons management: an association of editors who have special privileges over content, and an official organization that is responsible for fundraising and operations.

So we can imagine a triumphant community resource directory data commons, forged of a layered set of agreements about how shared data will be produced, managed, and used, among heterogeneous systems and for diverse purposes.

To establish and sustain this kind of commons, we will need to practice what Alexis de Tocqueville (1840) once described as the uniquely American "art and science of association," Theda Skocpol (2004) more recently described as "the democratic arts of combination," and Peter Linebaugh (2008) has identified simply as acts of "commoning."

The Cooperative Advantage

If the responsibility to (re)produce knowledge about a community is shared but diffuse, and if the output of organized production is to be truly free (as in speech and beer and, yes, puppies) then we will require some kind of mechanism for collective action, through which the resources (skills, time, money, data, knowledge) necessary to build and maintain the community resource data commons can be pooled.

For this purpose, at least at our table in D.C., I have explored the development of a community data cooperative.

A cooperative entity is owned and governed by its members. (Many co-ops are stores owned by their patrons; some co-ops are owned by their workers; cooperative housing property is owned by its tenants.) To survive, a co-op must be economically viable, just like any other entity in its field. The difference is that a co-op's decision-making process involves the democratic participation of people who have the greatest stake in its outcome, and as members they agree to equitably share in its various burdens, benefits, and responsibilities.

A "community data co-op" could serve a variety of stakeholders: foundations, local non-profits and other community anchors, possibly I&R vendors, conceivably even libraries and government agencies. (A co-op may include different classes of membership with different privileges and responsibilities; presumably, the primary class of members would consist of front-line workers who actually make referrals on a day-to-day basis.) Each stakeholder stands to benefit from a cooperative solution, and also has something valuable to contribute to the commons.

The challenge of cooperative development will be to successfully align these assets and interests through a set of reciprocal agreements. As such, the co-op might consist of three primary roles.

First, a co-op would organize the means of production of the "common data pool." So far, we've seen several different methods of producing this data: trained researchers can extract it; mass emails and letters can solicit it; front-line workers can generate it themselves as they do the work of making referrals. It can also be gleaned from IRS records, scraped from the web, or even required by funders. A cooperative strategy could integrate any of these tactics, aligning it all according to a common set of standards. And since—for the foreseeable future, anyway—verification of this data still requires the touch of human intelligence, the best solution may be one that directly involves those with first-hand knowledge of the field. This might even be the primary responsibility of membership in the co-op: instead of paying dues in cash, members could contribute their time to data management (time that is currently being spent ineffectively, to duplicative ends).

Second, the co-op could facilitate the circulation of this data through an ecosystem of services—including the internal systems of members like Bread for the City, open systems like Open211, and the enterprise-level systems of vendors like Aunt Bertha, Purple Binder, and even 211. Though the data would be open source, the co-op may require a license for commercial use and other kinds of premium services—presumably costing less than whatever the vendors would otherwise spend to collect the data themselves. Vendors could then reallocate their resources toward the development of services that add value to this data.

Third, the co-op would foster education. Cooperatives are committed to education as one of their core principles, and given that the data produced by this co-op would presumably be "open," education may be the primary benefit of membership: access to an array of opportunities for personal skill-building and organizational learning—anything from hands-on tech support to generalized data literacy training. Writing recently about the patterns of community technology development, Michael Gurstein (2013) called for innovation to be something that "is done by, with and in the community and not simply something that is done 'to' or 'for' the community." This may be such a strategy: generating community resource data through the generation of resourceful community. As such, a cooperative solution may not only yield better data—it is also likely to yield more effective use. Whereas Open311 demonstrates the paradigm that Tim O'Reilly famously dubbed "government as platform," here we can point to its corollary precept, community as platform, in which technology is not something that is made for people to consume, but rather made by people to share.

The Path Ahead

Now may be the right time to undertake a new approach to this problem. Several organizations have recently proposed new ways to enable the free and open circulation of interoperable community resource data. However, to achieve the promise of open data, we face challenges that are more political than technical.

As we do so, however, some essential questions have yet to be addressed:

- How might open, standardized community resource data be valuably synthesized with other kinds of knowledge bases—such as those used in crisis response, community needs assessment, philanthropy, or policy analysis?

- What is the proper role for government in the production and dissemination of data about the social sector? What about other community anchor institutions, such as libraries and schools?

- And finally, how can this work be grounded by the experiences and prerogatives of those with the greatest stake in its outcome: people in need?

The commoning path will require commitment, imagination, trust, and accountability. It almost goes without saying that this will be hard work; it may also simply be the right work to do.

About the Author

Greg Bloom was the Communications Guy at Bread for the City in Washington D.C. from 2008 to 2012. His recent work focuses on digital justice in D.C., including the development of community wireless networks and DiscoTechs (Discovering Technology Fairs). He is a founding member and "Chief Reality Officer" of Code for D.C., a volunteer civic hacking group, and he was lead organizer for Hack for D.C. during the 2013 National Day of Civic Hacking. Greg is a proud new member of CooperationWorks, and soon to be certified by its Cooperative Business Development Program (pending successful completion of an Excel test that he's pretty worried about, as he hardly knows anything about actually working with data). This research was made possible by a fellowship with Provisions Library, a residency at Elsewhere, the support of the Ralph K Morris Foundation, and lots of people who were generous with their time, brains, and/or couches. Supplemental research, commentary, and proposal will be published at gregbloom. org and communityresourcedata.codefordc.org.

References

Alliance of Information and Referral Systems (2009). AIRS standards for professional information & referral and quality indicators. Retrieved from http://www.airs.org/files/public/AIRS_Standards_6_0Final.pdf

Ashlock, P. (2012). Open & Candid: Phil Ashlock on Open311. Retrieved from http://openplans.org/2012/02/open-candid-phil-ashlock-on-open311/

The Aspen Institute. (2013). Information for Impact: Liberating Non-Profit Sector Data, in Aspen Institute's Program on Philanthropy and Social Innovation. Washington, DC: Beth Simone Noveck and Daniel L. Goroff. Retrieved from http://www.aspeninstitute.org/sites/default/files/content/docs/events/psi_Information-for-Impact.pdf

Fitch, D. (2009). Shared point of access to facilitate interagency collaboration. *Administration in Social Work, Vol. 33* (No. 2).

Gasser, U. & Palfrey, J. (2012). *Interop.* New York, NY: Basic Books.

Gurstein, M. (2003). Effective use: A community informatics strategy beyond the Digital Divide. *First Monday, 8.12.* Retrieved from: http://firstmonday.org/ojs/index.php/fm/article/view/1107/1027

Gurstein, M. (2013). Community Innovation and Community Informatics. *The Journal of Community Informatics, Vol. 9* (No. 3).

Levine, P. (2003). A Movement for the Commons? *The Responsive Community: Rights and Responsibilities, vol. 13.* Retrieved from: http://www.peterlevine.ws/responsivecommunity.pdf

Levine, P. (2007). Collective Action, Civic Engagement, and the Knowledge Commons. In E. Ostrom and C. Hess (Eds), *Understanding Knowledge as a Commons* (247). Cambridge, MA: MIT Press.

Montero, M. (2013) Social Consortium: A Partnership of Community Agents. *Global Journal of Community Psychology Practice, Vol. 4* (No 2). Retrieved from http://www.gjcpp.org/pdfs/Montero-v4i2-20130531.pdf

Nadeu, E.G. (2012). The Cooperative Solution. Retrieved from http://www.thecooperativefoundation.org/images/Cooperative_Solution_6x9-h_copy.pdf

New America Foundation. (2001). *Public Assets, Private Profits: Reclaiming the American Commons in an Age of Market Enclosure.* Washington DC: David Bollier. Retrieved from http://www.newamerica.net/files/archive/Pub_File_650_1.pdf

Ogden, M (2012, January). Open211 [Weblog]. Retrieved from http://maxogden.com/open211.html

Ostrom, E. & Hess, C. (Eds.). (2007). *Understanding Knowledge as a Commons — From Theory to Practice.* Cambridge, MA.: MIT Press.

Peuter, G. & Dyer-Witheford, N. (2010). Commons and Cooperatives. *Affinities: A Journal of Radical Theory, Culture, and Action, Vol. 4 (No 1).* Retrieved from http://affinitiesjournal.org/index.php/affinities/article/view/45

Skocpol, T. (2004). *Diminished Democracy: From Membership to Management in American Civic Life.* Norman, OK: University of Oklahoma Press.

Shank, N. (2004). Database Interoperability: Technology and Process for Sharing Resource Information. *Journal of Alliance and Information Referral Systems 2004.* See http://digitalcommons.unl.edu/publicpolicyshank/1/

De Tocqueville, A. (1840). *Democracy in America.* Retrieved from http://www.gutenberg.org/ebooks/816

Williams, K. & Durrance, J. (2010). Community Informatics. *The Encyclopedia of Library and Information Sciences, Vol. 3.* Retrieved from http://people.lis.illinois.edu/~katewill/williams-durrance-encyclo-community-informatics.pdf

CHAPTER 20

The Bigger Picture: Ten Lessons for Taking Open Government Further

By John Bracken

My job at the Knight Foundation is to identify people with promising ideas and help them execute them. Our primary tool for that is the Knight News Challenge, through which we've supported nearly a hundred projects, with more than $30 million over six years. We've supported several open government-related projects and groups like LocalWiki, the Open Knowledge Foundation, Ushahidi, EveryBlock, and Open Street Maps.

The code, insights, and talent networks we've supported through the News Challenge moved us to focus a recent iteration on open government. Our goal was to expand the table of people who engage with open government. In addition to practical open government applications, we hoped to uncover ideas about how the internet can change the ways in which citizens and governments interact. We wanted to involve more people in the use of technology to solve community problems, and we sought to expand the geographic footprint beyond what's become the standard open government metropoles of San Francisco, Chicago, and the Boston-New York- DC Acela nexus. Silently, I hoped that at least one of the winners would not even consider themselves as part of the open government movement.

During the application period, we partnered with locally based organizations to conduct events in fourteen cities, including less typical open government cities, like Lexington, Kentucky; Macon, Georgia; San Diego; and St. Paul, Minnesota. Out of the 860 submissions we received, several themes emerged that captured the open government zeitgeist. These included:

- Increasing citizens' direct participation in policymaking

- Strengthening policies for data transparency

- Making sense out of multiple datasets

- Understanding government spending and campaign contributions

- Making better use of public spaces and vacant land

After our analysis of the contest process and submissions, our assessment was that open government is generating more aspirational ideas than practical tools and approaches that address citizens' needs and wants. We learned a lot by talking directly with civic leaders, government officials, and hackers, particularly with those outside of the leading open government cities. I spoke with high-ranking government workers who were worried about the security and sustainability of open source projects, elected officials who were curious about citizen demand for data, and journalists who were dubious about governments' commitment to openness.

Our trustees ended up approving eight projects as winners. Not coincidentally, each of the eight had already demonstrated their idea and was able to talk to us about what was and was not working. Also, for the most part, they have been around the open government block for a while. (My hopes of supporting people entirely new to the field failed.)

Fundamentally, the eight winning projects are practical rather than aspirational. They address identified needs of citizens and governments. Despite our exhortations, few of the ideas that made it to the final rounds re-imagined democracy in the age of the internet. They are about building practical tools that citizen-consumers can use to more easily build businesses, reclaim abandoned land, and sell services to the government. They don't seek to engage citizens in re-imagining democracy or co-creating their communities. That could reflect the bias of the Knight Foundation and the investors, journalists, and developers who advised us, but the list may also be a reflection of where the open government movement is at this point in its development: in a field driven by aspiration, the value lies in practical businesses and services.

For a guide on moving more robustly from the aspirational to the practical, we might look to Kevin Costner. In the late 1980s and early 1990s, Kevin Costner was one of the biggest stars in Hollywood. Near the apex of his career, Costner starred in Field of Dreams, a 1989 fantasy-drama designed to make high school jocks weep. Prompted by the whispers of a disembodied voice, Costner's character plows under his cornfield, turning it into a baseball diamond for ghosts from the 1919 Chicago White Sox. "If you build it, he will come," the voice promises him.

"If we build it, they will come," has been open government's operative mode for the last few years. Like other social movements before it, open government is inspired by dreams of what might be, not on an evidence-based assessment of what people want or need. It's a movement based on the belief that by pushing out data, our fellow citizens will build things, government will be more efficient, and we will all live happier lives. Inevitably, we've been disappointed when those idealistic outcomes don't pan out and we realize that the vast majority of our neighbors lack the skills, wherewithal, time, or inclination to actively participate. Our aspirations for engagement have outpaced the reality—a status appropriate for such a young social project. As open government emerges into adolescence, though, we need to bridge the gaps between innovators and citizens, who are the ultimate users.

To make that leap, we need to consider a later Kevin Costner movie: The Postman. Based on David Brin's 1985 post-apocalyptic fantasy novel, this movie features Costner playing a drifter who dons the uniform and identity of a dead mail carrier. In so doing, he inadvertently becomes the personification of the disbanded US government. Costner's uniform and the act of distributing mail between previously disconnected towns rekindle a civic spirit among those he visits. (The movie was a dog, but Brin's novel is pretty great.)

How does open government move from building fields of dreams to delivering like a postman? How do we stop making baseball fields out of Iowa cornfields and start going town-to-town, knocking on doors, and building links, one community at a time? Now that we have the vision of it all down, it's time to shift into the practicalities of building useful tools. Here are ten things we need to prioritize to move from dreaming to doing:

Realistic Expectations

We need to learn how to build projects and businesses that bring value to customers, not just venture capitalist moonshots. Civic technology will not produce companies with a hundred times the return on investment. We need to be okay with that and build the financing and support services that will enable entrepreneurs' visions to become real and sustainable.

Delight

No one waits excitedly at the window for the postman to deliver us information about voting, taxes, or municipal budgets. Messages from loved ones, narratives in magazines, and holiday cards are what I look for when the mail arrives. We need apps and tools that are fun to use and don't feel like homework.

Drama

"We have 2,000 bills. Little bill bits," said California Governor Jerry Brown earlier this year. "You can't run a world on bill bits. That's not what moves people. There has to be drama. Protagonist and antagonist. We're on the stage of history here." We need to do a better job of taking civic data and presenting it to our neighbors in stories, visualizations, and culture.

Literacy

To appreciate the mail, it helps to be able to read. What are the skills and approaches citizens need to contribute to and benefit from open government, and how do we identify and develop them?

Research

What is the baseline for what does and does not work? How do we know how we're doing and determine what to do better? What are we measuring? How do we know whether what we're doing works, and how can we brag to others about it? How can we demonstrate an ROI to governments and potential investors? The fact that we don't have answers to these questions this late in the game is worrisome.

Models

When people ask us how to do open government, where can we point them? We need solid, well-documented success stories of real results.

Talent

When they need to hire, where do governments go? Programs like the Code for America Fellowship are a great start, but they aren't enough to form a workforce. We have a great set of leaders, but most of them could fit into one conference. We need to set up places for them to go when they leave government so we don't lose their experiences and networks to other fields.

Professional Development

Many people who take government jobs don't do so to be agents of change or to drive innovation. They often take them because they are good, solid jobs. Where do career government workers and civilians go to develop the skills we need to drive the movement forward from the inside out?

Leadership Transitions

We put a lot on the shoulders of individual government leaders to drive change. How do we build the systems so that the innovations built by a chief executive are not dismantled with their administration? What tools would help with transitions from one mayor or governor to another?

Risk Tolerance

How can we encourage and enable government leaders and workers to take risks that they are generally dissuaded from trying? We need to build a culture inside government that is tolerant of taking smart, well-calculated risks.

For open government to succeed, it needs to make its principles—transparency, openness, and data-driven decision-making—become synonymous with democracy. In order to fully benefit from the values of sharing and the wisdom of community, we need to move beyond placing our hopes in whispered promises toward doing the practical work of building useful, sustainable tools and a supportive ecosystem.

About the Author

John S. Bracken is the director of media innovation for the Knight Foundation. He oversees the Knight News Challenge, Knight's prototype fund, its journalism, and its technology investments. Bracken has over ten years of experience as a philanthropic investor in digital media, media policy, innovation, and global internet freedom, having previously worked at the Ford Foundation and the MacArthur Foundation.

CHAPTER 21

New Thinking in How Governments Deliver Services

By Mark Headd

Introduction

Open data programs provide a number of important benefits for governments and the citizens they serve. At the most basic level, these programs provide important insights into government activities—a fundamental ingredient for a well-operating democracy.

In addition to enhanced government transparency, these programs also provide a means for developing new applications and solutions—built on top of the data released by governments—that can be leveraged to deliver public services. These programs also highlight some of the long-standing problems with incumbent processes that are used by governments to procure technology solutions and services and provide insight into how these older processes might be improved.

Unlocking the Power of Open Data

The concept of "government as a platform"—an idea best, and most famously, articulated by Tim O'Reilly (2010), the founder of O'Reilly Media and a leading proponent of free-software and open source movements—often references the iPhone as an example of a platform done well. The decision in 2008 by Apple chief executive Steve Jobs to allow independent developers to build apps that would work on the iPhone "platform" has made the now ubiquitous device the success that it is. As noted in a 2012 *New York Times* article by David Streitfeld:

> The App Store opened in July 2008 with 500 apps. In an interview, Mr. Jobs laid bare the company's goal: "Sell more iPhones."

> Thanks to the multitude of apps, the goal came to pass. More iP-hones... were sold in the next three months than in the entire previous year, and that was just the beginning of the ascent. (Streitfeld, 2012)

The idea of turning a phone into an application platform has since been copied by other hardware and software companies, and it has informed the idea of turning government itself into a platform. Providing public access to government data in machine-readable formats (i.e., open data) is the foundation of the efforts being taken by governments around the world. They are essentially copying Apple's approach to stimulate innovative new apps and ideas that can run on their government "platform."

Open government data is at the heart of a change that is taking place in government. Since the inception of the internet and its now central role in how governments deliver services and information to citizens, governments have used data as an input into a finished product delivered by them for those they serve. Open data, for many governments, has now become the finished product that is delivered to its end-users—independent developers who can use open government data to develop innovative and valuable new solutions.

This kind of change in government can be long, complex, and fraught with risks. It requires a rethinking of government's traditional role of sole solution provider (the entity that builds, or contracts for, the customer-facing components through which public services are delivered) to that of a data steward. A 2012 report by the Center for Technology in Government noted the transformational dynamics created by open data programs:

> Open data initiatives disrupt government's traditional role as holder or owner of the data. In thinking about open data governance, we need to rethink government's role in relation to the entire set of new stakeholders. One possibility is to characterize government, as well as all other stakeholders, as stewards [of data]. (Helbig, Cresswell, Burke, & Luna-Reyes, 2012, p. 13)

The clearest example of how open government data can be used to encourage the development of useful new applications comes from the world of public transit. There are numerous examples of applications built using transit data released by governments with the GTFS specification, which is an open data format initially developed by Google in cooperation with Portland, Oregon's public transit agency. While initially designed to allow easy integration of transit data into the Google platform, the GTFS data specification has spawned a cottage industry of new transit apps. Websites like citygoround.org list hundreds of transit apps, many built using GTFS data.

These applications have fundamentally changed the way that riders on public transportation systems consume transit data, as well as the role of transit authorities in relation to how these applications are developed. In the past, the transit agencies themselves would have been the entity that designed, developed, and delivered the apps used by riders to get information—and many still do. However, an increasing number of transit agencies are getting out of the business of developing these kinds of customer-facing apps and are letting the new app market (fueled by the open GTFS data they release) meet rider demand instead.

In addition, some transit agencies—like the Southeastern Pennsylvania Transportation Authority, which serves the Philadelphia area—are now actively advertising apps built by independent developers to their riders.

Beyond Public Transit: The Limits of Open Data

This fundamental shift away from government as the sole solution provider to a data steward is now taking hold outside the world of transit data, fostering the growth of new ideas and solutions.

Leveraging open data to encourage the development of useful applications and services holds many benefits for governments. With this approach, new ways of building software and deploying solutions are developed without them having to make bets on specific technologies (something that governments do not do well). Independent developers operating outside of the normal government procurement process are often better positioned to leverage new advances in app development or service deployment.

Open government data is one way that governments can, in a sense, go around the traditional procurement process to encourage the development of useful software. However, this approach does have some limitations. Implicit in the idea of open data is the fact that governments can't dictate what users of the data actually do with it (provided they don't misrepresent the data or otherwise violate terms of use). Publishing open data and engaging outside developers can be a less-than-effective strategy if governments hope to achieve the development of specific tools or solutions.

The open data approach works best to generate emergent (rather than prescriptive), customer-facing applications that are related to particular kinds of data that have established communities or constituencies of enthusiasts (like transit data). Releasing open data and engaging outside developers to organically develop solutions is not the right approach for the development of all government IT systems. For example, this would be less than ideal for the development of a back-end accounting or financial management system, which requires specialized knowledge of government processes and would likely need to be built to exacting specifications. When governments have specific needs or detailed requirements for how a solution or app should be built and operated, standard government procurement is probably a better way to acquire this technology than hackathons or apps contests.

However, the government procurement process as it exists today is not ideal for acquiring optimal technology solutions that take advantage of the latest thinking on how software and services are developed and deployed. Viewed as cumbersome and complex, the process used by public sector entities to procure goods and services is often cited as a major barrier to introducing innovation—particularly the use of new technologies—into government operations.

Looking Ahead: Three Hard Truths for Government Procurement Reform

Advancing the innovation agenda within government often means confronting the harsh reality of the government procurement process. This is not a new problem, and there are a number of initiatives underway in governments around the country aimed at "streamlining" or "overhauling" the government procurement process to support the acquisition of new technologies and projects that engage smaller and more nimble companies with new solutions.

The City of Philadelphia, in particular, is engaged in some progressive efforts to use the government procurement process as a means to develop an ecosystem of smaller companies that offer innovative new ideas to longstanding city problems. If the goal of using the procurement process to stimulate (or at least not hinder) innovation inside government is to be realized, reformers in Philadelphia and elsewhere will need to face some hard truths about procurement reform.

In addition, advocates of procurement reform must expand their thinking about the nature of reform and their methods to bring about change by focusing on open government data as a foundational component for systematic change in how governments deliver services and information to those they serve.

Balancing Values

The arguments in favor of reforming the government procurement process bear a striking similarity to arguments used by advocates for overhauling the federal income tax system. Both sets of advocates point to the problem of unnecessary complexity as an element that can stifle innovation or even harm participants. In many instances, the same verbs are used when calling for reform—words like "overhaul" and "streamline" can be used almost interchangeably when talking about tax reform and procurement reform.

The federal income tax system is a useful reference for talking about procurement reform. It is often used by governments as a vehicle for achieving desired outcomes that (as many economists will quickly point out) have nothing to do with an efficient tax system. We imbue our tax code with certain provisions that, we hope, will help achieve outcomes deemed to have broad societal value.

A perfect example of this is the federal income tax deduction for mortgage interest. As a country and a society, we value homeownership over other kinds of investments, so our tax system "rewards" this investment with a special deduction. The objective is to encourage more home-ownership because it is highly correlated with desired outcomes, like higher property values and more stable neighborhoods. This deduction comes with a cost, however: it increases the complexity of tax forms, and it increases the effort required both to process these forms and to audit taxpayer compliance.

There are many other examples of income tax provisions that are specifically engineered to produce outcomes with broad social benefits—a myriad of deductions and credits for married couples, particularly those with children; deductions for contributions made to charities; and deductions for interest on student loans. Each of these examples shares two characteristics: they are designed to encourage specific outcomes, and they increase the overall complexity of the system. On an individual level, the cost of these broader societal benefits manifests as more time and effort to comply with income tax requirements.

Procurement processes are similar in many ways. Governments imbue these processes with requirements and other stipulations that they hope will lead to outcomes that are deemed desirable. Each of these requirements adds to the complexity of the process and the burden of firms that choose to respond to government RFPs.

For example, almost every government has purchasing requirements for minority- and women-owned businesses, and many have requirements that local companies receive preference over firms from outside the jurisdiction. The objective is to drive more government procurement dollars to minority- and women-owned businesses and to local businesses that create local jobs and pay local taxes.

There are also larger, overarching values embedded in the procurement process. For example, fairness and transparency are values that inform requirements like the public posting of bids and related materials, ample public notice of vendor meetings, and the clear specification of when and how bids must be submitted.

Risk aversion is another value that impacts the complexity and cost of the public procurement process. It is this value that informs requirements like performance bonds, vendor insurance, scrutiny of company financial statements, and requirements for financial reserves—all things that seek to reduce the risk assumed by governments from engaging with a company to provide a good or service. Each of these requirements can make the procurement process more complex and burdensome for bidders, particularly smaller companies.

All of this underscores the point that many of the factors that make government procurement processes complex and slow are also things that are intended to produce desired outcomes. These features of the procurement process were designed with a specific intent, and few people would argue with the laudable goals they seek to encourage. Yet, one of the side effects of these requirements is that they make the process slower, more complex, and harder for smaller and more nimble firms to participate in.

Efforts to overhaul or streamline the procurement process will undoubtedly run up against the provisions just discussed. Are there ways to streamline the procurement process that don't require provisions of this type to be relaxed or removed, or are there ways to relax these provisions without compromising the laudable outcomes they seek to encourage? This remains to be seen.

Nimbler Doesn't Always Mean Better

The great myth in government IT is that the private sector is always way ahead of the public sector in how technology is used.

In between two tours of duty in state and local government, I spent about ten years in the private sector working for both large and small technology firms. Before joining Code for America as Director of Government Relations in 2011, I worked for four different technology companies headquartered in places as different as Horsham, Pennsylvania; Blacksburg, Virginia; and San Francisco, California. I learned a lot about technology and how to be a software developer during this time, but I also learned that—as far as technology is concerned—the grass is not always greener on the other side.

There are plenty of examples of poor technology decisions in the private sector. We just hear about them less often because they are usually not a matter of public record or visible to the public through a budget submission or legislative hearing.

To be sure, governments around the world have issues with implementing technology, but some of the things I've seen in the private sector have been shocking—inexcusably bad decisions made by people who should know better, a complete lack of strategic thinking about how technology is used to benefit the company, and dragging old legacy technology along far past its point of usefulness simply because upgrading would be tricky and complex—the list goes on. The private sector has all of these problems and more. We just don't hear about them as much.

What my experience in the private sector made exceedingly clear to me is that it is entirely possible (and not very unusual) for private sector organizations, unshackled by complicated procurement processes like those used by governments, to make lousy choices and invest poorly in technology.

Simply making the government procurement process "simpler" won't guarantee that better IT decisions get made. Governments will still need to think more strategically about how they invest in technology and become better at learning how it can be used to make the delivery of public services more efficient and effective.

A Dearth of Makers Inside Government

My experience working as a software developer for several years, and continuing to work with other developers from a variety of disciplines for years after that, has affected the way I approach problems. Whenever I hear about an application or service or an idea someone has for one, I'm often privately thinking (as I think most people who have worked as developers are), how would I build something like that? This is probably true of most people who have built things for a living.

Understanding how things work and how to build them can be a useful skill when evaluating the level of effort required to perform a service or to solve a problem. This is something software developers do often—estimate the amount of time it will take them (or their team) to complete a series of tasks they have not yet begun. It's hard to do well. Even software developers who do this often will sometimes underestimate or overestimate the amount of time required to complete a task.

The ability to translate a problem into a series of steps that a person can imagine herself doing is the specific byproduct of making things. This is a problem in government, where, in general, there is a woeful lack of awareness about how things are made and what resources and materials are required to build things. In short, there is a critical lack of makers in government.

This problem is particularly acute when it comes to technology and how governments acquire it, even for needs that should be simple and relatively cheap, like content management systems for websites and web-based applications. The web is now an essential component of how governments deliver services and communicate with citizens, and yet, there are far too few people inside government (including those in the technology discipline) who have a solid understanding of how the internet works.

In just the last few years, the world of software development has seen a sea change that has transformed how web and mobile applications are built. Never before has it been easier or cheaper to build these applications. Yet governments continue to overpay for them (or the services of those firms that build them) because there is very little in-house knowledge of how these things are built.

This is not to suggest that effective websites and useful web applications are easy to build and don't require skill. They certainly do, but without a fundamental understanding of what the technologies behind these applications are, how they work, and how they are changing, governments cannot distinguish the skilled vendors offering reasonably priced solutions from the shysters.

In a way, it's not dissimilar from the experience many people have when going to an auto mechanic—if you don't know anything about how cars work, how do you know for sure if you're getting a fair price? It calls to mind the classic episode from the sitcom "Seinfeld," where George Costanza sums up the typical approach to auto repair like this:

Well of course they're trying to screw you! What do you think? That's what they do. They can make up anything; nobody knows! 'Why, well you need a new Johnson rod in here.' Oh, a Johnson rod. Yeah, well better put one of those on!

If the people who work for government don't have a clear enough sense of how things get made, they are ill-equipped to evaluate RFP responses from individuals or companies that want to do work on behalf of the government. This is especially important for technology procurement, where new software development paradigms can evolve rapidly.

Governments need to place an emphasis on recruiting and hiring people who have experience making things. In addition, governments need to focus on developing the "maker skills" of existing employees. This, by extension, will enhance the ability of governments to evaluate the estimates for work provided by respondents to RFPs.

Conclusion

Government open data programs and the independent apps they help generate provide tremendously helpful ways of fostering new approaches to old problems. They also support the application of new technologies and app development strategies for delivering public services.

However, even the most robust open data program is not a suitable replacement for a well-designed and properly functioning procurement process—one that fosters innovation and the risk that is inherent in it. Open data programs can—and should—complement well-designed procurement processes.

Open data programs have opened the door to new ways of thinking about how public services are delivered. They also help highlight some of the deficiencies in the existing processes used to acquire solutions by government and deliver services and information.

The job of overhauling existing government procurement processes to encourage innovation will not be an easy one, but one of the many benefits of open data is that it has led to this important discussion.

About the Author

Mark Headd is a writer, speaker, teacher, and thought leader on web development, open government and civic hacking. Self taught in programming, he has been developing telephone, mobile, speech recognition, and messaging applications for over ten years and has deep experience in communication technologies.

In August 2012, Mayor Michael Nutter selected Mark to become the City of Philadelphia's first Chief Data Officer, to lead the city's open data and government transparency initiatives. He previously served for three years as the chief policy and budget advisor for the State of Delaware's Department of Technology and Information, and as technology advisor to Delaware Governor Thomas Carper.

Mark has built open government software applications for the District of Columbia, the Sunlight Foundation, the New York State Senate, and the cities of New York, San Francisco, Toronto, Baltimore, and Philadelphia. He is an organizer, judge, sponsor, and participant in civic hacking events across the country, including Philadelphia and Baltimore.

References

Center for Technology in Government. (2012). The Dynamics of Opening Government Data. Albany, NY: Helbig, N., Cresswell, A. M., Burke, G. B., & Luna-Reyes, L. Retrieved from: http://www.ctg.albany.edu/publications/reports/opendata/opendata.pdf

O'Reilly, Tim (2010). Government as a Platform. In *Open Government* (Chapter 1). Retrieved from http://ofps.oreilly.com/titles/9780596804350/defining_government_2_0_lessons_learned_.html

Streitfeld, D. (2012, Nov. 17). As Boom Lures App Creators, Tough Part Is Making a Living. *The New York Times*. Retrieved from http://www.nytimes.com/2012/11/18/business/as-boom-lures-app-creators-tough-part-is-making-a-living.html?pagewanted=4

CHAPTER 22

Open Data and Algorithmic Regulation

By Tim O'Reilly

Regulation is the bugaboo of today's politics. We have too much of it in most areas, we have too little of it in others, but mostly, we just have the wrong kind, a mountain of paper rules, inefficient processes, and little ability to adjust the rules or the processes when we discover the inevitable unintended results.

Consider, for a moment, regulation in a broader context. Your car's electronics regulate the fuel-air mix in the engine to find an optimal balance of fuel efficiency and minimal emissions. An airplane's autopilot regulates the countless factors required to keep that plane aloft and heading in the right direction. Credit card companies monitor and regulate charges to detect fraud and keep you under your credit limit. Doctors regulate the dosage of the medicine they give us, sometimes loosely, sometimes with exquisite care, as with the chemotherapy required to kill cancer cells while keeping normal cells alive, or with the anesthesia that keeps us unconscious during surgery while keeping vital processes going. ISPs and corporate mail systems regulate the mail that reaches us, filtering out spam and malware to the best of their ability. Search engines regulate the results and advertisements they serve up to us, doing their best to give us more of what we want to see.

What do all these forms of regulation have in common?

1. A deep understanding of the desired outcome

2. Real-time measurement to determine if that outcome is being achieved

3. Algorithms (i.e. a set of rules) that make adjustments based on new data

4. Periodic, deeper analysis of whether the algorithms themselves are correct and performing as expected.

There are a few cases—all too few—in which governments and quasi-governmental agencies regulate using processes similar to those outlined above. Probably the best example is the way that central banks regulate the money supply in an attempt to manage interest rates, inflation, and the overall state of the economy. Surprisingly, while individual groups might prefer the US Federal Reserve to tighten or loosen the money supply at a different time or rate than they do, most accept the need for this kind of regulation.

Why is this?

1. The desired outcomes are clear

2. There is regular measurement and reporting as to whether those outcomes are being achieved, based on data that is made public to everyone

3. Adjustments are made when the desired outcomes are not being achieved

Contrast this with the normal regulatory model, which focuses on the rules rather than the outcomes. How often have we faced rules that simply no longer make sense? How often do we see evidence that the rules are actually achieving the desired outcome?

Sometimes the "rules" aren't really even rules. Gordon Bruce, the former CIO of the city of Honolulu, explained to me that when he entered government from the private sector and tried to make changes, he was told, "That's against the law." His reply was "OK. Show me the law." "Well, it isn't really a law. It's a regulation." "OK. Show me the regulation." "Well, it isn't really a regulation. It's a policy that was put in place by Mr. Somebody twenty years ago." "Great. We can change that!"

But often, there really is a law or a regulation that has outlived its day, an artifact of a system that takes too long to change. The Obama Administration has made some efforts to address this, with a process of both "regulatory lookback" to eliminate unnecessary regulations, and an increased effort to quantify the effect of regulations (White House, 2012).

But even this kind of regulatory reform doesn't go far enough. The laws of the United States have grown mind-bogglingly complex. The recent healthcare reform bill was nearly two thousand pages. The US Constitution, including two hundred years worth of amendments, is about twenty-one pages. The National Highway Bill of 1956, which led to the creation of the US Interstate Highway system, the largest public works project in history, was twenty-nine pages.

Laws should specify goals, rights, outcomes, authorities, and limits. If specified broadly, those laws can stand the test of time.

Regulations, which specify how to execute those laws in much more detail, should be regarded in much the same way that programmers regard their code and algorithms, that is, as a constantly updated toolset to achieve the outcomes specified in the laws.

Increasingly, in today's world, this kind of algorithmic regulation is more than a metaphor. Consider financial markets. New financial instruments are invented every day and implemented by algorithms that trade at electronic speed. How can these instruments be regulated except by programs and algorithms that track and manage them in their native element in much the same way that Google's search quality algorithms, Google's "regulations", manage the constant attempts of spammers and black hat SEO experts to game the system?

Revelation after revelation of bad behavior by big banks demonstrates that periodic bouts of enforcement aren't sufficient. Systemic malfeasance needs systemic regulation. It's time for government to enter the age of big data. Algorithmic regulation is an idea whose time has come.

Open Data and Government as a Platform

There are those who say that government should just stay out of regulating many areas, and let "the market" sort things out. But there are many ways in which bad actors take advantage of a vacuum in the absence of proactive management. Just as companies like Google, Microsoft, Apple, and Amazon build regulatory mechanisms to manage their platforms, government exists as a platform to ensure the success of our society, and that platform needs to be well regulated!

Right now, it is clear that agencies like the SEC just can't keep up. In the wake of Ponzi schemes like those of Bernie Madoff and Allen Stanford, the SEC has now instituted algorithmic models that flag for investigation hedge funds whose results meaningfully outperform those of peers using the same stated investment methods. But once flagged, enforcement still goes into a long loop of investigation and negotiation, with problems dealt with on a case-by-case basis. By contrast, when Google discovers via algorithmic means that a new kind of spam is damaging search results, they quickly change the rules to limit the effect of those bad actors. We need to find more ways to make the consequences of bad action systemic, rather than subject to haphazard enforcement.

This is only possible when laws and regulations focus on desired outcomes rather than the processes used to achieve them.

There's another point that's worth making about SEC regulations. Financial regulation depends on disclosure - data required by the regulators to be published by financial firms in a format that makes it easy to analyze. This data is not just used by the regulators themselves, but is used by the private sector in making its own assessments of the financial health of firms, their prospects, and other financial decisions. You can see how the role of regulators in requiring what is, in effect, open data, makes the market more transparent and self-policing.

You can also see here that the modernization of how data is reported to both the government and the market is an important way of improving regulatory outcomes. Data needs to be timely, machine readable, and complete. (See Open Government Working Group, 2007.) When reporting is on paper or in opaque digital forms like PDF, or released only quarterly, it is much less useful.

When data is provided in re-usable digital formats, the private sector can aid in ferreting out problems as well as building new services that provide consumer and citizen value. This is a goal of the US Treasury Department's "Smart Disclosure" initiative (see http://www.data.gov/consumer/page/consumer-about). It is also central to the efforts of the new Consumer Financial Protection Bureau.

When government regulators focus on requiring disclosure, that lets private companies build services for consumers, and frees up more enforcement time to go after truly serious malefactors.

Regulation Meets Reputation

It is true that "that government governs best that governs least." But the secret to "governing least" is to identify key outcomes that we care about as a society—safety, health, fairness, opportunity—encode those outcomes into our laws, and then create a constantly evolving set of regulatory mechanisms that keep us on course towards them.

We are at a unique time when new technologies make it possible to reduce the amount of regulation while actually increasing the amount of oversight and production of desirable outcomes.

Consider taxi regulation. Ostensibly, taxis are regulated to protect the quality and safety of the consumer experience, as well as to ensure that there are an optimal number of vehicles providing service at the time they are needed. In practice, most of us know that these regulations do a poor job of ensuring quality or availability. New services like Uber and Hailo work with existing licensed drivers, but increase their availability even in less-frequented locations, by using geolocation on smartphones to bring passengers and drivers together. But equally important in a regulatory context is the way these services ask every passenger to rate their driver (and drivers to rate their passenger). Drivers who provide poor service are eliminated. As users of these services can attest, reputation does a better job of ensuring a superb customer experience than any amount of government regulation.

Peer-to-peer car services like RelayRides, Lyft, and Sidecar go even further, bypassing regulated livery vehicles and allowing consumers to provide rides to each other. Here, reputation entirely replaces regulation, seemingly with no ill effect. Governments should be studying these models, not fighting them, and adopting them where there are no demonstrable ill effects.

Services like AirBnB provide similar reputation systems that protect consumers while creating availability of lodging in neighborhoods that are often poorly served by licensed establishments.

Reputation systems are a great example of how open data can help improve outcomes for citizens with less effort by overworked regulators and enforcement officials.

Sites like Yelp provide extensive consumer reviews of restaurants; those that provide poor food or service are flagged by unhappy customers, while those that excel are praised.

There are a number of interesting new projects that attempt to combine the reach and user-friendliness of consumer reputation systems with government data. One recent initiative, the LIVES standard, developed by San Francisco, Code for America, and Yelp, brings health department inspection data to Yelp and other consumer restaurant applications, using open data to provide even more information to consumers. The House Facts standard does the same with housing inspection data, integrating it with internet services like Trulia

Another interesting project that actually harnesses citizen help (rather than just citizen opinion) by connecting a consumer-facing app to government data is the PulsePoint project, originally started by the San Ramon, California fire department. After the fire chief had the dismaying experience of hearing an ambulance pull up to the restaurant next door to the one in which he was having lunch with staff including a number of EMR techs, he commissioned an app that would allow any citizen with EMR training to receive the same dispatch calls as officials.

The Role of Sensors in Algorithmic Regulation

Increasingly, our interactions with businesses, government, and the built environment are becoming digital, and thus amenable to creative forms of measurement, and ultimately algorithmic regulation.

For example, with the rise of GPS (not to mention automatic speed cameras), it is easy to foresee a future where speeding motorists are no longer pulled over by police officers who happen to spot them, but instead automatically ticketed whenever they exceed the speed limit.

Most people today would consider that intrusive and alarming. But we can also imagine a future in which that speed limit is automatically adjusted based on the amount of traffic, weather conditions, and other subjective conditions that make a higher or lower speed more appropriate than the static limit that is posted today. The endgame might be a future of autonomous vehicles that are able to travel faster because they are connected in an invisible web, a traffic regulatory system that keeps us safer than today's speed limits. The goal, after all, is not to have cars go slower than they might otherwise, but to make our roads safe.

While such a future no doubt raises many issues and might be seen by many as an assault on privacy and other basic freedoms, early versions of that future are already in place in countries like Singapore and can be expected to spread more widely.

Congestion pricing on tolls, designed to reduce traffic to city centers, is another example. Systems such as those in London where your license plate is read and you are required to make a payment will be replaced by automatic billing. You can imagine the costs of tolls floating based not just on time of day but on actual traffic.

Smart parking meters have similar capabilities—parking can cost more at peak times, less off-peak. But perhaps more importantly, smart parking meters can report whether they are occupied or not, and eventually give guidance to drivers and car navigation systems, reducing the amount of time spent circling while aimlessly looking for a parking space.

As we move to a future with more electric vehicles, there are already proposals to replace gasoline taxes with miles driven—reported, of course, once again by GPS.

Moving further out into the future, you can imagine public transportation reinventing itself to look much like Uber. It's a small leap from connecting one passenger and one driver to picking up four or five passengers all heading for the same destination, or along the same route. Smartphone GPS sensors and smart routing algorithms could lead to a hybrid of taxi and bus service, bringing affordable, flexible public transportation to a much larger audience.

The First Step is Measurement

Data driven regulatory systems need not be as complex as those used by Google or credit card companies, or as those imagined above. Sometimes, it's as simple as doing the math on data that is already being collected and putting in place new business processes to act on it.

For example, after hearing of the cost of a small government job search engine for veterans ($5 million per year), I asked how many users the site had. I was told "A couple of hundred." I was understandably shocked, and wondered why this project was up for contract renewal. But when I asked a senior official at the General Services Administration if there were any routine process for calculating the cost per user of government websites, I was told, "That would be a good idea!" It shouldn't just be a good idea; it should be common practice!

Every commercial website not only measures its traffic, but constantly makes adjustments to remove features that are unused and to test new ones in their place. When a startup fails to gain traction with its intended customers, the venture capitalists who backed it either withdraw their funding, or "pivot" to a new approach, trying multiple options till they find one that works. The "lean startup" methodology now widely adopted in Silicon Valley considers a startup to be "a machine for learning," using data to constantly revise and tune its approach to the market. Government, by contrast, seems to inevitably double down on bad approaches, as if admitting failure is the cardinal sin.

Simple web metrics considered as part of a contract renewal are one simple kind of algorithmic regulation that could lead to a massive simplification of government websites and reduction of government IT costs. Other metrics that are commonly used on the commercial web include time on site; abandon rate (people who leave without completing a transaction); and analysis of the paths people use to reach the desired information.

There is other data available as well. Many commercial sites use analysis of search queries to surface what people are looking for. The UK Government Digital Service used this technique in their effort to redesign the Gov.UK site around user needs rather than around the desires of the various cabinet offices and agencies to promote their activities. They looked what people were searching for, and redesigned the site to create new, shorter paths to the most frequently searched-for answers. (Code for America built a site for the city of Honolulu, Honolulu Answers, which took much the same approach, adding a citizen "write-a-thon" to write new, user friendly content to answer the most asked questions.)

This is a simpler, manual intervention that copies what Google does algorithmically when it takes search query data into account when evaluating which results to publish. For example, Google looks at what they call "long clicks" versus "short clicks." When the user clicks on a search result and doesn't come back, or comes back significantly later, indicating that they found the destination link useful, that is a long click. Contrast that to a short click, when users come back right away and try another link instead. Get enough short clicks, and your search result gets demoted.

There are many good examples of data collection, measurement, analysis, and decision-making taking hold in government. In New York City, data mining was used to identify correlations between illegal apartment conversions and increased risk of fires, leading to a unique cooperation between building and fire inspectors. In Louisville, KY, a department focused on performance analytics has transformed the culture of government to one of continuous process improvement.

It's important to understand that these manual interventions are only an essential first step. Once you understand that you have actionable data being systematically collected, and that your interventions based on that data are effective, it's time to begin automating those interventions.

There's a long way to go. We're just at the beginning of thinking about how measurement, outcomes, and regulation come together.

Risks of Algorithmic Regulation

The use of algorithmic regulation increases the power of regulators, and in some cases, could lead to abuses, or to conditions that seem anathema to us in a free society. "Mission creep" is a real risk. Once data is collected for one purpose, it's easy to imagine new uses for it. We've already seen this in requests to the NSA for data on American citizens originally collected for purposes of fighting overseas terrorism being requested by other agencies to fight domestic crime, including copyright infringement! (See Lichtblau & Schmidt, 2013.)

The answer to this risk is not to avoid collecting the data, but to put stringent safeguards in place to limit its use beyond the original purpose. As we have seen, oversight and transparency are particularly difficult to enforce when national security is at stake and secrecy can be claimed to hide misuse. But the NSA is not the only one that needs to keep its methods hidden. Many details of Google's search algorithms are kept as a trade secret lest knowledge of how they work be used to game the system; the same is true for credit card fraud detection.

One key difference is that a search engine such as Google is based on open data (the content of the web), allowing for competition. If Google fails to provide good search results, for example because they are favoring results that lead to more advertising dollars, they risk losing market share to Bing. Users are also able to evaluate Google's search results for themselves.

Not only that, Google's search quality team relies on users themselves— tens of thousands of individuals who are given searches to perform, and asked whether they found what they were looking for. Enough "no" answers, and Google adjusts the algorithms.

Whenever possible, governments putting in place algorithmic regulations must put in place similar quality measurements, emphasizing not just compliance with the rules that have been codified so far but with the original, clearly-specified goal of the regulatory system. The data used to make determinations should be auditable, and whenever possible, open for public inspection.

There are also huge privacy risks involved in the collection of the data needed to build true algorithmic regulatory systems. Tracking our speed while driving also means tracking our location. But that location data need not be stored as long as we are driving within the speed limit, or it can be anonymized for use in traffic control systems.

Given the amount of data being collected by the private sector, it is clear that our current notions of privacy are changing. What we need is a strenuous discussion of the tradeoffs between data collection and the benefits we receive from its use.

This is no different in a government context.

In Conclusion

We are just at the beginning of a big data algorithmic revolution that will touch all elements of our society. Government needs to participate in this revolution.

As outlined in the introduction, a successful algorithmic regulation system has the following characteristics:

1. A deep understanding of the desired outcome

2. Real-time measurement to determine if that outcome is being achieved

3. Algorithms (i.e. a set of rules) that make adjustments based on new data

4. Periodic, deeper analysis of whether the algorithms themselves are correct and performing as expected.

Open data plays a key role in both steps 2 and 4. Open data, either provided by the government itself, or required by government of the private sector, is a key enabler of the measurement revolution. Open data also helps us to understand whether we are achieving our desired objectives, and potentially allows for competition in better ways to achieve those objectives.

About the Author

Tim O'Reilly is the founder and CEO of O'Reilly Media Inc., thought by many to be the best computer book publisher in the world. O'Reilly Media also hosts conferences on technology topics, including the O'Reilly Open Source Convention, Strata: The Business of Data, and many others. Tim's blog, the O'Reilly Radar "watches the alpha geeks" to determine emerging technology trends, and serves as a platform for advocacy about issues of importance to the technical community. Tim is also a partner at O'Reilly AlphaTech Ventures, O'Reilly's early stage venture firm, and is on the board of Safari Books Online, PeerJ, Code for America, and Maker Media, which was recently spun out from O'Reilly Media. Maker Media's Maker Faire has been compared to the West Coast Computer Faire, which launched the personal computer revolution.

References

Lichtblau, E., & Schmidt, M.S. (2013, August 3). Other Agencies Clamor for Data N.S.A. Compiles. The *New York Times*. Retrieved from http://www.nytimes.com/2013/08/04/us/other-agencies-clamor-for-data-nsa-compiles.html

Open Government Working Group. (2007, December 8). 8 Principles of Open Government Data. Retrieved from http://www.opengovdata.org/home/8principles

The White House. (2012). As Prepared for Delivery: Regulation: Looking Backward, Looking Forward - Cass R. Sunstein. Retrieved from http://www.whitehouse.gov/sites/default/files/omb/inforeg/speeches/regulation-looking-backward-looking-forward-05102012.pdf

Afterword: What's Next?

By Abhi Nemani

The principle binary struggle of the 21st century is not left or right, but open societies versus closed.

—Alec J. Ross

The early history of the open data movement, as chronicled in these pages, tells us that data will certainly play a critical role in optimizing service delivery, creating new business opportunities, and setting new policy. Cities ranging from Asheville and Portland to Chicago and London have set up open data shops; millions of dollars of economic activity have been stimulated both at the local and national levels; and core civic services such as childhood welfare in Maryland and Public Works in Louisville are being constantly renovated through data. Beyond these tactical enhancements, cultural and social shifts are emerging as citizens build more trust in their government and become more engaged in its work.

Still, the legacy of the open data movement remains to be seen. The long-term success of our current efforts should be measured not only by their efficacy now, but by their ability to catalyze future action into new challenges and harder issues. While progress has begun in difficult areas such as personal data, platform integration, and inter-agency coordination, we have only just scratched the surface. As open data becomes mainstream, political and philosophical issues are coming to the fore. How can we design for inclusion? How can we reconcile privacy and openness? We must take on these questions next.

To address these challenges and realize future opportunities, a key lesson from these narratives must be taken to heart. Data is at best a tool—sometimes a blunt one—and tools are only as good as their operators. The open data movement must look not only beyond transparency as an end goal, but beyond any single constituency as operators. "How to open data" is not only a question for governments, and neither is "what to build with it" one for civic startups. New York City has pioneered some of the most impressive applications of data analytics, while BrightScope has opened up millions of rows of data. The Smart Chicago Collaborative, Philadelphia's Chief Data Officer, and SmartProcure have all used data to advance policy reform. Civic hackers and journalists have played a critical role in making data more meaningful and available.

There are countless other examples—many detailed in this anthology—of unexpected open civic data operators from all facets of our society. In this way, open data has served to blur the lines between our public and private lives, to reconnect the consumer, citizen, and civil servant. When looking ahead, this may be part of open data's greatest legacy: the emergence of a new kind of connective tissue that enables us to create governments of the people, by the people, that work in the 21st century.

About the Author

Abhi Nemani is the Co-Executive Director (Interim) at Code for America (CfA). For nearly four years, Abhi has led CfA's strategic development and growth, including the development of multiple new programs including the launch of a first-of-its-kind civic startup accelerator and the CfA Peer Network, designed to connect cities to help them work together. Abhi has been featured as a speaker at SxSW, the World Bank, and various universities and conferences around the world. He graduated magna cum laude from Claremont McKenna College with a honors degree in Philosophy, Politics, and Economics.

APPENDIX I:

Further Reading

Braybrooke, K. and Nissila, J. (Eds). (2013). *The Open Book*. London, UK: The Finnish Institute in London. Available at http://theopenbook. org.uk/

Hibbets, Jason (2013). The Foundation for an Open Source City. Available at http://theopensourcecity.com/

Lathrop, D. and Ruma, L. (Eds.) (2010). Open Government: Collaboration, Transparency, and Participation in Practice. Sebastopol, CA: O'Reilly Media. Available at https://github.com/oreillymedia/open_ government

Noveck, Beth (2010). *Wiki Government: How Technology Can Make Government Better, Democracy Stronger, and Citizens More Powerful*. Washington, DC: Brookings Institution Press.

Open Government Working Group. (2007, December 8). 8 Principles of Open Government Data. Available at https://public.resource.org/8_ principles.html

Socrata (2013). Open Data Field Guide. Available at http://www.socrata.com/open-data-field-guide-chapter/about/

Tauberer, Josh (2012). Open Government Data. Available at http:// opengovdata.io/

The Sunlight Foundation. (2010). Ten Principles for Opening Up Government Information. Available at http://assets.sunlightfoundation. com.s3.amazonaws.com/policy/papers/Ten%20Principles%20for%20 Opening%20Up%20Government%20Data.pdf

Townsend, Anthony (2013). *Smart Cities: Big Data, Civic Hackers, and the Quest for a New Utopia*. New York, NY: W. W. Norton & Company.

32591671R00179

Made in the USA
Charleston, SC
22 August 2014